LIVING THE CANADIAN DREAM

LIVING THE CANADIAN DREAM

How Canadian Tire
became Canada's store

Daniel Stoffman

**Published on the 90th anniversary
of the founding of the Canadian Tire Corporation**

Living the Canadian Dream
© 2012 Canadian Tire Corporation, Limited.
All Rights Reserved.

Canadian Tire Corporation, Limited

2180 Yonge Street
Toronto, ON M4P 2V8

Second printing

Photograph page vi : In 1967, Canadian Tire sponsored the
largest classic and antique car rally ever to be held in Canada.
Cars travelled for 11 days from both Ontario and the Maritimes
to Montreal's Expo '67, parading through communities on
the way.

Library and Archives Canada Cataloguing in Publication

Stoffman, Daniel
  Living the Canadian dream : how Canadian Tire became
Canada's store / Daniel Stoffman.

Includes index.
ISBN 978-1-77136-089-0

  1. Canadian Tire Corporation – History.   2. Billes family.
I. Canadian Tire Corporation   II. Title.

HD9745.C34C35   2012   338.7'616830971   C2012-906792-x

Publié en français sous le titre *Au cœur du rêve: Comment
Canadian Tire est devenu le magasin de choix au Canada*
ISBN 978-1-77136-096-8

Project management and book design
  by Counterpunch Inc. / Linda Gustafson and Peter Ross
Editing by Judy Phillips
Typeset in Goluska and Slate Pro, designed in Canada
  by Rod McDonald
Printed and bound in Canada by Friesens Corporation
Text printed on acid-free paper

PICTURE CREDITS

Every effort has been made to trace the
copyright owner of the visual materials
used in this publication. We apologize for
any unintentional omissions, and would be
happy to include acknowledgement in future
editions. Many of the visual materials are
from the Canadian Tire Archives; additional
materials are courtesy of Canadian Tire
employees and associate dealers. Thank you
to the individuals and companies that so
graciously granted permission to reproduce
their images:

Appleby Photo Studio: 49 (fourth row,
  middle)
Paul Arella/Canadian Tire Corporation (CTC):
  279 (left and bottom right)
Artistic Productions Ltd.: 76
Atlantic Photo Service: 182 (top)
Carson Au: 122
Bill Beaton: 134
Jack Bennett: 18

Reprinted with permission of Brunswick
  News Inc.: 63 (bottom middle)
Courtesy of the Canadian Pacific Railway:
  185 (middle right)
Cei Chinn Photography: 183 (right)
Cinesound Ltd.: 46
John Crawford Photographer: 49 (top
  left), 70
Courtesy of CTC Supply Chain: 145 (bottom
  right), 184, 185 (middle left and centre)
Bob Cunningham Photography Ltd.: 263
  (top right)
P. Doyle: 218
William Dunn Artistic Productions Ltd.: 83,
  227, 262 (top and bottom right)
John Evans: 212
Giffels Assoc. Ltd.: 179, 180
Gold Photography: 148 (middle)
Milt Goodman: 117, 119, 120, 121 (left), 211
Courtesy of Keith Gostlin: 271 (right)
Courtesy of the Graham and Forster families:
  252 (left)

Graphic Industries Ltd.: 114
Colin Hart: 203
Courtesy of James Hou/Winners Products
  Engineering: 278 (right)
Courtesy of Bob and Esther Hougham:
  133, 257
Andy Isaak/New Heights Aerial
  Photography: 184, 244–45
Cameron Jenkins/CTC: 108–09, 184 (top and
  middle row), 241, 254, 255, 260, 263,
  266, 272 (top and bottom middle), 280,
  289 (right), 295 (bottom right)
Chris Little/CTC: 205 (bottom row, right), 206
Anthony Macarri: 267, 285
Reprinted with permission of Maclean's
  Magazine: 167
Gary Manks: 137, 282 (bottom right)
Jason Maynes/CTC: 290 (top left)
Newton: 49 (third row, right)
Paul Orenstein: x
Perspective 5 Photography & Design
  Studio: 118

J.M. Radey: 50 (top row, second from left)
Ross Saito: 123
Lisa Sakulensky: 171
B. Sandford: 197, 198, 199
Stan's Studio: 49 (third row, middle)
Star newspaper service: 35, 143 (bottom left),
  173 (top right)
Jason Statler Photography: 112, 125
Joseph Stephen/CTC: 255, 269, 270
Studio C. March: 86
The Pridham Studios: 89 (top right)
The Telegram: 27
The Tenszen Studio: 68
Toronto Star Archives/GetStock.com: 63
  (bottom right)
Toronto Star Syndicate: 38 (top), 95
Kendall Townend: 201, 215, 273, 290
  (bottom), 292
Ben Webster: 252 (right)
Western Archives, Western University: 30
Courtesy of Justin Young: 228

This book is dedicated to the men and women who, over the past nine decades, have helped bring the Canadian Tire dream into reality.

Contents

Foreword

FOR A LONG TIME NOW I have dreamed of having the story told of how Canadian Tire came to be Canada's store and how it evolved into the icon it is in the life of Canada and Canadians. That dream has now become a reality with the publication of this book.

The Canadian Tire story is important for many reasons. Over the years, almost a million men and women have worked to make Canadian Tire a success. The company's history should be available to all our employees, and the contributions of the talented management teams that have guided our destiny should be acknowledged.

It is also important that the history of the company be recorded for the many past and current talented executives who have guided us on our journey through the decades.

As Canadian Tire has a rich history of community service, and is present in so many Canadian communities from coast to coast, it is fitting that those communities have the opportunity to learn how, from the beginning, the company stood ready to be of service.

The current and future business community in Canada can also benefit from an understanding of the history of Canadian Tire. Much can be learned from a company whose values have, for the most part, been preserved for over 90 years and whose evolution is unique. If one set out to design a new company I am not sure that anyone would come up with the Canadian Tire recipe. Our company defies casebook thinking. But it is a company that has flourished and prospered because of, and in spite of, its unique evolutionary journey.

It is the story of a forward-thinking family, the Billes family, who founded and nurtured the Tire for 90 years. And it is the story of how committed Martha and Owen Billes are to the future life of the Tire.

It is the story of leadership, innovation, and entrepreneurship, of ideas far ahead of the times in which they were conceived, of profit-sharing and unique relationships. In today's world these values are more critical than ever.

"Strive always to make things better" was one of A.J. Billes's maxims and that is what Canadian Tire has always tried to do. I have had the enormous privilege of serving Canadian Tire for many years and I have seen its relentless quest to explore new ways of serving Canadians better. This book chronicles that quest. And it provides a glimpse into its future. Yes, there have been bumps along the way to the present and more can be expected in the future. But the company's ability to overcome the challenges of those bumps provides the clues to how it will respond to future challenges on its way to greater excellence.

I had the great good fortune to have learned about the core values of Canadian Tire in the late 1980s by dropping into A.J.'s modest little office located just off the mailroom at home office. There, amid the dated furniture, including a well-used rocking chair, this modest and gentle man, with an ever-present twinkle in his eye, shared his experiences and his views with me. It was thus that I began my love affair with the Tire.

A.J.'s legacy is an important one in Canada, and although A.J. was honoured with the Order of Canada and was inducted into the Canadian Business Hall of

Fame, his humble demeanour and retiring ways militated against his publicly taking his place among Canada's business giants. But there is no question that he lives among them.

Her father's legacy has been carefully maintained by Martha Billes. Together with her son, Owen, she represents continuity and the protection that a controlling shareholder affords to the implementation of management's strategic imperatives. Both Martha and Owen are committed to the best in governance practices. Their highly disciplined approach to the Board's composition, its independence of thought, and its duty to challenge have greatly facilitated my work and that of my fellow directors. They constantly remind us to use our "gift of days" wisely.

This book records the first 90 years, but the Canadian Tire story is not finished. There are many more chapters to come as the company continues on its journey. The new world of retailing will present it with many opportunities to apply the strength of its brand, and its talent for innovative entrepreneurial initiatives, to the service of Canadians.

I am grateful to Daniel Stoffman for the charming way he has told the story of how Canadian Tire became Canada's store and to Linda Gustafson for her pictorial story and inspired design. Both embody the values for which the Tire stands. And words are inadequate to express my gratitude to all of you who shared your memories of the Tire with our author. You know who you are, and this book would not have been possible without you.

Maureen Sabia, O.C.
Chairman of the Board
Canadian Tire Corporation, Limited

CHAPTER ONE

Young men in a hurry

BILL BILLES and his younger brother, Alf, were already in business together before Alf had entered the first grade. Bill, the elder by six years, owned one of the largest paper routes in Toronto and little Alf wanted in on the action. Bill paid Alf five cents a week to help him deliver newspapers to homes in the city's east end. Five cents wasn't much, even at the beginning of the last century, but these weren't just any five cents. "He went to the bank and always insisted on shiny ones," Alf Billes recalled many years later. "They were more impressive, there's no question about it." And that wasn't all. When the day's work was done, Bill treated his employee to sweets from a bakery that advertised "yesterday's cakes" at a price of two for a penny.[1]

It was the beginning of a legendary business partnership. In 1922, the Billes brothers ventured into the automotive business. Their modest firm, Hamilton Tire and Garage,[2] morphed into a national retail chain, Canadian Tire Corporation. Through the Roaring Twenties, Great Depression, and World War II, the business adapted to the changing times, grew, and prospered. After the war, Canada's economy boomed and Canadian Tire boomed with it. Canadians bought automobiles and built houses in the suburbs. They needed auto parts and accessories, household

◀ Alfred Jackson (A.J.) and John William (J.W.) Billes, c. 1920s.

goods, hardware, hockey skates, and garden supplies. Canadian Tire supplied all that and more.

Then, in the 1990s, came the biggest challenge of all — the arrival of powerful new competitors from the United States. Another iconic Canadian retailer, Eaton's, collapsed in the face of the new competition and experts predicted the same fate for Canadian Tire. It was, they said, "a deer in the headlights." They were wrong. Canadian Tire not only stood up to the new competition but, remaking itself without losing its own unique personality, it emerged stronger because of it.

The Billes brothers have passed on, leaving behind a retail empire that has become a national institution. Canadian Tire's 490 stores span the country from Newfoundland to Vancouver Island. In addition, Canadian Tire Corporation now operates gas bars and convenience stores, a financial services company, specialty automotive stores, a clothing retailer, and a chain of sporting goods stores.

Like all businesses, Canadian Tire has had its ups and downs. But the ups have outnumbered the downs and, in 2012, as the company celebrates its 90th anniversary, it is not only thriving but seeking new challenges.

How did the Billes brothers and their successors do it? That's what this book is about.

▼

IN 1922, Toronto had a population of about 500,000. It also had 40,000 cars. That wasn't many — a ratio of 0.08 cars per person compared with today's ratio of 0.58 — but it was the largest concentration of vehicles in Canada. Although the majority of Canadians would not be car owners until after World War II, by 1922 car ownership was growing rapidly and would increase fourfold by the end of the decade.

The world was speeding up. Commercial aviation, which would do for long-distance travel what the car did for shorter trips, was in its early days but developing rapidly. It was also early days for modes of communication — telephone, movies, radio — that today we take for granted. The first talking pictures were released, the first commercial radio stations went on the air, and phone lines were strung across the country, all during the 1920s.

John William (Bill) Billes and Alfred Jackson (Alf) Billes were second-generation Canadians whose father, Henry Billes, arrived in Toronto from England before the turn of the 19th century and worked as a butcher for a wholesale meat company in the Toronto neighbourhood of Riverdale. He married Julia Constable,

▲ J.W. and A.J. Billes in their sister Elsie's wedding party: (from left) Melville Stuart Gooderham (groom), A.J., Elsie Billes, Melville Gooderham, Averil Billes, J.W., and Col. Albert Gooderham, May 14, 1935.

▲ The former Billes family home on Sackville Street, Toronto, 1976.

▲ Billes family portrait taken in 1903: (from left) J.W., Julia with A.J. on her lap, Evelyn, Averil on Henry's lap, Mae, and Harry.

▲ A.J. and J.W. dressed to the nines for their sister Elsie's wedding.

▲ Julia Constable Billes, 1935.

3
▼

the daughter of an innkeeper. Of their seven children, Bill was the third eldest and Alf the second youngest.

The family lived in a rented house on Sackville Street, where Julia made all the clothes for the family. One hot summer day, Henry Billes, a side of beef over his shoulder, dropped dead of a heart attack at the age of 59.[3] Alf, 16 years old, had to quit school to help support the family. Abandoning his dream of becoming a missionary, he took a job as a clerk at the Dominion Bank. Bill, who had completed an accounting course, was an adventurous young man. When his father died, he was riding the rails through western Canada. Bill had shown an entrepreneurial flair while still in school by buying vegetable and flower seeds in bulk and packaging them for sale. This sideline turned a profit of about $500 a year ($7,600 in 2012 dollars), the equivalent then of a workingman's annual wages. Bill Billes understood at an early age that it was better to run a business than work for one.

Back in Toronto, he looked for work in the automotive field, a promising young industry that fascinated him. He worked for Goodyear and Mack Trucks before joining the army in 1917. After a month in uniform, Bill was discharged, declared unfit because of a heart murmur.[4] He found employment with Riverdale Tire Corp., which billed itself in newspaper advertisements as "Canada's largest retail tire dealers." With stores in six cities, including three in Toronto, Riverdale Tire was in the business of buying surplus tires in the winter and selling them during the summer driving season.

Bill had bought his first car, a 1910 Model T Ford, in 1914.[5] Alf, on the other hand, didn't know much about cars and preferred to get around town on horseback. His favourite steed, Kenny, had been fired from his job as a police horse when he jumped over a backfiring Model T. Alf got Kenny cheap and rode him for years.[6]

In 1913, Bill negotiated a purchase of tires for his employer. Bill must have been proud of the deal because a Canadian Tire catalogue published in 1943 claims 1913 as the date the company was founded.[7] In fact, it was founded in 1922 when the brothers pooled their resources and came up with $2,000 to buy the branch of Riverdale Tire operating out of a garage at Gerrard and Hamilton Streets, across the street from the forbidding hulk of the Don Jail.

Bill gave incorrect dates for the founding of the company on several occasions, perhaps wanting to exaggerate Canadian Tire's status as a long-established firm. He also liked to claim that he was the sole founder, despite the undisputed fact that Alf was involved from the start. In 1944, Bill wrote a letter addressed to Fry & Co., the brokerage firm acting as underwriter of Canadian Tire's first public share offering.

▲ J.W. Billes, 1920s.

The letter, included in an information package issued by Fry to potential investors, stated: "Purchasing this business in 1922, I was sole proprietor until later joined by my brother, Mr. Alfred J. Billes, in the ownership and management."[8]

It is true that Bill had discovered the business opportunity. It is also true that he was the prime mover behind the decision to start a business. Alf Billes said years later that he enjoyed working in the bank and would not have gone into the automotive business but for the chance to work with the elder brother he idolized.[9] "It could have been any kind of business," he said, "and I would have gone with him. Because my brother was a born businessman."[10] Yet not only was Alf present from the beginning, he had contributed a greater share of the purchase price — $1,200 to Bill's $800. Bill, however, as the senior partner, owned 60 per cent of the company to his brother's 40 per cent.[11] (This division of ownership would have important repercussions much later in the company's history.) The money purchased the business but not the building, which was rented to the brothers by the owner of Riverdale Tire.

▲ A.J. Billes, 1920s.

There has been some confusion about the name of the business the brothers bought. In the letter published by Fry, Bill claims that Canadian Tire succeeded Hamilton Garage and Rubber, which had been established in 1909. Previous accounts of Canadian Tire's history have taken this to mean that the business the brothers bought was named Hamilton Garage and Rubber. But in fact it was a branch of Riverdale Tire Corp., as attested by that company's many newspaper advertisements at the time promoting the Riverdale Tire store at the corner of Gerrard and Hamilton.[12] So it must have been the Billes brothers who decided to call their enterprise Hamilton Tire and Garage, after Hamilton Street.

Bill and Alf had everything going for them. Through luck, more than foresight, they had chosen an industry that was about to undergo phenomenal growth. "I doubt that any of us fully appreciated what the automobile was going to do or whether it would even replace the bicycle," Alf Billes admitted many years later.[13] In addition to having good luck, they were smart, ambitious, and full of energy. The one thing they didn't have at the birth of Canadian Tire in September 1922 was very many tires. They lacked the capital to put in a stock of tires, and demand for tires declined toward the end of the year anyway, since most drivers put their cars away for the winter rather than struggle with cold engines and snow-covered roads. Instead the brothers sold replacement parts, mostly to a clientele of mechanics, and also offered indoor parking for about 20 cars. Their parking customers were businessmen, lawyers, and doctors living on the more affluent streets north of Gerrard. They did not have garages of their own, and the Billeses offered secure, heated car storage and protection from theft.

Someone had to be there 24 hours a day to keep the fire going and watch for burglars. The one doing the overnight shift wasn't supposed to sleep. "But we did anyway," Alf later admitted. "When we were needed, there was a bell outside. [Customers] were able to ring us, and we'd pop down."[14]

The brothers were tall, lean, and athletic. They were ready, if necessary, to defend their territory. Alf recalled the time three husky sheet-metal workers refused to move their truck, which was blocking customers' access to the garage. A fight started and one of the toughs knocked Alf down onto the muddy lane, breaking his jaw. "They were hard as nails," he later recalled. "But [Bill] was a much better fighter than I was. His fists would just fly." The brothers didn't win the fight, but the truck never blocked the lane again.

Difficult neighbours were the least of their problems. Within weeks of the opening of the business, the nearby Gerrard Street Bridge closed for several months of repairs. As a result, the traffic that was supposed to bring business to the garage disappeared. "We learned early that things didn't come easy," Alf said later.[15]

Nevertheless, enough cash was coming in to allow Bill to spend much of his time looking for good deals on tires. By spring, they had enough tires to go into the tire business for real. They opened first in a small storefront on Dundas Street but after a month decided to decamp to a better location, on Yonge Street at Gould, in the heart of Toronto's bustling downtown, just a few blocks from the stock exchange and central business district.

The business had a new name: Canadian Tire Corporation. It didn't matter that Canadian Tire would not become a corporation until 1927 and would not expand outside Toronto until 1934. By choosing "Canadian Tire Corporation" as the name of their enterprise, the brothers were announcing that they had big plans for the future.

The bad luck of the bridge closing near their first location was soon offset by good luck. After two winters of almost no snow in Toronto, some manufacturers of tire chains decided to unload their stock. "We bought tons and tons of chains at a ridiculous price," Alf later recalled. "The day they started to haul those chains to our shop it started to snow, and it snowed for three days. We made a small fortune on that."[16]

The brothers knew that tires could be a lucrative business because tires had to be replaced frequently. The tires were narrow and tall in comparison with those

today and came in four sizes. Poorly made by modern standards, they had difficulty withstanding the wretched road conditions. The uneven cobblestones on city pavements were hard on tires and the mostly unpaved rural roads were even worse. The flimsy tires were inflated to 60 pounds of pressure per square inch, and blowouts were frequent. Drivers had to know how to make their own tire repairs. Anyone venturing on an intercity trip would take a repair kit and blowout patches and sometimes a full change of tires as well. Even the best tires lasted only about 3,000 miles.

An early example of innovative Canadian Tire marketing was the brothers' decision to sell tires on credit, something none of their competitors did for the obvious reason that some customers wouldn't pay. When that happened, Alf and Bill would go to the culprit's home with a couple of burly employees — Alf called them "the boys" — and some wooden blocks. There, they jacked up the car and reclaimed the tires. Sometimes the owner of the car objected and fisticuffs ensued. When Alf married Muriel Moore in 1928, she informed him he would no longer be going on tire repossession outings with the boys.[17]

The roof over the store at Yonge and Gould leaked everywhere — which didn't hurt the tires, but it kept customers away when it rained, as it was no drier inside than out. Despite that problem, the brothers enjoyed a profitable year until fall, when tire sales dried up. So they closed the store. Alf went back to John Sloan & Co., the wholesale grocer where he had worked as a bookkeeper the previous winter.

The following spring, as driving season approached, they reopened Canadian Tire, this time farther north on Yonge Street, at Wellesley. Business was even better at that location and, foreshadowing big things to come, they ventured into selling non-automotive products for the first time. At the beginning of December, the Billeses were offered a line of imitation ivory combs, brushes, and mirrors on consignment. They put them on display but nobody was buying, probably because potential customers didn't think of looking for a hairbrush in a store called Canadian Tire. Then, about three days before Christmas, "the customers came," Alf recalled. "Undoubtedly, our prices were right. And by the time Christmas came around, we had practically no stock left."[18] Canadian Tire then closed for the winter, to reopen in the spring of 1924.

First they rented a storefront at Yonge and Wood, but that location lacked space to change tires. Next, they moved to 639 Yonge Street, at the northeast corner of Yonge and Isabella, just three blocks south of the major intersection of Yonge and Bloor Streets. This became Canadian Tire's first long-term location; the business would remain there for six years. It had room for more merchandise than previous quarters and the city raised no objection to Canadian Tire's installing tires on Isabella Street. It was here that, for the first time, Canadian Tire entered the gas retailing business when the city allowed the placement of a hand-operated gas pump on the edge of the sidewalk along Isabella.

The year 1924 was an important one for Bill for two reasons. His first child, Gwen, was born to Gladys, whom he had married the year before, having met her at a skating rink several years earlier. And, when the winter of 1924–25 arrived, he and Alf kept the store open. Canadian Tire would never close for the winter again. It was in business for good.

▲ Gladys Dickson and J.W., before they were married.

▲ Muriel Moore Billes on her wedding day, 1928.

ALTHOUGH CANADIAN TIRE had been calling itself a corporation for several years, it did not actually become one until 1927, when it was officially incorporated. The incorporation papers listed as shareholders the two brothers; Gordon Blakeley, shipper; Morley Hicks, manager; and Elsie Gertrude Billes, stenographer.[19] Elsie was the youngest of the seven Billes siblings.

Incorporation signalled that Canadian Tire was growing up. Once settled at Yonge and Isabella, first on the northeast corner and later in larger premises on the southeast corner, it transformed itself from a capital-starved new venture into a serious business run by a pair of innovative, self-confident entrepreneurs. These entrepreneurs, it should be noted, were still known as Bill and Alf — it wasn't until the late 1940s that, gradually, they became known as J.W. and A.J. respectively. Betty Stevens, a switchboard operator who joined the staff in 1948, helped the process along; she found that the initials came across more clearly than the names when she paged the two bosses on the intercom.[20]

At Yonge and Isabella, most of the characteristics emerged that would define Canadian Tire and spur its success in the decades to come: low prices, loyal employees, a broad array of products, flamboyant marketing methods, and multiple stores run by independent business owners called "dealers."

The guiding principle of the Billes brothers was to offer customers the lowest possible prices. To that end, Bill, using his by then extensive knowledge of the tire business, was always on the lookout for deals. In 1924, for example, he bought

▲ 639 Yonge Street, at the northeast corner of Yonge and Isabella, Canadian Tire's first long-term location.

▶▶ The Canadian Tire store moved across the street to 637 Yonge Street, at the southeast corner of Yonge and Isabella, in 1930.

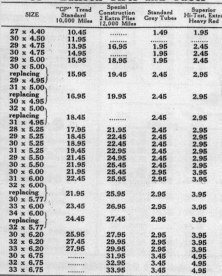

▶ The 1928 "catalogue," consisting of a folded price list, with a much-sought-after road map on the back side. Tires and tire accessories featured heavily.

"Our prices had to be good because we were the bad boys." — Alf

a large supply of slightly damaged tires from a former employer, Tiger Tire and Rubber, that had suffered a major fire.

Buying direct from the manufacturer was to become a key operating principle for Canadian Tire. Wholesalers, from Canada's earliest history and into the 20th century, dominated the retail distribution system. They were much bigger than the retailers who depended on them for credit. The wholesalers, not the retailers, had the financial clout and connections to travel to Britain and the United States to import goods. Timothy Eaton was as dependent as any merchant on the favour of the wholesalers when he opened a small dry goods store in St. Marys, Ontario, in 1861. But as his business grew, eventually becoming a national department-store chain, he was able to bypass them by dealing directly with manufacturers.[21]

Bill Billes continued what Timothy Eaton had started. He decided early that he didn't need the wholesalers. Canadian Tire could save money by bypassing them, and it could pass those savings along to the customer, thereby increasing its sales. High volumes, not high profit margins, would build the company. This strategy caused consternation among competitors, who threatened to boycott suppliers selling directly to the Billeses. The suppliers capitulated with the exception of one, Gutta Percha and Rubber, which continued to supply Canadian Tire at the same price as it sold to wholesalers. In return, Gutta Percha's advertising was displayed prominently across the front of 639 Yonge. Eventually, the other suppliers relented and "Direct Factory Distributors" became one of the slogans painted on the storefront. The phrase "Factory Distributors" also appeared in Canadian Tire's newspaper advertising.

"Our prices had to be good because we were the bad boys," Alf recalled years later. "The established competition didn't like us at all, and most of our suppliers wouldn't even admit that they sold to Canadian Tire."[22]

In a 1985 speech, Alf said he and his brother faced two choices in the early years of Canadian Tire: "Follow the leadership of the establishment and charge all that the traffic would bear, or add to our buying cost only what we thought would give us a reasonable return for our effort." Choosing the latter, they became "price cutters and outcasts of the establishment."[23]

The Billeses did not use suppliers' brands for most of their tire sales, preferring to use their own brand name, Super-Lastic. Canadian Tire's price for one tire was $12.95, of which $1 was profit. Nobody else was selling tires so cheaply. Canadian Tire made more money from a cheaper item, the tube; it was able to get seconds for only 75 cents and then sell them for $3.25. Alf Billes explained: "Why did I sell the tire so cheaply? I had to, to get the customer in. It wasn't skinning the customer in any way because the tube that I sold for $3.25 would sell for more than double that [somewhere else]."[24]

The best customers got even lower prices. Many of these were in the automotive business themselves, mechanics and garage owners who would drop off a list of parts they needed in the morning and come by later to pick them up. These customers got a 10 per cent discount.[25]

The first important Canadian Tire product line not directly related to cars was radios. The company first advertised radio batteries for sale in 1929 and radios and parts in 1930. A radio catalogue was published in 1935. It featured such models as "The Canadian," an electric floor model in a walnut console. The regular price was $198.50, but Canadian Tire offered it "direct from the factory" for $119.50. A six-tube model, also in a walnut console, cost just $39.50.

The expansion into radios illustrates what is still a key element of Canadian Tire's business strategy: try things and see if they work. Some things don't work; the first attempt at self-service, for example, was a disaster, as more goods were pilfered than sold.[26] The radio line, on the other hand, was a big success, and the department continued to expand until Canadian Tire, by 1937, was among the largest retailers of radios and radio parts in North America. Alf Billes was a radio buff himself. The country house he built during the 1930s at Shanty Bay, on Lake Simcoe, north of Toronto, was not equipped with a phone but it had an elaborate radio rig. When his family was at Shanty Bay, Alf and Muriel spoke twice a day by radio.[27]

In 1935, Bill Billes decided Canadian Tire should sell sporting goods. At first, it seemed an odd addition for a store specializing in automotive goods, but Bill's reasoning was that the boy who gets his first bicycle at Canadian Tire will buy tires there when he grows up.[28] Soon Canadian Tire became the place not only to get a first bike but also that precious first pair of skates. The sporting goods department expanded until it was carrying a full range of gear, including camping, fishing, and hunting equipment. By then, the relationship between automotive products and recreational equipment was obvious. The industry had begun promoting

▲ This Canadian Tire branded tire, thought to have been made in the late 1920s or early 1930s, was dredged up from the ocean bed off Yarmouth, Nova Scotia, in the 1960s. It was still inflated and in excellent shape.

▶ 1936 catalogue. The camping scene illustrates that the travelling motorist could fulfill all of his or her camping and motoring needs at Canadian Tire.

▲ A MotoMaster oil can from the early 1950s.

▲▲ An early advertisement for MotoMaster spark plugs, from 1936.

▲ In addition to highlighting the great value of the MotoMaster brand of oil, this 1948 advertisement provided consumers with useful information.

1935 The spring and summer catalogue is the first to list "Motormaster" dependable electrical products, featuring MotoMaster spark plugs. MotoMaster is Canadian Tire's own exclusive line.

1936 MotoMaster certified 2,000-mile oil is offered at 70 cents per gallon, $1.10 less than oil sold under highly advertised brand names. Canadian Tire guarantees that MotoMaster certified 100 per cent–pure Pennsylvania oil tests better than the average of 11 brands. Other MotoMaster products offered in 1936 include greases, grease, ignition parts, spark plugs, generators and armatures exchanges, radiators,

flywheel gears, piston rings, heaters, and thermostats.

1939 The "Moto-Master" trademark is registered.

1940 The MotoMaster product line continues to expand, to include liquid waxes and polishes, dry soaps for cleaning seat covers, bearings, motor weld compounds, hydraulic shock absorbers, and radiator hoses.

1948 New MotoMaster products include jacks, antifreeze and radiator chemicals, mirrors, headlamps, auto lamps, switches,

▲ Ads (clockwise from top left) from 1966, 1989, 2000, and 1989, demonstrating the evolution of MotoMaster as an automotive brand, from the product assortment to the packaging and logo.

fan belts, specialized lubricants and motor conditioners, engine valves, clutch plates and parts, mufflers and tailpipes, steering sets, carburetors, and replacement parts for Ford and Chevrolet models.

1986 MotoMaster tires are introduced and become Canada's best-selling replacement tires.

1987 The "built tough; backed tough" campaign heavily promotes the MotoMaster brand. More than 12,000 MotoMaster automotive products are available exclusively through Canadian Tire stores.

1997 A new MotoMaster advertising campaign uses the slogan "MotoMaster works here."

2012 MotoMaster continues to provide Canadians with reliable, affordable automotive products, including tires, motor oils, wiper blades, and batteries that meet or exceed the industry's highest standards, incorporate the latest technology, and offer top quality at great value.

▶ MotoMaster gear oil jug, c. 2012.

Interior of the London, Ontario, associate store, 1939.

car ownership as the best way to escape the crowded city for the pure air of the countryside. And Canadian Tire had the equipment you needed once you got there.

From the beginning, the Billeses displayed a knack for promotion. The Yonge and Isabella store was emblazoned with logos and slogans such as "Canada's Greatest Tire Sale" and "We Make Your Dollars Go Farther." Another slogan, "The Longest Run for Your Money," was accompanied by a drawing of a spinning tire with a smiling, running person embedded in it and a silver dollar speeding alongside. This logo was one of Alf Billes's favourites, yet its creator is unknown. One evening, Alf was busy serving a customer when a man who had been waiting handed him a piece of paper containing the sketch of the spinning tire and then walked out of the store. "I never saw him again," Alf recounted years later. "I always had a sad feeling that I was never able to compensate him in any way."[29]

Motor oil was an important product line for Canadian Tire from its earliest days. It sold motor oil under its own brand name, MotoMaster, and was in need of a logo for the can. At the time, Alf was working with an architect on designs for the Shanty Bay house, which features many gables. Alf was doodling one day and came up with an inverted isosceles triangle — an upside-down gable.[30] "Standing the triangle on its apex was significant to him," says his daughter, Martha. "He'd come from the wrong side of the tracks and worked his way up and created something. The instability of the triangle and yet the strength of it is the juxtaposition that was important, in his mind." The inverted red triangle, with a maple leaf on top, is Canadian Tire's trademark to this day.

Alf admitted he hadn't known much about automotive technology before going into the business. Once in, however, he was always looking for innovations that might save the company money or make some. A big seller for the store was heaters, then an accessory rather than standard equipment. They worked by heating water. The problem for Canadian Tire was that heaters wouldn't work in Fords because Fords lacked water pumps. Working with a mechanic, Alf devised a way around this problem. "We were installing heaters for one dollar, and that meant we sold a heater and we made money on installing it," Alf said. "And I'm not an engineer. Why hadn't Ford figured it out?"

He also devised an ingenious approach to reducing congestion at the entrance to the service department off Isabella Street. He drew plans for a turntable, so that the cars, once serviced, could be spun around, speeding up their exit from the garage. "That was typical," Alf recalled. "The service people, they were the ones that said, 'Here's our problem, now what can be done about it?' and I had the cooperation of all of them."

▲ The running tire logo appeared on the cover of each catalogue until the mid-1930s.

Bill Billes was parsimonious when it came to capital upgrades, so the turntable was built by the Canadian Tire service department. That suited the employees, since it kept them employed during the winter when demand for servicing was slow. "Canadian Tire never, ever laid off a person during the wintertime," Alf said. "Never in all the time we have been in business. And because we were growing rapidly, we needed to make changes in the building and this is how we kept them busy all during the winter.

"In those days it was typical, come Christmas, that the factories would be down maybe for a month or two months or three. But as far as we were concerned, people still had to eat during the wintertime. So we saved up the jobs. Instead of having some outfit to come in and do the job, we did it ourselves. I had the cooperation of the buildings department in City Hall. They'd pass my drawings, which weren't particularly qualified. And even our electrical work we did ourselves. And I learned from the inspectors."[31]

Alf loved gadgets and innovations. Once, on a trip with his buyers to the annual fall hardware show in New York, he announced he knew just the place to go for lunch. It turned out to be a long, narrow restaurant. "You placed your order and the food came out on a little electric train from the kitchen," recalls Tommy Rye, a Canadian Tire buyer who was on the trip. "You picked your food up as the train came past. Alf loved conveyer belts and all that sort of stuff."

For the Billes brothers, the most important business principle was a variation of the golden rule: if you treat the customer the way you would want to be treated, he will keep coming back. As a result, much of Canadian Tire's marketing program involved being nice to customers. One of the most successful initiatives was "road hazard insurance," launched in 1931, by which Canadian Tire undertook to insure its tires for one year against damage resulting from bad roads. Canadian Tire would either repair the damaged tire at no cost or replace it at a reduced price depending on how many months it had been in use.

This was a first in the industry and hugely popular among customers. Alf had conceived the idea while in charge of "adjustment," the official term for dealing with complaints from dissatisfied customers. The manufacturers guaranteed their tires against defects, but almost all problems were caused by bad road conditions and thus weren't covered by the guarantee. The result, recalled Alf, was that "every adjustment was a fight."

Adjustment was the most miserable aspect of the business. That's why Bill, who was president, had passed it on to Alf, his vice-president. "It was so hard on the

Guaranteed Savings

"Super-lastic" TIRES

25,000 MILE UNCONDITIONALLY GUARANTEED

Tire Facts!

DO you know that every $1.00 you invest in "Super-lastic" returns you $1.48 in actual tire miles and service? In the price chart below you will find two sets of prices given . . . . one is your cost on "Super-lastic, the other the regular retail price on other makes of equal quality. Learn true tire economy the "Super-lastic way"! Popularity! Just think, three, four, and as many as five hundred "Super-lastics" go into service in a single day. Popularity earned through value-giving . . . . you can't buy better tires at any place . . . . at any price . . . of any make . . so why pay more?

Remember . . . . we do not sell seconds, second hand or rebuilt tires. Every tire listed is a FIRST, new fresh stock and you must be satisfied or your money back (see back of order form . . . Satisfaction Guaranteed or money refunded).

Guarantee

ALL tires listed under cols. "B" and "C", also Giant Bus-Truck Tires, are guaranteed for 12 months on passenger car service or 6 months on commercial car service, against cuts, bruises, rim cuts, blow outs, faulty brakes and usual road hazards that would make the tire unfit for further service.

Should this condition develop with the tire, we will, at our option, either repair it, without cost to you, or replace it with a new tire making a charge to you at the rate of 1/12 the prevailing retail price on private car service and 1/6 the prevailing retail price on commercial car service for each calendar month, or fraction thereof, from date of purchase. Invoice to verify this date must be retained by purchaser, otherwise guarantee is void.

This Guarantee is not applicable to tires deliberately abused through neglect, or through fire, theft, running flat, or used on cars too heavy for that class of tire, worn out, or tires destroyed through faulty wheel alignment. Tires in which shoes are used or 30 x 3½ tires rim cut are positively not adjusted.

Standard manufacturers Warranty against defects in workmanship and material also remains effective during Bonded guarantee and thereafter for the entire life of the tire.

◀ The 1932 unconditional tire guarantee, a Canadian first.

constitution," Alf said. "There just had to be a better way. So I figured out that maybe we'd insure the tires. There was a lot of skepticism. People said it would cost us a fortune. Well, it didn't cost us a fortune."

Customers coming in expecting a fight were amazed when they didn't get one. And when they found out how little they were going to have to pay to replace a worn tire, they were "tickled pink," Alf recalled. "That's the basis on which most Canadian Tire problems were looked at: What would we want if we were in the other fellow's shoes?"[32] What was good for the customers was also good for Canadian Tire. Its main competition, Consolidated Tires, didn't match the guarantee, and it couldn't match Canadian Tire's prices either. Business boomed.

Free road maps were another favour to customers. Today, road maps are easy to come by. Back then, in the early days of the automobile, they were hard to find and expensive to buy. Why not, reasoned the brothers, make a gift of road maps to our customers, current and potential? And so, in 1926, Canadian Tire, wanting to build a mail order business, issued a one-page price list with road maps of Ontario and the Maritimes on the other side. They obtained a list of all car owners in those provinces and mailed the price list/map to all of them.

A one-page price list seems a small thing, yet in retrospect, it stands out as a turning point in the company's history. Mail orders flowed into Yonge and Isabella, and the one-page list was soon replaced by increasingly fatter catalogues. The booming mail order business caught the attention of aspiring entrepreneurs who saw an opportunity. Retail stores, they argued, could sell more Canadian Tire products more efficiently than a mail order operation could. And so the network of dealers, the foundation of today's Canadian Tire chain, was born.

"In those early days we had no ambition to have 400 Canadian Tire stores," Alf Billes said in 1992. "This was the farthest thing from our minds. We wanted to make our store in Toronto good for our Toronto customers, but we wanted to extend it from coast to coast by mail order. Then people saw the train or bus come in and there was stuff from Canadian Tire being unloaded. They said, 'Maybe we can get in between here.' These are the people that started the associate stores. We didn't go looking for them. They came to us."[33]

Bill wrote most of the catalogue copy, aided by Alf, who wrote the sections on tires and oil, his areas of expertise. Neither was given to understatement. The 1932 catalogue, for example, describing an improvement in inner tubes, called it "a crowning achievement in rubber chemistry ... a tube that laughs at old age." Much of the catalogue was filled with advertisements for car "accessories" that today are basic equipment, such as heaters and "windshield cleaners," meaning wipers. One year, apparently upset over rumours, probably spread by disgruntled competitors questioning the nationality and ethnic origin of Canadian Tire's owners and staff, Bill Billes published an open letter on the catalogue's inside front cover denying rumours that they were American, Jewish, German, or Italian. "The Canadian Tire Corporation ownership, management, and staff are Canadians of Anglo-Saxon descent," he wrote. "We are proud of the fact that we are an out-and-out Canadian organization."[34]

The catalogues were carefully designed, with lively artwork on the cover associating Canadian Tire with good times. A 1939 catalogue cover shows a happy young couple, with the man pushing his lady in a swing. Another, 29 years later, shows a beautiful girl in a bikini lounging on a beach towel while two men show off huge fish they have just caught. Meanwhile, an older man, embarrassed by the small size of his catch, hides his fish behind his back.[35]

The mail order operation illustrates another characteristic that made Canadian Tire a success: simple hard work. All staff members were expected to help fill the rush of orders that ensued whenever a new catalogue was issued. Every order was treated as a matter of urgency. Any order received by mail or telephone by 8 p.m. or even later would be rushed to Union Station for shipping on the next train.

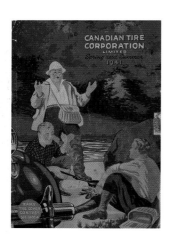

▲ The 1941 catalogue introduced a set of characters who would appear on every cover until the 1970s.

At 24 pages, the 1934 catalogue was the largest to date and the last to combine a price list with a road map.

▲ The branch stores at 1242 Bloor Street West and 458 Danforth Avenue both had gas pumps.

While many businessmen would be satisfied with one highly successful store, the Billes brothers were always restless. One store could not satisfy their ambitions. They knew they had a winning formula and were determined to expand it beyond Yonge Street. They were always game to try things, not all of which worked. In 1928, an experiment in branch stores failed. The idea was to complement the downtown store with one in the east end, on Danforth Avenue, and another in the west end, on Bloor Street West. The two stores, operated by managers employed by Canadian Tire, lasted about a year. "We didn't know how to run a branch store," Alf later admitted.[36] On the other hand, having garage owners sell Canadian Tire products did work. By the mid-1930s there were dozens of these "B" dealers throughout Ontario.

The failure of the branches coupled with the success of selling through garages led to an obvious conclusion: for whatever reason, the Billeses were better suited to distributing their wares through independent operators than being operators themselves of multiple retail outlets. In 1934, a Hamilton, Ontario, entrepreneur named Walker Anderson approached Bill with a proposal: he would open a store in Hamilton selling only Canadian Tire products. Anderson would own the store and pay Canadian Tire for his inventory. Canadian Tire, which had disdained the established wholesalers, would effectively become a wholesaler itself, shipping goods to Anderson, who would add an agreed-upon markup. Bill agreed but on one condition: Anderson could not name the store Canadian Tire. Instead, he should call it Super-Lastic Tire Sales.

The association would be clear to anyone who knew that Super-Lastic was Canadian Tire's brand. At the same time, if Anderson's enterprise didn't succeed,

the Canadian Tire name would not be tainted with failure. Anderson agreed. The deal was sealed with a handshake and he opened for business in a space that measured 30 by 25 feet. Other early associate stores, in London, Ontario, and in the town of Weston, just outside Toronto, also operated under the Super-Lastic banner. The fear of failure proved unfounded and eventually all the dealerships were renamed "Canadian Tire Corp'n Associate Store."

Hamilton is only 67 kilometres west of Toronto. But Anderson's store was the beginning of a system — dealer-operated Canadian Tire stores — that eventually would spread the company's name right across the vast expanse of Canada, from Atlantic to Pacific. The idea of owner-operated stores appealed to the two brothers because it was an affirmation of their concept of capitalist economics. From their own experience, they knew that, while a good employee will work hard, an owner will work harder.

Bill Billes rarely granted interviews to the press. An exception was one he gave to the *Financial Post* explaining why Canadian Tire relied on dealer-owners rather than using the branch-manager system favoured by other chains. "We believe in the principle of private enterprise," he said. "The dealer who owns his own business but profits from our better buying position, our advertising and our direction, has much greater incentive than a man on a salary, even if you include a bonus."[37]

The dealer network expanded rapidly and, by the end of the 1930s, there were 105 associate stores in Ontario, Quebec, and the Atlantic provinces. It could have expanded even more quickly but Bill Billes wouldn't let just anyone open a store just anywhere. For example, when two young men wanted to open a Canadian Tire store in Cornwall, on the St. Lawrence River near the Quebec border, Bill turned

them down. On the other hand, he told them that if they wanted to open a store in Ottawa, he would consider it. His reasoning was that Cornwall's industries might not survive the Depression, whereas the federal civil service never stops growing. They followed his advice and their Ottawa store, opened in 1935, was a success.

But that success didn't come easily. At the beginning, the owners of the Ottawa store, Neil "Mac" MacNish and Ed Leroy, worked day and night, sometimes sleeping under the counter to keep an eye on their $500 worth of stock. Leroy and his wife lived in one room at the rear of the rented premises. Things were going well until a fire destroyed everything. They didn't give up but instead reopened in a temporary location. Their next location for a time was one of the most modern in the chain. The partnership lasted until 1953, when they decided Ottawa needed a second Canadian Tire store. Leroy stayed in the original store and MacNish became dealer of the new one until his retirement in 1972.[38]

▲ Ed Leroy, Stan Hagen, A.J. Billes, Neil "Mac" MacNish, and Murray Rumple at the 1963 Dealer Convention, held in Toronto.

▼

TO OPEN more than 100 new stores in six years was amazing. To do it in the midst of the worst economic conditions in Canadian history was phenomenal. The Billes brothers, it seemed, were oblivious to the Depression. As early as 1930, just as the Canadian economy was plunging into uncharted depths, they demonstrated that they planned to ignore the collapsing economy. While other businesses were shutting their doors, Canadian Tire was outgrowing its premises. And so in 1930 the store was moved to larger quarters, directly across the street on the southeast corner of Yonge and Isabella. Three years later, it took over an adjacent building. The expanded store, bearing the impressive address 625–637 Yonge Street, took up most of a city block and featured a large clock over the entrance. It encompassed 35,000 square feet spread over three floors.

It was a brave move. To understand just how brave, it's necessary to appreciate the severity of the Great Depression. Triggered by the stock market crash of October 1929 and lasting until the outbreak of World War II, the Depression was an economic disaster. In its worst phase, half the working population of Canada was on some kind of temporary relief. The average yearly income was less than $500, yet the poverty line for a family of four was $1,000.[39] In 1933, close to a million people were unemployed out of a population of 11 million. Children went to school hungry or didn't go at all because their parents could not afford to clothe them. People fainted from hunger in the streets. Thousands of businesses went bankrupt.

▼

Why didn't Canadian Tire share in the suffering? One reason was its reputation for low prices, which were more important than ever during the hard times. Another was that its customers, the minority of the population that owned cars, were more affluent than the general population that didn't own cars. But perhaps the most important reason for the company's success during the 1930s was that everyone, including car owners, had to economize. This was bad news for the auto manufacturers and dealers but good news for Canadian Tire. Its spare parts and tires were in increasing demand as drivers tried to keep old cars on the road rather than buy new ones. The Depression also provided a plentiful supply of potential dealers wanting to own a piece of a business that was flourishing during the hard times.

Getting merchandise was a major problem for some retailers during the Depression years but not for Canadian Tire, which had built up good relations with suppliers. "Our idea was never to take the last penny out of the manufacturers' pocket and put it in ours. We knew that our suppliers had employees too," Alf Billes explained. "We really didn't feel the Depression seriously."[40]

But good workers were eager for jobs and worked hard to keep them, recalled Mayne Plowman, who later became a senior executive, in an interview in 2010. He had learned how to drive at the age of 10 as a farm boy in Manitoba. Then the hard times prompted his family to move to Toronto. In 1931, at the age of 17, he began work at Yonge and Isabella installing tires and car batteries. Later he worked as a counterman selling auto parts. Plowman worked 14-hour days to earn a base weekly salary of $35 plus another $50 or so in commissions — big money in the depths of the Depression.[41]

Myrel Pardoe also joined Canadian Tire during the Depression years. She was 16 years old when she was hired in 1932 as a summer replacement for a friend. Her job was to open mail for a salary of $8 a week. She made an extra $41 in bonuses that year and considered herself lucky to have a job.

When Myrel's friend rejoined the staff in the fall, Myrel feared she would be out of work. She went to J.W. and asked if she had to leave. Instead of letting her go, he gave her a raise and made her a permanent employee.[42] "There just weren't jobs," she recalled later. "People had no money. And so if you got a job you stayed at it."[43]

She certainly stayed at it: in April 2002, she was presented a pin commemorating her 70 years at Canadian Tire. She continued working part time until the fall of 2003; she died in 2004.

▲ Myrel Pardoe, Clifford Colvin, Elva Desmarchais, and Bill Preece each received a 25-year service pin and a cheque for $1,000 at the 1957 Pin Party.

AS PRESIDENT, Bill handled all buying and administered the company. Alf, as vice-president, was in charge of sales, including mail order, and service. The two worked smoothly as a team. "In all our years we never had a quarrel," Alf recalled. "Probably that was because he was the peacemaker. I always tried hard to get my way if I really felt it was best for the business." Yet if Bill was insistent in his opposition, Alf did not get what he wanted. Alf always deferred to his elder brother.[44]

Bill was the introvert, quiet and distant, whereas Alf was the gregarious one. Alf bubbled over with ideas for new ventures. Bill was more cautious, preferring a slow and steady path to growth.

The talents and energies of both were integral to the company's success. Alf had many ideas — not only the turntable to speed up the movement of cars in the service garage but also an automated car wash, a Canadian Tire gas bar, and on and on. Bill had one big idea: keep the balance sheet spotless. He hated debt and made sure Canadian Tire didn't have any. That's another reason he embraced the dealer system, and probably the most compelling one for him. Without the dealer system, Canadian Tire could not have expanded except on borrowed money. The beauty of collaborating with independent entrepreneurs was that they had to come up with capital to open the associate stores, thereby building Canadian Tire and increasing its revenues at no cost to the Billes brothers.[45]

Bill had a gruff exterior, yet he was kind and generous to employees. And he was scrupulously fair. On one occasion, as newly arrived merchandise was being unloaded from trucks, Bill decided to walk through the receiving department to get to his office. One of the workers didn't know him and yelled, "You're not supposed to be in here. Get out." Bill complied and entered the building by another door. Later, he surprised the employee by telling him who he was. Then he praised him for following the rules.[46]

Alf also had a rule: The customer was king. Gary Coniam, a retired employee, recalls telling a customer, shortly after joining Canadian Tire, that the store was closing at 6 p.m. "Don't ever say that to a customer," a more experienced clerk admonished him — Alf would consider it a firing offence.

Both brothers were imbued with a fierce work ethic. Martha Billes recalls driving past a golf course with her father one day. The course was busy and Alf remarked, "What a shame that all those people have nothing to do."[47]

They expected their employees to share their work ethic. The standard work day at Canadian Tire lasted from 8:30 a.m. to 10 p.m. for three days and 8:30 a.m. to 6 p.m. the rest of the week.[48] Often employees were expected to stay even longer.

One day, Mayne Plowman decided the job was too hard and that he would quit. Then, mopping the floor with other employees one night after closing, he noticed that Alf was mopping too. That impressed him so much that he decided to stay. He didn't leave until he retired four decades later.[49]

▲ Mayne Plowman giving a parts presentation at the 1960 Dealer Convention.

IN 1936, six years after moving to bigger quarters and with the country still mired in the Depression, Canadian Tire had a unique problem: its sales were growing too rapidly. When it moved into the premises on the southeast corner of Yonge and Isabella, the store had not needed all the space and had rented some of it out. Now the store was using every inch and was bursting at the seams. Residents of Isabella Street were in revolt and with reason. It was a struggle to get to and from their homes. Freight trucks, loading and unloading merchandise, blocked the street and sidewalks at all hours. Customers' cars waiting to get into the service department were lined up down the block.

There was only one solution: Canadian Tire had to move again. But this time it would be to a building big enough to last.

CHAPTER TWO

The roller skating years

THE GRAND CENTRAL MARKET, at the northeast intersection of Yonge Street and Davenport Road, opened for business on May 28, 1935. With its colonnaded facade and Spanish-style roof, it was a colourful addition to the Toronto streetscape. Intended as an uptown version of downtown's century-old St. Lawrence Market, it would, its promoters hoped, add some spark to Toronto's depressed economy.

Full-page newspaper advertisements invited every Torontonian to attend the opening ceremonies presided over by Duncan Marshall, the provincial minister of agriculture. "From the farm to the table" was Grand Central's motto, and 80 merchants stood ready to accommodate shoppers.

But the customers never came. In the dirty thirties, people weren't looking for new places to shop. Within a year, the Grand Central Market stood empty.[1]

The vacant building caught the attention of Alf (or A.J., as he later became known) Billes, who was looking for a new location for Canadian Tire's flagship store and the corporate office. It wasn't ideal, having been designed as a food market, with huge freezers and coolers on the lower level.[2] But it had two big advantages: it was just five blocks north of the existing store and it was massive — so big, in fact, that many employees doubted they would ever use all of its 69,000 square feet.

◀ Clerks on roller skates at the Yonge and Davenport store, 1940s.

▲ The Yonge and Davenport store, 1960s.

Bill (J.W.) Billes, ever the cautious one, was reluctant to move. But he couldn't deny that Canadian Tire had outgrown the Yonge and Isabella space, and so A.J. prevailed. The price for 837 Yonge Street was right — $130,000, some $45,000 less than the cost of building it several years earlier.[3] It was the first time Canadian Tire had owned real estate.[4] Eight years later, Canadian Tire bought 940 Yonge, a three-storey building on the west side of the street, and a third building on nearby Pears Avenue.[5] This assembly of buildings would house the flagship store, warehouse facilities, and corporate offices for almost three decades to come.

The Canadian Tire office workers had no problem making the move. They loaded their papers and equipment onto their wheeled office chairs and pushed them five blocks north to Davenport Road.[6] Renovating the market building to accommodate Canadian Tire wasn't so easy. A bowling alley was converted into a shooting range where hunting rifles could be tested. A theatre was transformed into a display department where new methods of exhibiting goods could be tried out. The mezzanine floor was rebuilt to accommodate "home office," as the corporate offices came to be called. The heart of the business, the retail operation, was on the main floor. On either side of a display of products were two immense counters running the entire length of the store, behind which clerks stood ready to take orders. As at Yonge and Isabella, customers would come to the counters and ask for

something they had seen on display or in the catalogue. The clerks would then go and retrieve the requested items.[7]

After the new location opened for business in 1937, a problem soon became apparent: the stock areas behind the counters were so vast that it was taking too long for the clerks to get back with orders. This was worse for the clerks than for the customers. Both those serving customers in person and those working on mail orders were on commission, and they complained that the long distances were reducing their earnings.

Then A.J.'s wife, Muriel, had an idea. Roller skating was a popular form of entertainment for young people at the time. As a teenager, Muriel Moore had loved the sport and often frequented skating arenas with relatives and friends. Why not, she suggested one day, speed up service by putting the countermen on skates?[8]

It was a brilliant plan. Soon sales clerks were racing about the place with car parts and other products under their arms or balanced on their shoulders. Not only was service speeded up, thereby boosting sales, but people were coming to Canadian Tire just for the entertainment value of seeing clerks on skates. "There were some visitors from the States who came in and asked, 'Is this the store where the clerks are on roller skates?'" recalls Fred Sasaki, who began his Canadian Tire career on skates and went on to become treasurer of the company.

Michael Levy, a retired Toronto schoolteacher, grew up near the store and frequented it. He says the neighbourhood kids all looked up to the countermen on skates. "They were so cool!" he exclaims. "I remember seeing one of them skating really fast with a muffler pipe in his arms and a cigarette dangling from the corner of his mouth. How cool was that?"

"They were amazing," adds Silverio Ferrari, a computer technician who also grew up in the area and visited the Canadian Tire store often. "They skated real fast and would often come within an inch of each other, but they never collided. It was like a ballet."

The survivors of that era all have skating stories to tell. Recalls Sasaki: "One time, the maintenance people left some little hoses on the floor. I was skating with merchandise in my hands and I tripped over a hose and fell. A.J. was standing right there. He didn't say anything, but I was embarrassed."

Although the store's terrazzo floors were difficult to navigate, the clerks became such expert skaters that mishaps were few. Bill McCullough, who went on to become a buyer, spent six years on skates. "You got so adept that you could roller skate better than you could walk," he recalls. "And you would carry heavy bins up and down stairs with your skates on."

▲ Ralph Codner, 1950s.

Skating ability became a required skill for aspiring Canadian Tire sales clerks. When Alan Warren, who later became a Canadian Tire executive and dealer, first applied for a job at 837 Yonge, A.J. asked him, "Do you know how to roller skate?" Taken aback, Warren sputtered, "Well, I have roller skated." That was true, but a more accurate answer to A.J.'s question would have been "no." Still, he got the job and, after some lessons from Ralph Slee, a fellow employee, became adept enough on skates.

Employees had to skate well to survive. "If you couldn't, you starved to death because you were on commission," recalls retired employee Keith Pickering, who donned skates when he joined Canadian Tire in 1947. He earned $3.90 for every $100 worth of goods he sold. "Much of it was small stuff," he adds, such as light bulbs for the home or car. "You had to sell quite a lot. There weren't many big items."

Elderly ex-employees credit the years of skating for their good health. Mayne Plowman was on skates for 15 years. Interviewed at the age of 96, he said, "Wearing those roller skates was good for our feet. It was good exercise. I don't have a problem with feet or legs or anything now. I put it down to roller skates." Bill McCullough, who was on skates six days a week for six years, was in good health

when interviewed at the age of 89. "My doctor laughed like the devil when I told him I was on roller skates six days a week and he said, 'That probably had a lot to do with your strong heart.'"

One other store, in Laflèche, Quebec, equipped its clerks with roller skates. Employees also used skates at the distribution centre on Sheppard Avenue in Toronto.[9]

Putting sales clerks on roller skates was a good way to make the best of a bad system. The process of buying something at Canadian Tire could be awkward and time-consuming in the 1930s and 1940s. The customer would look at the display and then go to the counter and say, for example, "I'd like to buy a hammer. I liked the one at $2.95." Sometimes the clerk would accompany the customer to the hammer display to confirm his choice before going to fetch it in the stock area. Then he would write up the quantity, the part number, a description, and the price of all items purchased; add it up; and collect the money from the customer. If the clerk made a mistake and undercharged, the clerk paid for it.[10]

Having customers jostling each other to get the attention of sales personnel behind a vast counter never made any sense, asserts Bill McCullough. The take-a-number system had not yet been invented and there were no orderly queues. On Friday nights, it was chaos at the counters. It got so busy that J.W. and A.J. would often help out, although they never put on skates.[11] A clerk would say, "Who's next?" and a dozen customers, all crowding around the counter and waving their hands for attention, would shout, "I'm next, I'm next." It's amazing, McCullough thinks, that nobody decided to have the customers take numbers. Perhaps it's not so amazing. Many good ideas — like having countermen wear roller skates — seem obvious only in retrospect.

Unlike the auto parts and hardware items, Canadian Tire's assortment of sporting goods was elaborately displayed. "The bicycles were all lined up and your job every morning once you were on the counter there was to go out and dust these bicycles and keep everything neat and tidy," relates Keith Pickering, who sold sporting goods. "During fishing tackle season, there were big displays behind the counter, and we had the lures rotating inside a window."

The sporting goods salesmen were not on commission, so Pickering could spend plenty of time with customers. An avid fisherman himself, he would advise on good fishing spots and put together a package for a young novice. "I'd bring the lures out, and tackle boxes, and I'd pick a rod for them and a reel. You had to serve the customers."

▲ The grand counters at the Yonge and Davenport store filled only a portion of the building, c. 1937.

◀ Customers at the automotive parts counter in the Yonge and Isabella store.

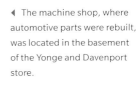

◀ The machine shop, where automotive parts were rebuilt, was located in the basement of the Yonge and Davenport store.

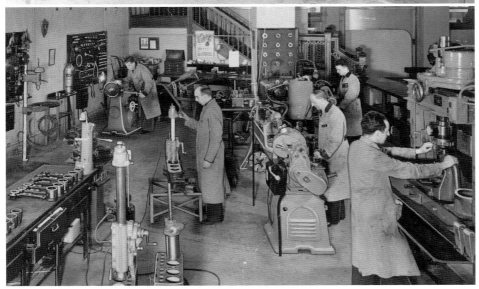

▲ A clerk helps a customer make his selection.

CARD NO.

CHECK NUMBER AND PRICE ..take to cashier..

DO NOT BEND OR MUTILATE IN ANY WAY

CANADIAN TIRE CORP'D LTD.

▲ Blank self-selection card.

The Billes brothers never stopped searching for ways to win the favour of customers and potential customers. When King George VI and Elizabeth, the queen consort, arrived in Toronto in 1939, the first official visit to Canada by a reigning monarch, Canadian Tire erected a massive viewing stand across the entire Yonge Street frontage of the store so that customers could view the royal couple as they passed by. It was also the year Canadian Tire ventured into Quebec for the first time, opening stores in Rouyn and Trois-Rivières. And it was the year that the world plunged once again into war.

▼

THE DEPRESSION had brought hard times to most businesses, yet Canadian Tire sailed through it. World War II, on the other hand, kick-started the economy, as the Canadian government poured vast sums of money into the war effort that began on September 10, 1939, with the declaration of war against Germany. The war years, however, were tough times for Canadian Tire. The problem wasn't lack of demand but lack of supply.

"During the war our supply was cut off," recalled A.J. "What tires were in inventory you weren't able to sell. The only people who could get a tire were in some way connected to the war effort, and they got the permits and used up the tires we had in stock."[12]

Canadian Tire could have boosted prices on goods that were in short supply, but that would have conflicted with its golden rule policy of customer relations. "A lot of our old customers have written and told us about how they couldn't have run their car during the war if it hadn't been for the fact that we were able to supply them with parts," A.J. recalled later. "We could have doubled prices on a lot of things, but we didn't. We thought we were entitled to the same margin of profit as we always enjoyed. And that didn't hurt us."[13] To help its customers keep their vehicles going, Canadian Tire published instruction booklets on car maintenance and repair.

J.W., using his connections in the tire industry, was sometimes able to get "reliners," shells of old tires that could be placed inside worn ones to keep them on the road for a few months longer. "We sold them for a buck each," recounted A.J. "We could have got three dollars easily. People lined up for blocks."[14] Mac MacNish, one of the two Ottawa dealers, said later that motorists would gladly have paid $10 a pair during the war for reliners.[15]

▼

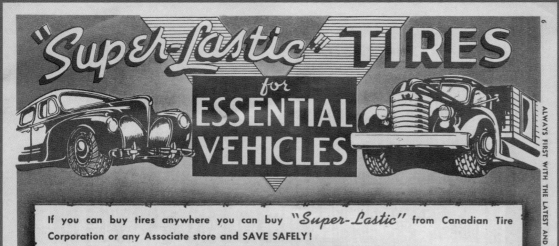

"Super-Lastic" TIRES
for ESSENTIAL VEHICLES

If you can buy tires anywhere you can buy "Super-Lastic" from Canadian Tire Corporation or any Associate store and SAVE SAFELY!

You are privileged to use your official order to buy tires wherever you wish. No one dealer has any preferred claim on YOUR permit.

Should present restrictions on tire sales be modified, during the life of this catalogue, then "Super-Lastic" will be immediately made available according to any new Goverment regulations.

Dealing with wartime restrictions and tire rationing, Canadian Tire continued to keep prices fair and used its catalogue to inform customers about eligibility and availability of tires.

TIRE SIZES RELEASED TO ELIGIBLE CLASS "B" VEHICLES

FARMERS, RURAL MAIL CARRIERS, WAR WORKERS UNDER TRANSIT PLAN, ETC.

SIZE	War Tires 4-Ply	Pre-War Tires 4-Ply	6-Ply
700/15		22.45	12.40
550/16		9.92	
600/16	16.65	See Next column	
625/16	20.80	See Next column	
650/16	20.80	See Next column	
700/16		18.80	22.75
750/16			32.75
525/17	15.30		
525/18	15.30		
550/18	14.00	8.75	
475/19	14.00	8.75	
500/19	12.55		
450/20	12.55	7.98	9.20
475/20		7.98	9.20
500/20		7.98	9.20
440/21	12.40		
450/21	12.40		
525/21		9.95	

THOSE ELIGIBLE TO BUY

While certain types of vehicles are generally considered eligible, new rulings are regularly issued to tire rationing representatives embodying changes to govern existing conditions. Your regional tire rationing officer is appointed to fairly interpret these rulings and to give you information governing your particular case.

Generally speaking, tires in this section (B) are available to FARMERS who do not own a truck, WAR WORKERS registered under the transit plan, RURAL MAIL CARRIERS and other ESSENTIAL USERS.

We and all our associate stores carry official application forms for tire permits and shall be glad to assist you with your tire problems.

TIRE SIZES AVAILABLE TO CLASS "A" VEHICLES

600x16

CTC JUNIOR 4-ply, XX28	$8.50
CTC SPECIAL 4-ply, XA28	$9.85
CTC SPECIAL 6-ply, XB28	$11.90
Master Super-Lastic 4-ply, XE28	$13.98

625-650x16

De-luxe, 4-ply 625/16, XG37	$15.65
De-luxe, 4-ply 650/16, XG38	$16.85
New Super-lastic, 4-ply 625-650/16, XC38	$13.70
Snow and Mud, 650/16, 4-ply, TW38	$18.85

WHO IS ELIGIBLE?

Tire sizes in this group are only available to those considered highly essential. The list includes certain professional groups, police, fire fighters etc. As in the case of "B" users full information is available through your local tire rationing officer.

MODIFICATION

Effective May 12th, 1943, these sizes in 4 ply only, were also made available to certain class "B" vehicles. Your nearest rationing officer has full details.

INNER TUBES

A complete range for every tire.

SIZE	CTC SPECIAL Regular Red Cat. No.	Price	SUPER-LASTIC Heavy Red Cat. No.	Price	SUPER-LASTIC Hi-Speed Black Cat. No.	Price
700/15					XL55	2.89
550/16					XL49	2.29
600/16	XJ50	1.67	XK50	1.84	XL50	2.29
625/16	XJ50	1.67	XK50	1.84	XL50	2.29
650/16					XL51	2.89
700/16					XL51	2.89
750/16					XL52	3.95
525/17	XJ4	1.59	XK4	1.75	XL4	2.29
550/17	XJ4	1.59	XK4	1.75	XL4	2.29
600/17	XJ4	1.59	XK4	1.75	XL4	2.29
650/17	XJ4	1.59	XK4	1.75	XL4	2.29
375/18					TL7	2.25
525/18	XJ2	1.44	XK2	1.59	XL2	1.95
550/18	XJ2	1.44	XK2	1.59	XL2	1.95
600/18	XJ5	1.74	XK5	1.88	XL5	2.35
650/18	XJ5	1.74	XK5	1.88	XL5	2.35
700/18					TL53	3.05
475/19	XJ3	1.45	XK3	1.62	XL3	1.97
500/19	XJ3	1.45	XK3	1.62	XL3	1.97
525/19	XJ5	1.74	XK5	1.88	XL5	2.35
550/19	XJ5	1.74	XK5	1.88	XL5	2.35
600/19	XJ5	1.74	XK5	1.88	XL5	2.35
650/19	XJ5	1.74	XK5	1.88	XL5	2.35
700/19					TL53	3.05
450/20	XJ1	1.29	XK1	1.43	XL1	1.67
475/20	XJ1	1.29	XK1	1.43	XL1	1.67
500/20	XJ1	1.29	XK1	1.43	XL1	1.67
525/20			XK10	2.10	XL10	2.60
550/20			XK10	2.10	XL10	2.60
600/20			XK6	2.10	XL6	2.58
650/20			XK6	2.10	XL6	2.58
440/21	XJ1	1.29	XK1	1.43	XL1	1.67
450/21	XJ1	1.29	XK1	1.43	XL1	1.67
500/21	XJ8	1.53	XK8	1.74	XL8	2.10
525/21	XJ8	1.53	XK8	1.74	XL8	2.10
600/21			XK6	2.10	XL6	2.58
500/23					TR6	2.60

Don't risk tire failure. Be sure to include tubes in your application if needed.

Because of the shortages of merchandise, no new dealerships were allotted during the war. Available merchandise was shared among the existing dealers at the normal price. The hugely successful radio department was closed for the duration of the war, as radios were needed for military purposes. Fifty Canadian Tire employees joined the Canadian forces; seven of them were killed in action.

The division of authority between the two brothers continued as before. J.W. was president and in charge of buying and administration, while A.J. supervised sales and service. J.W. was the boss but, A.J. recounted much later, "He pretty well gave me my head. I looked after all the moving of merchandise, and he was the office man. I didn't interfere with his office, and he didn't interfere with my store."

J.W.'s office was upstairs, whereas A.J.'s was downstairs, on the same level as the store. The hiring process in those days was informal: people looking for work would wander in off the street and show up at A.J.'s office, the door of which was usually open. One such person was Fred Sasaki, who, one day in 1944, read in a newspaper ad that Canadian Tire was looking for warehouse employees. He went to see A.J. During the interview, Sasaki said he hoped his being Japanese would not present a problem.

A.J. said, "It doesn't matter to me if you are Japanese. As long as you work hard, that's all I care about."[16]

In 1944, with Canada and its allies at war with Japan, Japanese ancestry was an issue for many employers. On the evening of December 7, 1941, hours after the Japanese attack on the American naval base at Pearl Harbor, two Mounties interrupted dinner at the Sasaki home in Vancouver and arrested his father, the owner of a log and lumber export business. All males of Japanese origin between the ages of 14 and 45 were ordered to move at least 100 miles from the Pacific coast, and many were interned in camps.

Fred Sasaki was then in his final year of commerce at the University of British Columbia. He went to Calgary, where a sister lived. His UBC professors, sympathetic to his plight, sent him the course materials. "I wrote my exams at the University of Calgary in a big hall by myself," he recalls. "I was fortunate enough to pass with first class honours, and I got my bachelor of commerce."

Sasaki's father was interned in a camp, first in Alberta, then in Ontario. After a year, he was sent to peel potatoes as a cook's helper in a lumber camp in northern Ontario. Meanwhile, Fred's mother and sisters were in a camp in the B.C. interior.

The federal government had set up an office in Toronto to help displaced Japanese relocate and find jobs. Sasaki reported there and was told to go for an interview the next morning at a chemical plant. He did so and, after waiting an hour, was told,

▲ Fred Sasaki delivering a profit-sharing presentation to employees, late 1950s.

▶ Fred, late 1970s.

"Sorry, we can't hire you. If we did, the other workers would go on strike." His next attempt was at a chain of bakery shops, where he was hired on the condition that the other employees be told he was Filipino, not Japanese. The boss said, "After you work here a few months and they find out what you are like, then you can tell them that you are Japanese and I think everything will be okay."

Sasaki took the job, which involved unloading 100-pound sacks of sugar and flour. "After a few months, I told the other employees that I was Japanese and they accepted me," he relates. But he wanted to find an employer who might eventually appreciate his business credentials; in addition to his UBC degree, these included three years serving Japanese-speaking customers at a Royal Bank branch in Vancouver's Chinatown.

So his next stop was Canadian Tire. He worked in the warehouse for two years and then was promoted to stock keeper in the parts department. One day, the representative of an auto parts supplier based in Midland, Ontario, asked about his background and Sasaki described his educational qualifications. On his next visit, the man said that his office manager/accountant had quit and asked if Sasaki would be interested. Sasaki decided to take the job and told A.J. of his decision. A.J., not wanting to lose the personable young man, talked it over with J.W., who agreed to offer Sasaki a job as an accounts payable clerk.

It was a more junior job than the one available in Midland but by then Sasaki's family had been reunited in Toronto and he didn't want to leave them, so he decided to stay at Canadian Tire. He stayed for 45 years, becoming a trusted executive, a key figure in the growth of the company, and one of the few to develop a close relationship with both J.W. and A.J. Billes.

Ralph Codner also played an important role in the early years at 837 Yonge. "He was a tiny, tiny man with a big smile on his face," recalls Martha Billes, who as a child often visited her father at the store. Codner was bursting with energy, always on the move, and rarely sat down, even to eat. He had joined Canadian Tire in 1941, becoming head of the accessories department and then manager of the store. Because it was the only corporate-owned store and because it was attached to the executive offices, 837 Yonge had a special importance. It was where new ideas about display, product lines, and other merchandising techniques could be tried out before being urged upon the dealers. Later, Codner became chief purchaser for the corporation.

Another key player was Les Wheeler, who was in charge of advertising. As an account executive with a Toronto advertising firm, he had tried everything to land

▶ Ralph Codner and Mayne Plowman at the 1955 children's Christmas party.

▲ Installing Ralph Slee's colossal Santa Claus — then the largest in the world — 1956.

the Canadian Tire account. He even designed Canadian Tire ads and sent them to J.W., but J.W. refused to see him. Then the company went ahead and placed some of Wheeler's ads in Toronto's *Star Weekly*, among other publications. One day, in 1947, J.W. called Wheeler and asked if he would like to come work for Canadian Tire. He did and, in addition to creating newspaper ads, relieved J.W. of responsibility for the catalogue. Under his direction, it became a slick, professionally designed publication. It also became steadily thicker. In 1956, Wheeler created the first eight-page flyer. The Canadian Tire flyers became a huge success, sparking a dramatic increase in sales.

Another well-known name from the early years was Ralph Slee, whose specialty was store layout and displays. One of his more memorable displays was a colossal Santa Claus, seven storeys high, erected in front of the store in 1956. It almost collapsed on the street in a rainstorm.[17]

Other key employees busied themselves maintaining good relations with the associate dealers. Norman Jones, the first permanent employee the Billeses had hired while still at Yonge and Isabella, offered help and advice to dealers from home office, while Joe Haggas drove across Ontario, Quebec, and the Maritimes to see them in person. Ernie Hanson, meanwhile, was the one dealers called when they needed goods in a hurry.[18] In 1941, the first Dealer Convention was held so that all the associates and home office executives could discuss problems and share ideas. The annual Dealer Convention, now an important Canadian Tire institution, serves the same function.

Various members of the Billes clan worked at Canadian Tire over the years. Among the earliest were Mae Tuckman, a sister of the two founders, who worked in the pricing office; J.W.'s daughter, Gwen, who was on the switchboard; and his son John, who worked in the store and, later, in the accounting department.

▼

ALEX BARRON, like all successful salesmen, was persistent. Working for the Toronto brokerage firm Fry & Co. in 1939, he was trying to sell his services as a financial advisor to J.W. Billes. But J.W. was having none of it. Barron made repeated phone calls but couldn't even get through to J.W.'s secretary. Then, out of the blue, he received a call inviting him to come and meet J.W., who proceeded to turn over his personal investment portfolio to Barron's supervision.

Barron had moved to Toronto at the age of 17 from Paris, Ontario, to work as a stockbroker. His smooth manners and impeccable three-piece suits belied his small-town roots and inspired confidence in clients. Obviously, he made a strong impression on J.W. In 1944, under Barron's guidance, J.W. made an important decision: he decided to offer shares of Canadian Tire to the public. It was a surprising move at first glance given that J.W. had always been close-mouthed about the company's finances; issuing shares meant opening the books to the public. On the other hand, he had long been fascinated with the stock market, where he had both lost and made money. He had made enough during the 1930s to buy himself a yacht, the *Jogwendi*, named for his children, John, Gwen, and Dick.[19]

Issuing a limited number of shares was a way to cash in on the success of the company without losing control of it. As J.W.'s letter in the prospectus issued by Fry & Co. stated, Canadian Tire was a hugely successful company: "In 20 years of business, up to 1941, the company had an unbroken record of increases in annual and monthly earnings, and the sales each year exceeded those of the previous year, and each month, exceeded those of the corresponding month of the previous year." The war, J.W. went on, had cut into revenues thanks to the tire shortage and restrictions on motoring. But "earnings have remained substantial and we feel that with the coming of peace we can count on a resumption of the steady growth of the pre-war years."

All of the two brothers' existing shares were converted into 100,000 common (voting) shares, of which J.W. owned 60,000 and A.J., 40,000. Each of them sold 7,500 shares to the public at $10 each. By 1946, the shares were worth $39.50 apiece.

▼

THE END of the war in 1945 did not immediately end the tire shortage at Canadian Tire. Gutta Percha went out of business, and Goodyear stopped supplying private distributors such as Canadian Tire. Dunlop, a long-time supplier, announced it needed all its tires for English cars that were going to be manufactured in Canada. That never happened, but Dunlop's tires were not popular with Canadian Tire customers anyway, so the relationship ended.[20]

A.J., who was in charge of the tire business, found the solution to his problems in Ohio. James Hoffman, president of Ohio-based Mansfield Tire and Rubber, said he would be happy to supply the company with as many tires as it needed. Not only that, he would be prepared to build a plant in Canada so Canadian Tire would not have to pay import duties. It wasn't long before a new factory making Mansfield tires bearing Canadian Tire's Super-Lastic brand was built in Barrie, Ontario. "It was one of the earliest factories with automatic equipment, which others didn't have, so we had some excellent prices," A.J. said. "And it was an excellent tire."[21]

Although the era of scarcity was drawing to a close in the postwar years, J.W. and A.J. never lost their distaste for wastefulness. Alan Warren recalled in an interview before his death in 2010 that, when A.J. hired him, he was given a pencil. A.J. said that when the pencil was less than three inches long, he would get a new one free of charge. But if the pencil were misplaced or left at home, he would have to buy one from the Canadian Tire office. "I never paid for a pencil all the time I was there," Warren recalled in his memoirs. "It's amazing how it sharpens your focus on controlling your own expenses when it comes out of your pocket. This has stood me in good stead all of my business life, as did many of the lessons I learned from A.J."[22]

J.W.'s prediction that the war's end would see a revival of Canadian Tire's growth could not have been more accurate. The postwar baby boom was a bonanza for Canadian Tire. Larger families needed larger houses, triggering a construction boom in the suburbs that led to the development of the first suburban shopping malls. The suburban lifestyle depended on the car. Dad needed one to get to work. Mom needed one to ferry the kids about and travel to and from the shopping mall. Thus was born the two-car family.

▼

▲ Gladys, J.W., A.J., and Muriel Billes (flanked by dealers) at the 1953 luncheon held in celebration of the company's 40th anniversary.

The two-car family in its bungalow with a big backyard and two-car garage needed stuff. Lots of stuff — for the car and the house and the backyard. The suburban family needed tools to keep the house in good repair, equipment for the kitchen, toys and sports gear for the kids.

The challenge for Canadian Tire was to become *the* place where all of that could be found. Tommy Rye understood the implications sooner than most. He was a buyer and decided that plumbing supplies were a natural extension of the existing line of hardware. Dealers resisted, saying they didn't have the space, but Rye prevailed and plumbing became an integral part of Canadian Tire's offering. Rye then proposed that the store carry toys. Why? For one thing, Canada was teeming with kids in the 1950s and, for another, toys would help draw the half of the population Canadian Tire had overlooked — women — into the stores. He was right again.

Rye had grown up on Collier Street, around the corner from the Canadian Tire flagship store and home office. He joined the company in 1941 at the age of 14. "I started in the purchasing department," he recalls, "checking off the packing slips after the stuff came in and then checking off the purchase order. If it wasn't busy I had to go down to the receiving department to work on unloading trucks. I worked everywhere in the company. You would work anywhere they needed you. I don't think they had titles until about 1960. My title was just 'employee.'"

Rye joined the air force as a navigator but the war ended before he was shipped overseas. Back at Canadian Tire in 1946, he became a buyer. Previously, J.W. did all the buying himself, but now it was too much for one person. Being a buyer could be more exciting than it sounds. Rye might have to go to the suburbs to get a special order that a customer needed in a hurry — for example, a muffler assembly consisting of muffler, exhaust pipe, and tailpipe. He would go by motorbike. "It was great riding a motorcycle down Yonge Street with all that stuff over your shoulder," he remembers. "I guess it was dangerous, but in those days you didn't think of it."

From the very earliest days of the company, J.W. Billes had been on the lookout for goods he could offer to his customers at low prices. The postwar period offered some unusual opportunities. A manufacturer that had a contract to supply the military with tire pumps had 100,000 pumps left over at the end of the war. J.W. decided to buy about 70,000 of them. "People thought he was crazy," Rye recalls. "We had tire pumps for a long, long time. But we made money on them." It was just another example of Canadian Tire's knack for underselling the competition. "There wasn't that much in competition in those days except the service stations and little garages, and they hated Canadian Tire," Rye said. "They called it 'Canadian trash.'"

One of the oddest purchases he made, in collaboration with Ralph Codner, was of a large quantity of disposable summer dresses constructed of a heavy paper that felt like cloth. They sold for 88 cents each. "We picked them up at a ridiculous price and they walked out of the store," Rye recalls. "Most people thought if they wore it once they would get their money's worth."

By 1956, Canadian Tire comprised 150 associate stores selling some 15,000 products, and distribution — warehousing all those products and getting them to the stores on time — had become a critical part of the business. At Yonge and Isabella, the warehouse was on the third floor and A.J. and his "boys" could often be seen hauling tires up three flights of stairs. At Yonge and Davenport, products were stored in three locations: a five-storey warehouse behind the store and two nearby buildings. It was obvious that Canadian Tire needed a new, purpose-built warehouse that could accommodate its rapid growth.

The company acquired a 41-acre site on Sheppard Avenue East and a ground-breaking ceremony, with J.W. wielding the shovel, was scheduled for November 13, 1956. However, when the time came, J.W. was in the hospital. It might have been expected that A.J. would replace him but, out of deference to his brother, A.J. refused and insisted that J.W.'s wife, Gladys, do the honours.[23]

The 225,000-square-foot building opened in 1957. Some employees who later played important roles in building Canadian Tire started their careers roller skating around 837 Yonge; others did the same at the Sheppard Avenue Distribution Centre.

▲▲ Employees of the Niagara Falls store, *c.* 1956.

▲ Employees of the Quebec City store, 1960s.

▶ Associate stores: (from left, top row) Hanover, Ont., 1941; Walkerton, Ont., 1942; St. John's, Nfld., 1956; (second row) Windsor, Ont., 1952; Goderich, Ont., 1949; Valleyfield, Que., 1955; (third row) Parry Sound, Ont., 1959; Orangeville, Ont., 1949; Hull, Que., 1959; (fourth row) Kincardine, Ont., *c.* 1965; Saint John, N.B., 1953; Hamilton, Ont., 1968; (bottom row) Prescott, Ont., 1966; Bathurst, N.B., *c.* 1950; Fenelon Falls, Ont., 1969.

▶ Stores and service bays: (from left, top row) Sudbury, Ont., *c.* 1952; Fenelon Falls, Ont., 1947; Belleville, Ont., 1946;
Belleville, Ont., 1946; Forest, Ont., 1955; Alliston, Ont., 1956; (second row) Kingston, Ont., *c.* 1955;
Stratford's delivery van, *c.* 1945; Windsor, N.S., *c.* 1950; Charlottetown, P.E.I., *c.* 1948; Alylmer, Que., 1964;
(third row) Stratford, Ont., 1967; service bay at Yonge and Davenport, 1937; Arnprior, Ont., 1968;
(fourth row) Yonge and Davenport, 1965; Alliston, Ont., *c.* 1976; Belleville, Ont., 1968; Val-d'Or, Que., 1978;
(bottom row) Belleville, Ont., *c.* 1965; unidentified service bay, 1977; Campbellford, Ont., 1975;
Antigonish, N.S., 1989.

▲ Sheppard Avenue warehouse
groundbreaking, November 13,
1956. Gladys Billes is seated at the
wheel of the grader, while A.J. Billes
holds the golden spade.

One of them was the late Arch Brown, who went on to run what was then the biggest Canadian Tire store in the country, in Barrie, Ontario.[24]

Before donning skates at the warehouse, Brown had a promising career with General Motors, where he was the youngest person ever to rise to the post of district manager. Brown was a friend of J.W.'s son Dick and had sailed on the *Jogwendi*, J.W.'s yacht. One day, Dick, an executive in the corporation, called and offered him a job at Canadian Tire. Brown said he wanted to be a dealer, not a corporate executive. Dick Billes promised that if Brown stayed for five years and did a good job, the corporation would finance his first store. Brown agreed and left GM.

"My mother broke down and started to cry because she thought I was doing so well at GM," Brown recalled. "She thought I was throwing away my career to work at a discount store."

The lure of owning one's own business is powerful, and Brown was just one of many talented individuals who left promising careers at major companies to become Canadian Tire dealers. "I saw so many people in GM who were in their late 50s and early 60s and just hanging on by their fingers. I saw in many cases those fingers being stepped on and down they would go. I swore I wouldn't be put in that position. That was the main reason why I left, and why I emphasized to Dick that I wanted a store and didn't want to be at home office in administration."

Al Cox joined Canadian Tire in 1952. Working for Parker Pen at the time, he one day walked off the street and into A.J.'s office and was hired on the spot. His first

job was "slugging" — loading trucks — at the warehouse behind the Yonge Street store. When the Sheppard Avenue Distribution Centre opened, Cox worked there as a dispatcher. Later he became one of the company's first computer programmers.

The state-of-the-art Sheppard Avenue facility was a big step forward from the makeshift warehouses Canadian Tire had relied on until then. When John Kron joined the company as vice-president of distribution during the 1960s, he found a way to make it even better. The building had two storeys, which meant a lot of extra work to get goods from the upper level down to the truck bay. Kron devised a ramp with an indoor railway to which pallets could be attached to bring boxes of merchandise down to the shipping area with less labour.[25]

The building was often invaded by flocks of pigeons, an unsanitary nuisance that had to be removed. "So the guys used to catch them, put them in cartons, and ship them out on a truck," Cox recalled with a chuckle. "And, of course, when they opened the box at the store in North Bay or wherever, the damn pigeons would fly out."

J.W. Billes never got to see the Sheppard Avenue warehouse. He died just three days after the groundbreaking ceremony in November 1956, a month and a half short of his 60th birthday. His doctor had prescribed Chloromycetin, a powerful antibiotic, to treat a throat infection. In rare cases, this drug can trigger pernicious anemia, leading to death.[26] Dick Billes believed that is what happened to his father.

A.J. blamed J.W.'s early death on overwork and chain smoking. There is no doubt

▶ Aerial view of the completed Sheppard Avenue warehouse, *c. 1961.*
▲ Al Cox with Canadian Tire's first home office computer system, *c. 1960.*

J.W. Billes, 1954.

that J.W. was a workaholic. "J.W. never moved from his office from the time he came in [to] the time he went home," recalls retired employee Art Arai. "He was always at his desk." Mac MacNish, the Ottawa dealer, had a vivid memory of a business trip to Toronto in 1935. As he was walking past the Canadian Tire building at 10:30 p.m., he glimpsed J.W. at his desk poring over some papers. He knew J.W. was a tireless worker who often kept at it into the night, but he was surprised nevertheless: it was New Year's Eve.

J.W.'s energy was boundless. "We would work in the store from 8 a.m. until 10 at night and then, when the snow was around, we would close the store and go up to Rosedale golf course and ski," A.J. once recalled.[27]

J.W. was a complex man, a brilliant business strategist, tough but fair. "J.W. once said that the success of Canadian Tire is a four-way street," said Arch Brown. "There are the supplier, the corporation, the dealer, and the customer. It had to be good for all four."[28]

Norman Jones, the first permanent employee ever hired by Canadian Tire, became the first to attain 25 years of service, and J.W. decided he should be rewarded. A party was held in Jones's honour during which J.W. stood to congratulate him. He said that normally someone with 25 years service to an employer would get a watch. J.W. then pulled up the sleeve of his jacket to show the watches all the way up his arm — he had collected them from others at the party. "If you've worked 25 years and you haven't got a watch, you didn't deserve one," he said. "But you deserve something." He then handed Jones a pith helmet filled with travel brochures and said, "I want you to take this, figure out where you want to go, and take an extra month holiday." After that, the three weeks extra holiday plus $1,000 cash for 25-year employees became a Canadian Tire tradition.[29]

"A lot of people looked at J.W. and said he was a gruff old man," said Tommy Rye. "But he wasn't. He didn't show it often, but he had a heart of gold. If you got to know him, he had a different personality."

But he could also be strict and uncompromising. Fred Sasaki, who worked closely with him and whose desk was just outside his office at 837 Yonge, recalls overhearing a conversation between J.W. and his son Dick one Saturday morning.

"Dick wanted to go to university, but J.W. insisted that to learn the merchandising business he didn't need a university education. It was quite a discussion, and it lasted a while. Dick really wanted to go, but J.W. insisted that he learn the business. I think that Dick should have gone to university but J.W. was quite stubborn about it."

▲ Mayne Plowman presents A.J. with a 25-year service pin at the first Pin Party as J.W. watches on, 1954.

J.W.'s plan was that Dick would work in the accounting department under Sasaki's tutelage for a year and then proceed to work in other areas until he knew the business. But that didn't happen and Dick stayed in accounting. "I guess his father thought that if he went to different areas under A.J.'s control that it may not work out," says Sasaki.

Instead, Dick served as secretary to the board of directors for four years. His father may have been grooming him as his successor, although that was never explicitly stated. The day after J.W. died, Dick moved into his office. But to occupy the president's office and to be the president are two different things. At the age of 28, Dick had neither the experience nor the knowledge to run Canadian Tire. A.J. considered the job his and the board of directors agreed.

▼

J.W.'S SUDDEN DEMISE on November 16, 1956, was a blow to Canadian Tire. He had overseen the company's growth from a two-man operation in an old garage to a national powerhouse in automotive products and one of the largest retailers in the country. He was aggressive yet cautious at the same time and his knowledge of the business was unrivalled; he kept details of thousands of products stored in his head.[30] The only major misstep he had made was his unusual will, which would prove troublesome to both the company and the Billes family.

His younger brother was a seasoned entrepreneur and an imaginative marketer. He was also an expert on tires. But was he qualified to be the ultimate boss of a rapidly growing, increasingly complex enterprise such as Canadian Tire? The jury was out.

One thing was obvious: A.J. had no intention of abandoning his thrifty, unpretentious ways. He refused to occupy J.W.'s large second-floor office, instead remaining in modest quarters on the ground floor of 837 Yonge.[31]

▼

A.J. AND HIS BROTHER never quarrelled,[32] but they did have their disagreements. Sometimes A.J. was able to convince his brother of the rightness of his case — for example, on the need to move to larger premises. But J.W. had the final say. Two of A.J.'s proposals J.W. had blocked were the translation of Canadian Tire's mail order catalogue into French and the entry of the company into the gas retailing business. J.W. did not want a French catalogue. On this issue, A.J.'s was the voice of pragmatism. The company by now had millions of existing and potential customers in Quebec, many of them unilingual francophones. It was good business to address them in their own language. So one of A.J.'s first acts after taking the helm was to commission a translation of the catalogue, to be issued for the fall and winter of 1957–58.

As for the English catalogue, it promised "everything for the two-car family." But something all drivers depended on wasn't sold by Canadian Tire: gasoline. At Yonge and Isabella, there had been a single pump. However, since the move to Yonge and Davenport, Canadian Tire had not sold gas because J.W. did not want to antagonize the big oil companies. A.J. disagreed; he thought it made no sense for the largest automotive retailer in the country not to be in the gasoline business.

And so a Canadian Tire gas bar opened in 1958 outside the corporate store at Yonge and Davenport. About the same time, another opened in Hamilton, adjacent to the first associate store.[33] The choice of Toronto as the site of the first gas bar was based on careful study. Unlike Montreal and Ottawa, which already had

▲ The first French catalogue, fall/winter 1957–58.

independent discount gas stations, Toronto was dominated by the big companies, all of which offered the same high prices. In Toronto, A.J. reasoned, he could make a splash by challenging the big companies and, by putting Canadian Tire's name in the limelight, draw more customers to the stores.

However, he knew J.W. had been right in not wanting to go to war with the oil giants because, while Canadian Tire was big, they were bigger. "The oil companies sold gas at a fantastic margin of profit," he said. "I couldn't resist it, but I didn't dare cut prices."[34] The solution was a stroke of genius: charge about the same as the oil companies for gas but give customers 5 per cent off in the form of coupons that could be spent only in Canadian Tire stores.

Thus was born Canadian Tire money. It allowed the company to undercut the oil companies without advertising lower prices and at the same time to boost traffic in the stores. Canadian Tire money has been a mainstay of the company's marketing strategy ever since. The first bills, valuable collectors' items today, carried the smiling tire and running dollar image given to Canadian Tire by the mystery artist who had dropped into the Yonge and Isabella store years before.

A.J. had been thinking about discount coupons well before the gas business was launched. He and his wife, Muriel, during a holiday in the United States, had seen them being handed out at Shell Oil stations and thought Canadian Tire

▲ Pears Avenue gas bar, Toronto, 1961.

▲ A sketch of the first Mor-Power gas bar under construction, 1958.

should do the same.[35] Muriel was familiar with store coupons because she did her grocery shopping at the Loblaws store at Yonge and St. Clair Avenue in Toronto. Loblaws gave its customers gold stamps that could be glued into books. Fill up a few books and you won a lamp or card table or some similar prize. Muriel didn't like the sticky coupons and she pressed A.J. to have Canadian Tire come up with something better.[36]

Ralph Slee, head of the display department, and his assistant, Bernie Freedman, created the designs. The first series of coupons was on poor-quality paper that tended to fall apart when folded. The next was printed on real banknote paper by British American Bank Note Co., printers of Canadian currency.[37] It featured Sandy McTire, a cheerful Scot sporting a tam-o'-shanter. Scots were supposed to be thrifty and so Sandy was an appropriate symbol for a store that promised the lowest possible prices.

It happened, however, over Muriel's strenuous objections. The banknote company, recalls Martha Billes, "said we had to get plates. Plates were awfully expensive and we always did everything on the cheap. Surely somewhere there were rejects. There were two plates that were perhaps suitable. One was the goddess Diana with two or three wolfhounds. She was nude from the waist up with flying scarves across the appropriate places. She would have been perfect for a stock certificate of the era, which was probably what she'd been for.

"The other one was a Scotsman with a hat on. These plates, and pictures printed from them, were circulated around. My mother thought that a Scotsman was terrible because there was no Scots blood in the Billes family, certainly not on my mother's side. It really rankled and went against her Methodist upbringing. But corporate decided it was going to be the Scotsman. My mother was really quite distraught about this but she did accept the money and we did embrace it as our own. There was a lot of infighting, discussion, gnashing of teeth to get the money actually created. The [corporate executives] were absolutely thrilled because they were worried about counterfeiting and the banknote company said, 'We'll always supply you the grade that the government moves out of. So when the government moves up to another grade of linen, then we'll move you up so you'll be able to follow them if you choose to.'"

When the Toronto gas bar opened in November 1958, the cashiers at first were extra generous with the coupons, handing out Canadian Tire money worth 25 per cent or more of gas purchases. As the word got out, there were lineups at the pumps all day long.[38] The gas bar was so busy that corporate employees, including

A.J. Billes, pitched in to pump gas. Spies from the oil companies sat in cars across the street.[39] The coupon system fit perfectly with the Billes brothers' strong belief that cash was good and credit was bad; unlike oil company gas stations, Canadian Tire gas bars did not issue credit cards. The coupons were a reward for paying cash. "We were trying to show people that credit costs money," said A.J.[40]

The oil companies were unhappy — but not so unhappy that they refused to supply Canadian Tire. The primary supplier was U.S. oil giant Texaco.[41] However, the threat of supplies being cut off was always present. In 1960, the oil companies decided to teach Canadian Tire a lesson. It started with price cutting. "It was a gas war," says Martha Billes. "The big guys filled the city with cheap gas and pushed the price down and down. They were quite determined to put us out of business."

A.J. was equally determined that they wouldn't succeed. He ordered the creation of a special coupon. It was labelled "Gas War Savings Coupon — Redemption Deferred" and would be redeemable only after the gas war was over and prices had risen above 49 cents a gallon. The front showed the oil companies in the form of Hercules wielding a ball and chain, with oil refineries in the background. Down in the corner was a tiny Canadian Tire gas bar employee offering savings to his customers. On the back, A.J. urged his customers to join him in solidarity against the bullies: "With your help, together we will defy the giants and win the gas war. Standing alone, pitted against giants, Canadian Tire Corp. hasn't a chance, but — shoulder to shoulder with you, the customer — we will win this war. Our mutual cause is morally and economically right."[42]

Fighting the oil giants wasn't cheap. At the height of the war, one of the gas bars was losing $25,000 a week. "It got to the point where the oil companies were selling gasoline at a price below our cost," A.J. recalled later. "They could have continued and actually put us out of the gasoline business. But I wasn't going to take it if I didn't have to. So I said to the customers, 'Keep coming, we're going to give you a good deal. You won't be able to cash the coupon now, but you'll be able to cash it in the future when the war's over.'"[43]

In June 1960, the oil companies cut off Canadian Tire's supplies. But still A.J. wouldn't give in. He bought 60 million gallons of gas from the Soviet Union, a bold move at the height of the Cold War. And he pushed ahead with plans to build more gas bars. By 1961, there were 16 Canadian Tire gas bars and more in the works.[44] By then, the gas companies had grown tired of selling gas cheaply and had to concede that the Canadian Tire gas bars were a fact of life. The gas war was over.

▲ Gas bar signage informs customers about how and where to redeem their gas and store coupons, 1960s.

Canadian Tire money

▲ Sandy McTire, first appearing in 1961 when the store cash bonus coupons were introduced, became synonymous with the company's emphasis on savings and value.

◥ A cash-paying customer is delighted to receive cash bonus coupons, also known as Canadian Tire money.

CANADA is the only country with two currencies. One of them is issued by the Bank of Canada, the other by Canadian Tire.

One evening, A.J. Billes and his second wife, Marjorie, were enjoying dinner during a holiday at a Bermuda resort when the conversation turned to the non-official currency, best known as "Canadian Tire money."

A.J. claimed that not only were most Canadians familiar with Canadian Tire money, many of them carried it in their wallets. That couldn't possibly be true, replied a non-Canadian doctor sitting at their table.

"About half the people here are Canadians and I'll bet most of them have got a coupon in their wallets right now," replied A.J.

"Nonsense," declared the doctor.

"We went around and found that almost every Canadian had a coupon in their wallet and those that didn't said they had some at home," A.J. recalled later.*

The doctor, added Marjorie, was annoyed at being proven wrong.

Canadian Tire money originated in 1958 when the company opened its first gas bar. Rather than advertise lower prices than the oil companies, A.J. decided to offer coupons worth 5 per cent of a gas purchase, redeemable only in merchandise at Canadian Tire stores. In 1961, the company began issuing the money in the stores as well. In that year, British American Bank Note Co., one of the Royal Canadian Mint's official printers, was hired to print the coupons. From then on, they looked and felt just like real currency — all the more reason for customers to collect them and spend them.

Some, like Thayer Bouck, collect

A gas war savings coupon, issued for a brief period in 1963 at the height of the gas war. The text on the reverse encourages customers to lend their support by accumulating these coupons.

A special coupon for use at a lubritorium.

A selection of Canadian Tire money. The earlier bills were signed by Fred Sasaki and A.J. Billes and featured the tire and dollar logo on the front. The 1958 notes had a rural scene on the back. Over the years there have been many series and versions of coupons, distinguished by colour, size, style, and authorized signatures. A number of these were created to commemorate special occasions, such as the 1976 Montreal Summer Olympics.

Josefina Abeleda surrounded by Canadian Tire money in the coupon department, 1979.

Canadian Tire money but never spend it. Bouck is president of the Canadian Tire Coupon Collectors Club, founded in 1990. He owns 50 binders filled with 54 years of Canadian Tire money in a variety of designs and denominations. Collectors look for rare notes such as "replacements," which have unusual serial numbers because they were issued to replace a series of notes that were damaged during the printing process. Such a coupon would be worth about $100, says Bouck, a retired math teacher. Rare bills from the original 1958 series can be worth as much as $2,000.†

Another sought-after rarity is the "Saski" note. All Canadian Tire coupons are signed by the CEO and the treasurer but, on one occasion, the printer could not find treasurer Fred Sasaki's signature, so he wrote it himself, spelling it incorrectly as "Saski."

There are countless stories about Canadian Tire money. Jim Ryan, when he was president of the petroleum company, was at a gas bar one day as part of a regular program of meeting customers. A man who operated a courier service showed up with $12,000 worth of Canadian Tire money in bundles. He wanted to convert it to regular currency, so Ryan paid him $10,000 for it.

Although most of the bills are in small denominations, such as 5, 10, or 25 cents, they can add up to large sums. Former dealer Reg Quinn kept a bill-counting machine at the back of his store because customers often arrived with as much as $100 worth of Canadian Tire money. "They would have stacks and stacks of it. Above a certain limit, we'd have the cashier call a manager and we would take it into the back to count."

There are also innumerable stories of dishonest Canadians trying to pass the coupons abroad. On one occasion, however, it was a dishonest Mexican who wound up with a pocketful of Canadian Tire money. In a park on the outskirts of Oaxaca, he pointed a knife at a tourist and demanded money. The tourist opened his wallet and handed him a wad of bills bearing the likeness of Sandy McTire. The thief, satisfied, departed.‡

In 2004, the Canadian Imperial Bank of Commerce was embarrassed when an employee in New Brunswick somehow confused Canadian Tire money with the official currency and loaded some into an automated teller machine. The bank customer who was expecting $20 bills was not amused when he got Canadian Tire notes worth a few cents each instead. The bank apologized and issued a refund.**

A PROFIT-SHARING PLAN FOR CANADIAN TIRE CASH CUSTOMERS

UP TO 5% IN CASH BONUS DISCOUNT NOTES ON ALL PURCHASES*

They look like money...
They feel like money...
and can be spent like money at all
Canadian Tire Associate Stores!

Now, When You Make a Cash Purchase at most Canadian Tire Associate Stores, you get profit-sharing CASH BONUS DISCOUNT NOTES to a value of up to 5% of your total purchase. These notes can be used as CASH, for any subsequent purchases of ANY merchandise listed in the Canadian Tire Catalogues, newspaper advertisements, or displayed in Canadian Tire Stores. You can spend them in part payment (together with actual money), or save them up until you have enough to buy anything you need with nothing but CASH BONUS DISCOUNT NOTES. That bench saw, new tire, vacuum cleaner, or anything else you have wanted for so long can be YOURS without spending a dime, because your Canadian Tire Store will accept these notes as hard cash!

Q. How is This Profit-Sharing Plan Possible?

A. Canadian Tire has been able to negotiate substantial freight-cost savings in some areas, and now we wish to pass this saving on to YOU, the customer, in the form of CASH BONUS DISCOUNT NOTES.

Q. Will the 5% CASH BONUS DISCOUNT be Obtainable at All Canadian Tire Associate Stores?

A. At the present time more than 65% of the Canadian Tire Associate Stores give 5% in CASH BONUS DISCOUNT NOTES. Others give 4% or 3%, while some, because of extra high freight costs, are not yet able to participate in this PROFIT SHARING PLAN. See the back cover of this catalogue for the actual percentage given at your nearest C.T.C. Store. If there is no percentage shown, please be patient — we are working on a saving for you too!

*NOTE: Since Canadian Tire's CASH BONUS DISCOUNT NOTES are available only in denominations of 3¢ and up, there is a minimum purchase requirement of 59¢ in stores offering 5%; 69¢ in stores offering 4%; and 79¢ in stores offering 3%.

▲ The 1961 fall/winter Canadian Tire catalogue introduces store cash bonus coupons, which previously were distributed at gas bars only.

▲ ◥ Promotional signage of the 1980s and 1990s.

▲ Commemorative coupons issued for Canadian Tire's 50th and 75th anniversaries.

Canadian Tire cash buys dream wheels

It took 15 years and $1,053 in colourful bills to meet teenage goal

KENYON WALLACE
TORONTO STAR

HE SAVED HIS MONEY — Norman Byers, 9, of Mispec is the proud owner of a new bicycle which he bought with $103.16 in Canadian Tire money he saved up over five years. Norman started with about $16 in the discount coupons from his grandmother, Thelma Byers, which his grandfather, the late Stephen Byers, had saved. He bought his bike at a sale the store was having. The total price came to about $118, and his family helped with the difference. He is the son of Alfred and Maryanne Byers.

◀ ▲ Over the years, people have saved and redeemed Canadian Tire money for various purposes: Norman Byers (left) bought his dream bicycle in 1984, at age nine; Brian McPherson, in 2011, after 15 years of coupon saving, was able to fulfill his childhood dream of owning a ride-em lawnmower.

Canadian Tire money is Canada's oldest loyalty program. In recent years, loyalty programs have become an important part of the arsenal of major retailers, and Canadian Tire's is evolving with the changing times. In 1995, the Options MasterCard was introduced, giving customers the ability to collect money on the card, and not just at Canadian Tire but anywhere in the world that accepts MasterCard.

In 2012, Canadian Tire began testing a new loyalty program, based on the Canadian Tire Advantage loyalty card. A card does something coupons can't — it tracks customer purchasing patterns so that the company can market directly to individual customers. If a customer's purchases reveal a strong interest in fishing, merchandise related to fishing can be promoted to that customer. Eventually, says CEO Stephen Wetmore, the Advantage card may be accepted at all stores in the Canadian Tire family so that, for example, money earned buying auto parts at Canadian Tire or apparel at Mark's could be redeemed for hockey gear at SportChek.

As for the ever-popular paper money, it was in the news again in 2012 when Corin Raymond, a Toronto singer-songwriter, raised more than $3,000 of it to record a new album at The Rogue Studios in Toronto. Rogue has been accepting the money for 20 years. "I started doing it because I realized we will always need coffee, toilet paper or light bulbs," explained James Paul, owner of the studio. Raymond raised the money from fans during a cross-country tour, returning to Toronto with a knapsack stuffed with coupons.††

Canadian Tire money is only given for cash purchases and the stores dispense much less of it than the 5 per cent of the purchase price customers got years ago. As the use of cash declines, so will the amount of Canadian Tire money in circulation. But as long as some customers still use cash, Canada's alternate currency will continue to have a place in our wallets. During an interview, CEO Stephen Wetmore pulled a freshly minted five-cent note out of a drawer and proudly pointed to his signature. He joked, "That's the reason I took the job, right? To get my name on Canadian Tire money."

Petroleum became a separate division of Canadian Tire and continued to challenge the status quo. Arch Malcolm, the division's first head, was an innovator in the service station business. At the Yonge and Davenport location in 1958, Canadian Tire introduced North America's first "lubritorium" where drivers could get a quick lube and oil change, performed by servicemen working in a pit underneath the vehicle.[45] It was more convenient than leaving the car for the day at a general purpose garage. Lube and oil operations have since proliferated across North America, but Canadian Tire's was the first.

Malcolm also pioneered the idea of customers pumping their own gas to keep labour costs down. The Canadian Tire gas bar on Main Street in Hamilton may have been the first self-service gas station in Canada.[46] By the end of 1974, Canadian Tire had 54 gas bars, several of which had been converted to self-serve.

A marketing technique A.J. especially liked was to give the customer happy surprises. "We pulled some dandies with the gasoline bars," recalled Arch Brown. "One of A.J.'s rules was that the customer always had to benefit. We would put on our gas pumps the same price as we put on our signs, but we charged the customer less than that. That's when we would see tremendous crowds. You could see the customers coming and smirking to themselves, thinking, 'These guys are stupid, they're giving money away.'"[47] They weren't stupid, of course. There is no better advertising than lineups outside your store. Marketing is all about attracting attention, and Canadian Tire, under A.J.'s leadership, was very good at it. When power lawnmowers first came out, a Canadian Tire team took two of them up the street from the flagship store to a small park on Yonge Street and started cutting the lawn. No one had ever seen a power lawnmower before and a crowd gathered to watch. It wasn't long before a city Parks Department official showed up. "What's going on?" he wanted to know.

"We're cutting your grass for you," explained Alan Warren, then a tire salesman.

"Says who?" asked the city official.

Attention had been paid. The Canadian Tire crew returned to the store, mission accomplished.[48]

▼

ONE DAY, Pops Desjardin, who had been in charge of maintenance of the Canadian Tire facilities for many years and had recently retired, came to see A.J. Billes with a complaint. "He was so annoyed that people wouldn't believe him, that he

"The best way to keep a man steadfastly earning profits for you is to tell him first that you will share your profits with him." — A.J. Billes

was damn near a millionaire," A.J. recalled.[49] A.J. told him to enjoy the problem because it was a nice one to have. Its cause was Canadian Tire's generous profit-sharing plan.

Profit-sharing, the system by which employees share in the profits of the company beyond their weekly paycheques, was of great importance to A.J. He wanted Canadian Tire's staff to think of themselves as owners of the business, not just employees of someone else's business. He was sure that owners worked harder and more carefully than employees. Profit-sharing, A.J. believed, increased productivity by as much as 20 per cent. Moreover, employees who are owners are less likely to join labour unions, and A.J. hated labour unions.[50]

So profit-sharing wasn't just an act of generosity; it was in Canadian Tire's own self-interest. "From the janitor to the president, you were a part owner of the company and you gave your best effort," says retired treasurer Fred Sasaki. "In my view, that is the fundamental reason why Canadian Tire is so successful."

But A.J. was motivated by more than self-interest. For him, profit-sharing was essential to the healthy functioning of the capitalist system. "For the fundamental good of the greatest number of people, capitalism appears to have no equal," he told a group of dealers-in-training in 1975. "But greed can and is eroding its effectiveness and could some day destroy it. Greed leaves a vacuum that politicians quickly fill with their brand of socialism....[51]

"The best way to keep a man steadfastly earning profits for you is to tell him first that you will share your profits with him ... Capitalism can be saved for the greatest good for the greatest number of people. It can and will be saved through enlightened self-interest."[52]

The Billeses started profit-sharing in the early years of their business by awarding bonuses twice a year to employees based on their performance. But cash bonuses, while a good incentive, don't turn workers into owners. Although J.W. supported the idea of profit-sharing, he wasn't convinced that it should take the form of stock ownership. He preferred to issue bonuses, sometimes in the form of government bonds.[53] But A.J. pushed for stock ownership and, after J.W.'s death, he forged ahead with a plan for the corporate employees who worked at home office and the distribution centre.

The plan, introduced in 1957, worked like this: Every year, the board decided on how much of the annual profit to put toward profit-sharing. If it was 20 per cent, each employee would get the equivalent of 20 per cent of his or her salary in Canadian Tire shares. The employee could take cash instead, but it would be much less than the value of the shares. Employees who left the company would get a portion of their shares depending on their length of service; after 10 years of service, they got all of them. In addition to the regular annual profit-sharing, an employee could use up to 10 per cent of his or her salary to buy more shares, in which case the company would contribute shares equal to half the employee's additional purchase.

For those who stayed, the shares were untouchable until enough of a nest egg had been built to provide a full salary for 15 years after retirement. Then the employee could cash in some of it for special purposes, such as a child's education.

As the years passed, the amount of shares in employees' hands built until, in 1975, they owned 16 per cent of the Class A non-voting shares and 12.2 per cent of the common (voting) shares.[54]

Not only was the plan uniquely generous but the performance of the Canadian Tire stock made it all the more profitable for employees. By 1971, a share that had been worth $25 eight years earlier had become, after several splits, 15 shares worth $525. Many Canadian Tire employees retired rich. One executive, a man who had joined Canadian Tire without completing high school, had shares worth $6.4 million. A janitor earning about $12,000 a year retired in the early 1970s with $300,000 — about $1.8 million in 2012 dollars.[55] A switchboard operator who worked for Canadian Tire for 18 years had a weekly salary of $85 when she retired. A lawyer working on her estate after she died found a document saying she owned Canadian Tire stock worth $150,000, or about $874,000 in 2012 dollars. "Please confirm that a decimal point has been misplaced," he wrote. It hadn't.[56]

IN 1961, Canadian Tire sold its store at Yonge and Davenport to Fred Billes, A.J.'s eldest son. There were those who considered Fred unqualified to run the store, including his cousin Dick, who said J.W. would never have allowed it.

The store, which had been managed by Peter Montgomery, who later became a dealer in Brampton, was a money-loser because it was paying more than its share of operating costs, such as electricity and heating. Corporate executives treated it as their store and often used it to test new products and store layouts. Upon taking over as dealer, Fred insisted that more of the operating costs be assigned to the corporation. Corporate would have to pay rent for its share of the building and could no longer grab product off the shelves whenever it wanted. Corporate officials were not pleased.[57] "My brother Fred was very hard-nosed," observes Martha Billes. "He didn't mind taking them on."

The sale of the main store signalled the company's total commitment to the dealer system and left Canadian Tire, now with no corporate-owned stores, as a rarity among franchised chain operations, a status it still maintains. Also in the 1960s, Canadian Tire branched out into a new field, financial services, a business that would become an increasingly important part of its revenue stream in the years to come.

The Billes brothers built Canadian Tire on cash. They did not ask their suppliers for credit and they encouraged customers to pay in cash. But every company has to change with the times. It was a sign of those changing times when, in the 1960s, Canadian Tire entered a business that is all about credit.

The origins of Canadian Tire's financial services business go back to 1961 when Bruce Wilson formed Midland Shoppers Credit in Welland, Ontario. Midland was in the factoring business: A merchant is owed money by a customer, but the customer can't pay right away. The merchant wants the money now, so he sells the debt to the factor, who pays him a discounted amount. The factor collects the full amount from the customer later. The difference between the full amount and the discounted amount is the factor's profit.

One Friday afternoon at the Welland Club, a private club for business leaders, Wilson got to talking with Grant Adams, a Canadian Tire dealer. Adams was complaining that he had so much money tied up in accounts receivable that he couldn't afford to build the service bays he needed. On Monday morning, Wilson called Adams and said, "Grant, if you want to sell those receivables and build your service bays, then you and I should get together."

Adams's store became Wilson's first Canadian Tire client and others soon followed, selling their receivables to Midland for a 10 per cent discount. The arrangement with Midland meant that dealers could offer credit to more customers than before. The Canadian Tire credit card did not yet exist, so each customer had to set up an account with the store. Despite this inconvenience, customers were eager to use credit. Sales increased, since those customers with only $20 cash in their

▶ Grant Adams in his Welland, Ontario, store, the first to implement self-service, 1958.

pockets were no longer limited to buying $20 worth of merchandise. As a result, stores using Wilson's services were performing better than stores that weren't.

Dean Muncaster, a young vice-president at home office, was impressed. In 1966, he invited Wilson to meet him in Toronto. Muncaster wanted Midland to service the credit of all the Canadian Tire dealerships in southwestern Ontario. Wilson didn't have the financial clout to this on his own, so he sold a majority interest in the company to Canadian Tire. By 1968, Midland was serving most of the Ontario stores. It then became a subsidiary of Canadian Tire, with Wilson remaining as head of Canadian Tire Acceptance Ltd.

Before the deal was completed, Wilson had a long talk with A.J. "Of course, he was a cash man, a proponent of cash money," Wilson recalls. "So it was kind of interesting. We spent the whole afternoon going back and forth."

By the time that conversation with Bruce Wilson took place, A.J. was no longer president of Canadian Tire. The discussion of the virtues of cash versus credit is symptomatic of the reason why: A.J. came from a simpler time, a time when, if you wanted to buy something, you saved up your money first. Those days were ending.

Soon Canada would be awash in credit cards, including Canadian Tire's own. The age of buy now, pay later had arrived.

Many other things were changing. Canadian Tire was growing at a breakneck pace and becoming ever more complex. The universities were launching business schools to teach bright young people how to manage such complex organizations. Canadian Tire had always been managed by people who had moved up through the ranks. Some of them, starting out on roller skates at 837 Yonge, had not even finished high school. These were the people who had built Canadian Tire, and they had done their jobs well. But the world had changed. Wisely, A.J. decided it was time Canadian Tire had professional management.

It wasn't that A.J.'s lack of a university education had hindered him in the past. In some ways, it had even helped because it made his "Prairie farmer" act all the more convincing. Arch Brown recalled overhearing a conversation between A.J. and a senior official of Imperial Oil over a gasoline contract. A.J. was saying things like, "Do you really mean that? Gosh, that's unbelievable." It was almost, Brown said, "as though he had a straw in his mouth. He just acted like he was a Prairie farmer, and the Imperial Oil guy let his guard down. Then all of a sudden A.J. sprung the trap, and the fellow didn't know what had hit him."

Despite the pressures of running a fast-growing company, A.J. never abandoned his famous open-door policy. "It didn't matter if you were the janitor or vice-president," recalls retired buyer Ron Down. "If you wanted to talk to him, you knocked on his door and asked for a few minutes. I don't think he ever said no. You could go in and talk to him about anything."

A.J. was developing diabetes and his doctor had ordered him to slow down. But, at age 64, he was still full of energy and had no intention of retiring. Leaving the president's duties to someone else would give him plenty of time to work on the project closest to his heart — profit-sharing, which to his dismay had not yet been adopted by the dealers. Leaving the top job would also give him a chance to get more involved in the company's core product. A.J. knew more about tires than anyone and just because he was co-founder and a major shareholder didn't mean he couldn't also be a tire buyer. "I am," A.J. announced happily at a board of directors meeting on June 17, 1966, "going back with the staff."

▲ A.J. Billes, c. 1963.

▶▶ The Hanover, Ontario, store's sporting goods display showcases the recently expanded Mastercraft line of baseball equipment in addition to fishing and camping supplies, 1950s.

CHAPTER THREE

The Dean of Canadian Tire

THE MUNCASTERS were a Canadian Tire family. Of seven brothers raised on a northern Ontario farm, five became Canadian Tire dealers. The most successful was Walter Muncaster who, in 1939, became manager of the Sudbury store. Six years later, a second mortgage on his house and a personal loan from J.W. Billes enabled him to buy the store.[1]

Walter Muncaster went on to become one of the most influential Canadian Tire dealers. He was a founder of the Canadian Tire Dealers' Association, which represents the interests of the dealers to the corporation. About a dozen of his employees went on to become dealers themselves.[2] Muncaster's store was among the first to successfully introduce self-service, removing the sales counter and letting customers handle the goods and bring their own purchases to the checkout.

"My dad figured you want to look at the merchandise — you want to feel and touch it," recalled Walter's son, Dean, in an interview before his death in March 2012. "Buying a hammer without being able to touch it didn't make sense to him at all. So he said, 'Let's put this stuff out.'" The Billes brothers had tried self-service in their Yonge and Isabella store in Toronto but gave up on it because of too much theft. But Walter Muncaster was committed to the concept and this time it worked.

◀ Dean Muncaster with Alex Barron,
long-standing chairman of the board, 1973.

▲▲ Walter Muncaster, in 1939, demonstrates his support for the war effort by decorating his car with a "bomb" aimed at Adolf Hitler.

▲ A young Dean Muncaster conducts a business session at the 1960 Dealer Convention.

▲ The newly expanded Sudbury store ready to open in 1952.

▲ Arch Brown, A.J. Billes, and Dick Billes, with their wives Helen, Muriel, and Norma respectively, at the 1960 Dealer Convention banquet.

Self-service reduced labour costs and boosted sales. In 1956, Walter Muncaster's store became the first to reach annual sales of $1 million.

Dean Muncaster was an employee at his father's store from an early age. After school and on Saturdays, he stocked shelves, helped customers, and installed tires. When Dean was 18, his father went away for a month and left him in charge of the store and its 40 employees. "It was challenging. I ended up having to think seriously about firing my brother-in-law," he recalled with a laugh.

Muncaster went on to study business at the University of Western Ontario in London and then at Northwestern University in Chicago, where he obtained a master's degree. While at Western, he wrote a paper on Canadian Tire. He did not remember what the paper said or whether it was he or his father who sent it to A.J. Billes in 1957. But A.J. must have been impressed because he invited the 24-year-old graduate in for a talk and hired him.

Muncaster was the first Canadian Tire employee hired directly out of university and the first with an MBA. Others would follow in his footsteps, both as executives and consultants. By the late 1950s, Canadian Tire had become one of Canada's largest retailers, offering a wide array of products and services to millions of people from a steadily growing number of stores. To grow and prosper, such a company needs information, massive doses of it. Extracting and analyzing information was what Muncaster had been trained by two business schools to do.

Before Muncaster's arrival, home office knew the sales and profits of each store, but not much else. It lacked the information needed to judge accurately the comparative performance of stores, to know which ones needed extra help or maybe a new dealer. One of Muncaster's first tasks was to introduce more sophisticated performance measurements, such as sales per employee, sales per square foot, and inventory turns (the number of times the inventory is sold per year). These kinds of data are elementary in retailing today but were not yet widely used in the 1950s.

"The basic thing I was trying to do was identify what made certain stores more profitable than others," said Muncaster. "Why did some stores have better sales growth than others? When we had the answer to that question, we could implant it in the minds of the less successful dealers."

He found "a huge spread" between the top-performing stores and the under-performers, the main difference being the ability of the dealers. Some of them were making as much money as they wanted and saw no need to make changes or work harder. That was fine for them but not for the corporation. Muncaster's work enabled home office to set benchmarks that all dealers were expected to achieve.

After three years of working for A.J. in Toronto, Muncaster decided, in 1960, to return to Sudbury to help run his father's store. The reason? The job he really wanted was president and he didn't think it was available; when A.J. retired, Muncaster thought, the top job would go to a Billes. "It didn't appear to me that there was any way in which I was going to be able to run the operation if Dick was still there," he explained.

Dick Billes, J.W.'s son, seemed to be the most able of the offspring of the two founders. As vice-president of purchasing and a board member, he was also the most experienced. He was intelligent, serious, and conservative — too conservative, in A.J.'s opinion. J.W.'s other adult children were not involved much in the company. In contrast, two of A.J.'s children, Fred and David, were board members. The eldest, Fred, had made it clear that he wanted the top job. He was handicapped, however, by a mercurial temper that resulted in embarrassing outbursts of profanity. "Fred was without question a very smart person," recalls Biff Matthews, a lawyer who later represented him in a takeover battle for the company. "Fred also understood people very well. He would have made the right decisions and that would have been good for Canadian Tire. But he was a bit rough — he had sort of a truck driver persona. I don't think he had the manner to be the CEO of a public company."

A.J.'s two other children, David and Martha, were too young and inexperienced to be considered for a major position in the company. Anyway, David, a mechanical engineer, wanted to build racing cars and had no interest in working for Canadian Tire. As for Martha, in those days a woman's place was thought to be in the home, a view her parents shared. Her early career at Canadian Tire had consisted of a part-time job on the switchboard and another as a cashier at the gas bar; she had turned down an offer to work in the company cafeteria.[3]

The move back to Sudbury did not mean Muncaster was cutting his ties to home office. He was appointed to the Canadian Tire board that same year and he stayed there. He also continued to be involved in dealer selection. Back in Sudbury, he busied himself with a pet project: devising a better product numbering system. The objective, he said, was to get a deeper understanding of the value of a store's inventory by product classification. With that knowledge, the dealer could ensure he had his money invested in items his customers actually wanted to buy.

Back then, most retailers relied on the product identification markings supplied by the manufacturer. Muncaster's system made it easier to track the profitability of the thousands of different items in the store. Let's say the item was a hammer. With this new system, there were two digits for the product classification

▲ Fred Billes with his wife, Barbara, 1965.

(hand tools), two more for the item classification (hammers), and two more for the specific model of hammer. After the system was developed in Sudbury, it was introduced throughout the chain.[4]

It wouldn't be the last time that an important technological advance originated in a dealership. In the late 1970s, two Ontario dealers, Reg Quinn and Don Graham, introduced computerized cash registers to give them better control of inventory. On their own initiative, they hired two University of Waterloo graduates in programming. It took them a year to build the software and get it running.

Quinn and Graham had produced the company's first automatic ordering system based on sales, to replace the then existing manual system. The result was more timely ordering of products and better-stocked shelves. The corporation liked it so much that it bought the software from Quinn and Graham and introduced it in stores across the country.

▼

SHORTLY BEFORE CHRISTMAS 1961, A.J. and Muriel went off on a Caribbean cruise. Before leaving, A.J. ordered the Canadian Tire stores in Toronto to stay open on Boxing Day. But the dealers didn't want to open and so Dick Billes countermanded A.J.'s order. A.J. heard about it, came back early from his holiday, and again ordered the stores to stay open. He told Dick never to do such a thing again. For Dick, who was barely on speaking terms with his uncle, it was the breaking point. He quit his job at Canadian Tire and, three months later, asked the board to fire A.J. and appoint him president in his uncle's place. The board declined. Dick then went to work as a consultant for Shell Oil, which was considering launching a chain of automotive and hardware stores to compete with Canadian Tire.

With Dick out of the picture as a potential successor to A.J., Dean Muncaster saw no reason to remain in Sudbury. He returned to the corporation full time in 1963 and was made vice-president of purchasing, systems, and development. Although he denied that his eventual appointment to the presidency was a done deal when he came back, his unofficial title was heir apparent.

"Dick wasn't there any longer and I hadn't seen anything between 1960 and then that led me to think that Freddy was automatically going to become president," Muncaster recalled. "So I probably felt I had a reasonable shot at it."

Asked to assess Fred Billes, Muncaster said, "Fred was about as far away from a linear thinker as you could imagine. You would be sitting there talking about

▲ In Gibraltar and Egypt: exotic ports of call on A.J. and Muriel's 1962 Mediterranean cruise.

something and all of a sudden there's Fred way over here with an idea. It might be good and it might be awful. But he was quite bombastic and profane, which didn't sit that well with me, not that I'm a fuddy-duddy. I'm not sure how bright he was but intuitive for sure, which I guess people would say is the exact opposite of me. I'm not very intuitive. I'm rational." Muncaster immediately set to work on three areas he considered in need of attention: an insufficient number of stores in the rapidly growing big-city suburbs, stagnant sales growth, and declining profit margins. He thought the business needed to be run more efficiently and with a greater sense of urgency. When he returned to home office in 1963, he recalled, "The June flyer came out in July and the merchandise arrived after that. That got my attention pretty quickly."

When A.J. announced at the 1966 annual meeting that he was "graduating" to the tire department, the board immediately appointed Muncaster president and CEO (all Canadian Tire presidents have also been its CEO). The 33-year-old seemed the perfect choice, recalls Martha Billes: "A really young buck with a brush cut. Not quite fresh out of university but he had been raised with Canadian Tire, his father was a dealer, and he knew everything about Canadian Tire. He really knew what he was doing."

Not only were Muncaster's qualifications impeccable, his timing was perfect. His entry into the job, and his 20-year tenure in it, coincided precisely with the entry of the baby boomers into the workforce. Canada, on a per capita basis, had the world's loudest post–World War II baby boom, with boomers accounting for one-third of the total population. The burst of fertility lasted 20 years, from 1947 to 1966; at its peak, Canadian women produced, on average, four children each.[5] When Muncaster ascended to the presidency, the first wave of boomers, those born in 1947, was turning 19. Many of them were about to buy their first car and rent their first apartment. Canadian Tire had the parts they needed to keep those old cars running, and it also had the toasters and frying pans they needed for their apartments. In the ensuing years, wave after wave of boomers would marry, have children, and buy houses, triggering a real estate boom of historic proportions. They would be prolific consumers and, for most of them, a Canadian Tire store would be only 15 minutes away.

▼

ONE OF THE NEW CEO'S first priorities was to recruit people like him into the executive ranks — young university graduates with a sophisticated approach to business management. The first of these to arrive, and the most influential, was Rich Hobbs, whom Muncaster had met at the University of Western Ontario, where they had belonged to the same fraternity. A year later, another Western alumnus, John Kron, joined as vice-president of distribution. In 1968, Bill Dawson, a former dealer with a special knack for retailing, became vice-president of marketing and a key member of Muncaster's management team.

No part of Canadian Tire was left untouched by Muncaster and his team. They respected the legacy of J.W. and A.J., but they also understood that the retail world was changing and that Canadian Tire, to remain competitive, must be at the leading edge of that change. So they introduced new technology and brought store designs into the modern era. And they transformed Canadian Tire's approach to marketing, distribution, and dealer selection.

Hobbs was like Muncaster in many ways. Both had worked in the stores and both were well versed in modern business theory. Both were committed to modernizing and expanding the company. Both were ambitious and supremely self-confident — if Muncaster ever stepped down as president and CEO, Hobbs was ready to step in.[6] However their personalities were different: whereas Muncaster was calm and soft-spoken, Hobbs was hot-headed and argumentative.

Hobbs grew up in the east end of Toronto, the same territory that produced Bill and Alf Billes. "We used to call it the gashouse district," he said. "It was a fairly poor part of the city."

After graduating from Western, he obtained a fellowship to study business for one year at Columbia University in New York City. Then he went back to Western to teach. It was 1958 and he was making $4,000 a year. He loved teaching but didn't see it as a career; a requirement for advancement in the academic world is publishing research papers and that wasn't one of Hobbs's strengths. He was still in touch with Muncaster, who was working at home office and whose uncle, Victor Muncaster, was having trouble with the Canadian Tire store in Sault Ste. Marie, where he was the dealer.

"His uncle was a really unsophisticated guy, like most of the early Canadian Tire people," says Hobbs, now retired and living near Gravenhurst, in Ontario's Muskoka region. "The store was getting too big for him and he was having a great deal of difficulty, emotionally, with managing it."

Muncaster asked Hobbs if he would consider taking on the management of his uncle's store. Hobbs talked to Victor, who offered him $10,000, good money in those days and a hefty increase over his university salary. "I turned him down," Hobbs recalls. "I said what I would do is take $5,000 and 50 per cent of any increase in profits

▲ Rich Hobbs, 1969.

that I made in future years. He agreed and then he went to Florida. I didn't see him for the first year. It was wonderful for me because it gave me a free hand to run things." It was the beginning of several years managing and owning Canadian Tire stores. The experience persuaded Hobbs, when he later became vice-president of dealer relations, that the existing system for selecting dealers was flawed. While he agreed with the principle that dealers should invest everything they had in the store, he didn't think the amount of their wealth should be an important criterion of selection. Also, Canadian Tire liked its dealers to have a strong connection to the local community; to reinforce this connection, dealerships were sometimes passed from father to son. Hobbs thought merit, not relationships, should be the deciding factor.

The Sault Ste. Marie store's annual profit had been $37,000 before Hobbs's arrival. Two years later, it was $95,000 and Victor Muncaster wasn't happy that Hobbs was due half the increase, the then substantial sum of $29,000. Hobbs left and applied to Canadian Tire for a store of his own. The selection committee, whose members included Dick Billes and Arch Brown, turned him down because he didn't have enough money to buy a store.

"That experience was important in developing my philosophy for the selection and training of dealers," Hobbs says. "My point was you don't need money, you need people who know what they're doing. Finally I just said, 'Look, give me the worst store you've got. Wherever it is, I'll do it.' They said, 'Okay.'"

The store was in Orangeville, a rural community north of Toronto. It was a tiny storefront operation, with only about 1,000 square feet of retail space. Sales were $80,000 a year and dropping. The young dealer had inherited the store from his father but had done little to increase business. Hobbs bought it with a borrowed $10,000 — $5,000 from the mother of a friend and $5,000 from the mother of the young dealer he was replacing. After taking over, Hobbs found he could get more sales just by expanding the inventory and upgrading customer service. But because the store and market were so small, the total revenues were not enough to produce an adequate income for the dealer. Hobbs, who was married with two children, was paying himself $50 a week at first, later raised to $90. He was barely getting by. His car was a wreck — the driver's side door was bolted on after it kept falling off — but it was all he could afford.

He told the dealer selection committee that unless he had a bigger store within two years, he would leave Canadian Tire. Two years later, in 1960, while Hobbs was contemplating other job offers, he was asked to become temporary manager

▶ A creative sporting goods display at the Hamilton store in 1966. Occasionally, Canadian Tire stores would participate in themed-display competitions.

SOLID FOAM PLASTIC

Decoys

ea. 1.19

"My management people were all doing their jobs well. My job every day was to go in and find something I could improve." — Rich Hobbs

of Canadian Tire's original associate store, in Hamilton, because the first-ever associate dealer, Walker Anderson, had died. As soon as he did so, Canadian Tire invited him to buy the store. Hobbs couldn't afford it, however. But after a complex negotiation with Anderson's estate, he was finally able to complete the transaction with no down payment. That was fortunate, as he had no money to make a down payment.

The store's sales and profits were stagnant, and Hobbs was able to improve them by removing a series of bottlenecks. These were all minor problems, but the cumulative impact of fixing them boosted sales significantly. One of the bottlenecks was that only one person was doing the inventory management; he was doing a good job but wasn't able by himself to keep the store fully stocked. Also, a shortage of cashiers was causing lineups, which in turn caused congestion in the parking lot, which in turn limited the number of people who could visit the store.

"Think about the store as a glass of water," says Hobbs. "When it is full, water just runs over the side. When a store gets to a certain capacity, it can't do any more business. So sales increase at the rate of inflation and that's about it."

Hobbs built a new service department and used the vacated space for sporting goods. He hired more cashiers and stopped allowing people living nearby to use the parking lot. Once these simple changes were implemented, Hobbs found himself at loose ends. "I was getting bored because I didn't have enough to do," he relates. "My management people were all doing their jobs well. My job every day was to go in and find something I could improve."

He decided to apply his talents to a broader canvas. Muncaster brought Hobbs into the corporation as director of merchandising and retail operations. Later he became vice-president of dealer relations but continued overseeing retail operations. He also was named to the board of directors. Unofficially, he held another position too — whenever there was an unpleasant task to be done, such as firing a dealer, Muncaster assigned it to Hobbs.

Muncaster and Hobbs set about overhauling the dealer selection system, with

◀ Negotiations between dealers and home office are the subject of a comedy skit at the 1963 Dealer Convention.

Hobbs's own career as the template. He had started in a small, unprofitable store and turned it around. That success gave him the chance to move to a bigger store. He obtained the bigger store not because he had money but as a result of his demonstrated skill as a retailer. This system became the norm for all dealers entering Canadian Tire.

It was one of those great ideas that seems obvious — but only after someone thinks of it first. Why not systematically put your top performers in charge of your most important stores? Professional sports has always operated this way. A young baseball player, for example, starts in the low minor leagues and, if he does well, is moved up to more advanced levels of competition. Eventually, if he is among the select few who are good enough, he gets called up to the major leagues. For Hobbs, Orangeville was the rookie league. Hamilton was the big leagues.

Muncaster had discovered that the difference between top-performing stores and poor performers was the ability of the dealer. Hobbs's idea of emphasizing merit over money was a way of reducing the number of poor performers. However, there were problems in implementing it, Muncaster recalled. "The father-to-son transfer was no longer acceptable. The sons would have to demonstrate on their own that they were able to do the job. That caused A.J. a fair bit of difficulty." The other issue was financing: if merit, not wealth, were to be the primary criterion of dealer selection, then some of the dealers chosen to move up would need financial help. So it was decided that, after the dealer had put up all of his own equity and obtained as much as he could in bank loans, Canadian Tire would finance the rest.

"That allowed us to move the best people, sometimes fairly quickly, into the big stores," Muncaster said.

Peter Edmonson, another University of Western Ontario classmate of Muncaster's, came aboard in 1972 as director of dealer relations. His job was to stabilize the finances of the dealers. "We had built a number of stores in the early 1970s and, as a result, were moving dealers quite quickly from the small stores to their next stores," he recalls. "Some of them had no equity because they had not made any money in the small stores. So there was a lot of so-called negative equity." His methods for turning negative equity into positive included loans, forgiving debt, and forgiving rent.

Canadian Tire developed a testing process for choosing new dealers from among the many applicants. "We found that some of the people without retail experience scored really well," recalled Muncaster. Thus, several former IBM executives, including Roger Thompson and Grant Wallace,[7] became dealers. The selection process analyzed how successful they had been in the past and how committed they were to making a career as a Canadian Tire dealer. The process was designed so as not to eliminate people without retail experience, many of whom went on to great success with Canadian Tire.

Another innovation was a formal training program for new dealers, lasting six months — two months each in a large, medium, and small store. "These guys would train with at least three different dealers in that time," says Hobbs. In each store they would learn something different. For example, in a big store they would specialize in a particular department such as automotive or sporting goods. In a small one, they would have to deal with the entire product line.

In interviews of new applicants, it was emphasized that not only the dealer but his family had to understand and accept the new system. The new applicants were not necessarily persons with retail experience; some, like Thompson and Wallace, were coming from senior positions in large corporations headquartered in major cities. Their families weren't always ready to move to small towns.

"Often we had cases where even if the man wanted to do it, his wife couldn't," recalls Hobbs. "She could be from a big city and he had been an IBM executive or something and suddenly they're going to Port Aux Basques, and that's tough."

During the training period, trainees were paid only $100 a week. They accepted it knowing that greater rewards lay ahead. "We had a thousand applicants a year, from all walks of life, coming in," said Hobbs. "They came because of the earning potential. I wanted bright, aggressive people. I wanted people who wanted to become rich. To an

◀ Early stores, like this one in Yarmouth, Nova Scotia, were typically located on the main street. In the 1960s they began to relocate to malls and suburban areas.

▶ The openings of new Canadian Tire stores have been great occasions for celebration. Maurice Soulard, the proud dealer of the new Hull, Quebec, store, is on the left.

extent it created problems: it made them an elite group of guys who were sometimes prima donnas. There were some negative aspects to that, but in terms of how it made Canadian Tire run, it was great. We had guys in there who wanted to succeed and were willing to sacrifice to do it, and they could see that it could happen."

In professional sports, if a big league player doesn't perform well, he gets sent back down to the minor leagues. That doesn't happen in Canadian Tire. What did begin to happen under the regime of Muncaster and Hobbs was that, for the first time, poor performers had their franchises terminated. "Some dealers were not being honest in their dealings with the corporation. There were dealers who weren't good at running stores, stores that were dirty, they weren't treating their customers well, they didn't have the creativity or the drive," said Hobbs. "So we had a lot of situations that were difficult, particularly in Quebec and eastern Canada. We didn't have a lot of new store expansion the first two or three years I was on the job because as we were training new dealers we were using them to replace existing dealers that we were disenfranchising."

Quebec and the Maritimes presented particular problems for cultural reasons. In Quebec, retailing was not considered a prestigious profession, so it was difficult to entice highly qualified people to operate Canadian Tire stores. André LeBlond, a university-trained executive, was hired to recruit new Quebec dealers, which he did successfully.

In the Maritimes, some of the established dealers felt they should be left to run their stores as they saw fit. Ontarians, they said, would never be accepted on the east coast and should not be sent there. As all of the new applicants were coming from Ontario, Muncaster and Hobbs decided to reject that advice.

The Ontario natives sent to the Maritimes did well. "Now we had the Maritime dealers' attention," Hobbs recalls. "So they started to pull up their socks and a lot of changes came about in the Maritime provinces. For a time, they led the other provinces in sales and updating of their stores."

Stripping a dealer of his store was not a step to be taken lightly. Hobbs would first visit a store and tell the dealer that certain things needed to be improved. If nothing had changed by the second or third visit, the franchise might be cancelled. It seems a harsh remedy but sometimes there was no other viable option. One Toronto store, for example, had a long-standing reputation for poor customer relations. The dealer, recalls Hobbs, "ran one of the worst stores we ever had. He wouldn't give refunds to customers for faulty merchandise. The staff would swear at the customers — tell them to get the hell out of the store. This went on for years."

Initially, Hobbs sent veteran executive Ralph Slee to the store to fire the dealer, but that turned out to be a mistake. After three visits, Slee still hadn't fired him. "Ralph was a very gentle, kind person. Every time he went out to see the dealer about retiring him, the dealer would give him hell about all the things he thought the corporation wasn't doing and Ralph would come back with his tail between his legs."

Martha Billes recalls that both her father and mother were "absolutely aghast" when they learned that Slee had been given such an assignment. "Ralph Slee was an artist. He was the nicest, sweetest, kindest soul you could ever imagine. He was a sweetheart. Why would you send him out to fire a dealer? It was totally out of keeping."

And so Hobbs invited the dealer in for a chat, also attended by Muncaster. It was a brief chat.

Hobbs said, "The store isn't being run very well."

The dealer said, "Well, I'm doing the best that I can."

Hobbs replied, "Fine, we'll be making a changeover at the end of the month."

The dealer said, "Okay," and that was the end of the conversation.

Hobbs does not remember much opposition from the dealers as a group to the tougher approach to underachievers. A good dealer was embarrassed to have a poor one in the same area, as it reflected badly on his own store. A customer experiencing poor service in one Canadian Tire location might assume that was the norm for all.

In the 1970s, Muncaster and Hobbs decided it was time to revamp the image of Canadian Tire. But, although he was committed to change, Muncaster had the

1926 One of the earliest Canadian Tire logos appears in the initial catalogue, which features a cartoon of a tire running hand in hand with a dollar, along with the slogans "We make your dollars go farther" and "The longest run for your money." This logo is used on catalogue covers from 1926 to 1933, adorns the side of the first Yonge and Isabella store, and is prominent on the first Canadian Tire money. The drawing was presented to A.J. Billes by an anonymous customer, who left the store before A.J. had a chance to thank him and ask his name.

1929 A.J. superimposes the logo from Eldred Pennsylvania Oil onto a triangle.

1934 The triangle and maple leaf appear together in ads for Mor-Power batteries. The triangle shape is also used for such products as Canadianize Wax Polish. The lone maple leaf inscribed with the letters *CTC* (shown here as part of the Mor-Power label) first appeared in newspaper ads in 1923 and then again in the 1926 catalogue.

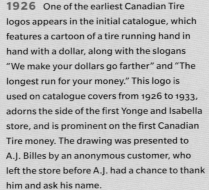

1935 The encircled maple leaf inscribed with the letters *CTC* appears in the 1935 catalogue. It is later incorporated into the "Tested Proven Products" logo, which makes its entrance on the 1936 catalogue cover and is then increasingly used on product packaging and store windows.

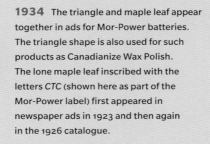

1940 Canadian Tire introduces the original version of the current logo, consisting of an orange triangle with a green maple leaf at the top, inscribed with the letters *CTC* — similar to the Mor-Power batteries logo. The word *Canadian* in the company name, Canadian Tire Corp'n, flows along a curve within the triangle. J.W. Billes had the logo designed by William Punkett of Oakville, Ontario.

1950 The logo is modified by rounding the corners and changing the lettering to black. The logo-shaped exterior signs hanging at Canadian Tire stores include the wording *Associate Store*.

1960 The logo retains its rounded corners but returns to white lettering and a green border.

1967 The logo is rejuvenated, with the help of Bernie Freedman, by widening the triangle, now painted red, and using a more modern typeface. The company name is written on straight lines, and the maple leaf is stylized, with no lettering. This logo is still used today and is referred to as the Classic logo.

2012 Today, the Icon logo — just the triangle with no wording — is highly recognized by consumers. It is used interchangeably with the Classic logo.

▲ ▶ Logos and signage evolved gradually over the years, with local variations, regardless of home office policies. The Muncaster years were the first to witness the standardization of store designs and larger formats. Associate stores (from left, top row) Galt, Ont., 1939; Cambridge, Ont., 1941; Amherst, N.S., *c.* 1950; (second row) Sudbury, Ont., 1959; Paris, Ont., 1968; (third row) Collingwood, Ont., 1956; Abbotsford, B.C., 1982; Wetaskiwin, Alta., 1983; (fourth row) unidentified gas station, 1986; Charlottetown, P.E.I., 1985; (bottom row) Waterdown, Ont., 2009.

Initially, Canadian Tire's home office did not provide dealers with standard signage, although they were told to name their stores after the Super-Lastic house brand of tires, rather than "Canadian Tire." By 1939, stores had begun displaying standardized hanging signs that identified them as official Canadian Tire associate stores. Nevertheless, through the 1940s and 1950s, store facades were as varied as the buildings themselves. By the 1960s, the company began rolling out standardized store formats and standard, modernized signage.

▲ Bernie Freedman of the display department helped design the Canadian Tire money and, later, redesigned the company's logo. Here he prepares a storefront display to commemorate the royal visit of Queen Elizabeth II, 1959.

sense not to fix what wasn't broken. Most Canadians living east of the Manitoba-Ontario border knew what Canadian Tire was all about and recognized its logo, the inverted red triangle with the green maple leaf on top. Apparently, that didn't impress a public relations firm commissioned to suggest improvements to the company's image. Its advice? An upside down triangle is unstable, so better get rid of the triangle. And, while you're at it, lose the name too because "Canadian Tire" doesn't accurately reflect the product mix.[8]

Muncaster sent the PR firm packing. Then, working with Canadian Tire's own designer, Bernie Freedman, he modernized the logo, replacing "Canadian Tire Corp'n." with plain "Canadian Tire" and taking the letters *CTC* out of the maple leaf.

In the early 1980s, the company began working with a Detroit-based advertising agency, W.B. Doner, which came up with the slogan "There's more to Canadian Tire than tires." Canadian Tire also had by this time a huge in-house advertising operation, employing hundreds of copywriters, artists, proofreaders, and translators.[9]

Canadian Tire's Quebec dealers wanted to advertise on television, but the corporation wasn't interested. "So we did it ourselves," recalls retired dealer Adam Bucci, who ran the store in Terrebonne, northeast of Montreal, for 30 years. "For a long time, the corporation was against television advertising. They thought it was too expensive. Then when we in Quebec proved it to be so powerful they got on the bandwagon." Canadian Tire's first national television campaign ran in 1977. It was aimed at do-it-yourselfers with the slogan "You can do it."

In the late 1960s, Canadian Tire still reflected its origins as a group of independent stores, some of which had originally been garages known as "B" dealers. The earliest associate stores had not even been allowed to use the Canadian Tire name. Not surprisingly, differences persisted in their signage, colour schemes, and advertising. One of the advantages of a franchised chain operation is that the customer knows what to expect when he or she enters one of its outlets, no matter where it is. Canadian Tire was not exploiting that advantage.

New signs were installed gradually over a three-year period. Canadian Tire paid for half the cost. "The philosophy was that we should look like a chain store," said Hobbs. "Canadian Tire customers should be able to go into a store in any part of the country and be at home, be familiar with the merchandising, where the products are located, the systems and the customer service, the warranty programs."

Under Muncaster's regime, Canadian Tire began to make price-cutting a more prominent part of its merchandising system. J.W. had disliked holding sales, be-

lieving that his stores should always offer the lowest possible price consistent with quality. He did not think prices should be lowered during the life of a catalogue, as the price in the catalogue already represented the wholesale cost plus the lowest possible markup.

Les Wheeler, the advertising specialist, argued that if suppliers cut their prices, Canadian Tire should be able to pass the saving along to its customers and advertise the special price as a limited-time sale. But J.W. insisted that it wasn't up to suppliers to dictate Canadian Tire's prices. A.J. was less dogmatic in opposing sales but he also felt the catalogue price should be respected.

Muncaster, even before he became CEO, authorized an increase in sales promotions, which jumped from only 2 in 1964 to 13 in 1970. Ralph Codner, the chief purchaser, was given additional authority to select new products and make special purchases, confident that Wheeler's advertising skills would sell whatever he bought. "There was very little I could tell these two experts about the art of merchandising," Muncaster said at the time.[10]

Under Muncaster, Canadian Tire's position in the marketplace remained as it always had been. "We believe that we're in the hard-goods department store business with some very particular limitations," Muncaster said in 1974. "We're basically in low-dollar-value merchandise. We're not a big ticket house. We have excluded the major appliances, furniture, things of that sort. And we keep out of specialized areas that we think somebody else would be able to do better than we can ... I think of boats and outboard motors and snowmobiles."[11]

One thing that did change was the company's approach to real estate. Previously, the dealers had owned or leased the real estate. Then A.J. Billes initiated a policy whereby the company would either own the property or be the lead tenant and sublet it to the dealer. Under Muncaster, this policy was applied to all new stores and, by the end of his tenure, the majority of buildings in the chain were corporate-owned.[12] Owning the building eliminated the possibility that a dealer could dump Canadian Tire and rebrand his store.

Real estate ownership became a key to Canadian Tire's expansion through the latter decades of the 20th century. When Canadian Tire bought land for a new store, it would often buy twice as much as was needed at the time. The real estate investments were largely financed by the sale of non-voting shares.[13] The foresight of management in the 1970s and 1980s made the expansion in the 1990s much easier and cheaper than it would have been otherwise. The excess land allowed Canadian Tire to build an entirely new store with no disruption to business. On

This large Montreal-area store under construction in 1972 was part of a new shopping centre development.

completion, the old store was razed to become the parking lot of the new one.[14]

"Everyone in the industry said we were crazy," recalls Steve Bochen, who arrived at Canadian Tire from Eaton's in 1967, a year after Muncaster had been appointed CEO. "We snuck up on our competition — we snuck up on Eaton's, we snuck up on Sears, and blew by them eventually because we used non-traditional approaches. Everybody in the industry said, 'You're not in the real estate business, you're in retail.' I think we thought we were in both."

Bochen became vice-president of personnel and later vice-president of distribution. He was another of Muncaster's university-trained executives, having attended the University of Michigan on a hockey scholarship. The move from Eaton's, a fading department store chain, to rapidly expanding Canadian Tire was a bit of a culture shock. "The people at Canadian Tire weren't typical corporate people. They were more entrepreneurial types. It was a wonderful environment because it was like running your own business."

Muncaster believed his key executives should have maximum freedom to make decisions. This meant that Bochen could make a decision to spend $1 million without seeking approval from the top. But at the same time, he might check with Muncaster over a $40,000 expenditure if he wasn't sure it was in line with company goals or his own mandate. Business schools called this management system "loose-tight," meaning that executives were given broad authority within clearly defined areas. The consulting firm McKinsey & Co., which made a study of Canadian Tire, called Muncaster the all-time best practitioner of the loose-tight system.

Muncaster wasted no time in pushing the Canadian Tire brand westward. Months after he became CEO, the company's first outlet west of Ontario opened in the Winnipeg suburb of Fort Garry. The company had been slow to go west, discouraged by the failure of eastern-based grocery chains to gain a foothold there.[15]

It was no secret that many westerners resented the economic dominance of central Canada. Did that mean they would refuse to shop at Toronto-based Canadian Tire? Muncaster thought not; the failure of eastern grocers, he concluded, was due to the dominance of the Safeway chain in the west, not anti-eastern sentiment.

Nevertheless, he decided to move cautiously. The first store ran for 18 months before any decisions were made about opening more western outlets. At the end of that time, management concluded that the Prairies were indeed Canadian Tire country, populated by value-conscious do-it-yourselfers. As a result, additional stores opened in Manitoba, Saskatchewan, and Alberta. But it wasn't until 1980, with the arrival of a store in Langley, British Columbia, that the company could boast of covering Canada from coast to coast.

Muncaster's changes paid immediate dividends. In the first seven years of his presidency, revenues rose from $97 million to $306 million. Profits more than quad-rupled, from $3.7 million to $16 million. Improved store management, removal of underperforming dealers, and a broadened product mix with more emphasis on housewares all helped. So, of course, did the addition of stores and the arrival of a whole new group of consumers — the early baby boomers — into adulthood.

Fred Sasaki, who had been a key advisor and confidant to both J.W. and A.J., went on to play the same role for Muncaster. He had been appointed treasurer after the death of J.W. and remained in that job when Muncaster became president, adding the title of vice-president of finance.

"He is a prince of a guy," Muncaster said. "He had incredible loyalty to A.J., and I can understand it completely. He feels rightly that A.J. rescued him from what happened to Japanese people during World War II."

Sasaki was 92 years old when he was interviewed in his suburban Toronto home in 2010. The hallway was full of boxes of his possessions — he was about to leave

▲ Brandon, Manitoba, store, c. 1973.

the house he had lived in for 52 years for a nursing home. His memory was as sharp as his opinions were blunt. Sasaki credits the great success of Canadian Tire to A.J.'s decision to bring in a professional manager to be president. This was done in the knowledge that none of the two founders' offspring was up to the job. J.W., Sasaki believes, would not have made the same decision.

The general view in the company was that Fred would not be suitable as president because of his personality. "I guess it was mainly his temper," said Sasaki. As for Dick Billes, "compared to Dean Muncaster, it was like night and day. If Dick had been appointed president, the company would not be what it is today.

"A.J. did the right thing by bringing in a neutral person. You have got to hand it to him that he made that decision. To see Dean Muncaster's potential when Dean was so young, that was quite ingenious of A.J. Dean was the right person. He had the right background with his education and having worked in his father's store."

▼

IT IS NOT SURPRISING that Canadian Tire, which sells many products that appeal to the technical-minded, was an early adopter of computer technology. A.J. Billes, who loved innovative technology, led the way in the 1950s when he approved the first point-of-sale system for tires. Of course, A.J. wasn't attracted to technology for its own sake. But if something could make the company and its retail outlets operate more efficiently, and thus more profitably, he was all for it, even if it meant some short-term disruption. The point-of-sale system was called SVC, which stood for "stock voucher card." Every time a tire was shipped to a store from Canadian Tire's distribution centre, an IBM punch card would go with it. Once the tire was sold, the store would mail the card back to Toronto, where it was fed into an IBM RAMAC 650 computer and a new tire would be ordered. As the system became more sophisticated, it issued reports that gave the dealers up-to-date information on the sales performance of different tires.[16]

The IBM punch cards were also used for a time at the flagship retail store. It was A.J.'s idea that customers could look at displays of products and pick up punch cards that contained details of the product. When customers had all the cards they wanted, they would go to the cashier, who would feed the cards into a processor that then printed out three copies of the invoice — one for the customer, one for the cashier, and one that would go to a station to be collected by the clerk who would retrieve the items. The purchases arrived at a redemption counter

▶ Customers making their shopping selection from the punch card display, 1960.

▲ Warehousing and fulfillment systems: (clockwise from top left) the tire department at Yonge and Davenport in 1951; the Pears Avenue warehouse in 1955, a few blocks from the home office store; the Sheppard Avenue Distribution Centre, 1959; and the state-of-the-art Brampton Distribution Centre, 1973.

where a checker would confirm the order against the customer's invoice and bag the purchases.

This system worked better in theory than in practice. In a typical scenario, a couple would come into the store accompanied by a small child whose idea of fun was to wander about the store collecting cards. His mother would relieve him of the cards and stick them back in the closest holder. Customers would then arrive at the redemption counter to discover that none of the items that had arrived matched what they thought they were buying. The customers were then sent back to the display areas to pick a new set of cards, making sure that the descriptions on the card matched what they wanted.

On busy days, chaos reigned — both at 837 Yonge and at a few other stores that had installed the system. The punch cards didn't last long before they were replaced by modern self-service.[17]

Al Cox, who had started his career at Canadian Tire loading trucks, went on to become one of the company's first computer programmers. In 1960, he qualified as a programmer on the company's IBM 650, one of only a handful installed across Canada at the time. This early computer, which was used for invoicing and inventory management, filled a room and required two five-ton air-conditioning units to keep it from overheating. It had 64 kilobytes of memory, a fraction as much as that of a $400 laptop computer today. Canadian Tire rented it from IBM for $19,000 a month.[18]

▲ Management information systems employees at home office, 1979.

In 1974, Muncaster engaged Gary Philbrick, an American management consultant with expertise in both computers and retailing strategies. His assignment was to review all the company's computer and management information systems and make recommendations for future improvements. It was supposed to be a two-month job but Philbrick wound up staying eight years.

The problem Philbrick quickly identified was a lack of control over inventory. Put simply, there was too much stuff piled up in the distribution centres and too much stuff in the stores. Canadian Tire needed new systems to maximize sales by reducing the amount of slow-selling items in the stores and ensuring that products in demand were always in stock.

He got a shock when he visited the state-of-the-art distribution centre that the company had opened in 1973 in Brampton, west of Toronto. Muncaster and John Kron, the vice-president of distribution, were proud of this high-tech, "high-bay," automated warehouse. Before having it built, the pair had travelled to Germany to see how the new technology was being used by manufacturers to store and retrieve sub-assemblies. Canadian Tire was the first Canadian company to apply the same technology to individual products, pulling pallet loads automatically out of the high-rise stacks.[19] With 65 million cubic feet of space, the new distribution centre was among the largest in the world.

Soon after arriving at Canadian Tire, Philbrick went to Brampton to see how this technological marvel was working. Muncaster and Kron had told him that it would be five to seven years before another warehouse was needed.

"I went to meet the young man who was running the computer part of it," recalls Philbrick. "I'm talking to him and he says, 'Excuse me, I've got to shut the system down now.' And I said, 'What? It's the middle of the day.'" More than 100 trucks were waiting to be unloaded but only 40 slots in the warehouse were available to unload them. The distribution centre was full.

Philbrick went to see Muncaster and Kron. He said, "You told me that you built that warehouse to last five to seven years. I must have misunderstood you, because you must have meant five minutes." Muncaster and Kron couldn't believe their spanking-new distribution centre was overflowing, but a phone call to the site confirmed Philbrick's news. However, the news wasn't all bad. There was nothing wrong with the new warehouse, he told them. The problem was simple: there was too much inventory, too many boxes of items that weren't selling fast enough.

Merchants tend to fall in love with the items on their shelves. That was easy to do at Canadian Tire, since the stores were profitable. Despite that, their turn-over rate was low. "Some of those stores had six months' merchandise in the store at one time," recalls Philbrick. "They were in love with the merchandise. Their idea was 'stack it higher, pile it deeper. The more merchandise you have, the more you'll sell.'"

The Pareto Principle, or the 80-20 rule, applies to many things in life, including merchandising, but it seemed some dealers weren't aware of it. "Eighty per cent of your sales come from 20 per cent of your merchandise," Philbrick says. "You needed to match up the inventories with what people were buying. And that meant you were just going to have to get rid of lot of stuff that wasn't selling and not let it get back in."

Home office had been sending a monthly report to dealers called PSIT, for "product sales and inventory trends," but it didn't give them all the information they needed. Philbrick replaced it with a report known as the GMROI, which stood for "gross margin return on inventory." This computer-generated report told dealers which classifications — for example, hand tools — produced the best gross margins.

▲ The Hamilton store before and after Gary Philbrick's recommended merchandising improvements: (clockwise from top left) the automotive department in 1966; a customer trolling the "strike zone" in 1974; and the nicely stocked sporting goods section featuring popular items, 1977.

"The dealers who were doing really well were the ones who had their inventory dollars invested in the things people really wanted to buy," commented Muncaster. It seems obvious, but it isn't until the data is collected.

"What I was proudest of, I changed the vocabulary of that dealer organization," Philbrick says. Before, if you asked a dealer how he was doing, he might say "fantastic" or "lousy." After implementing Philbrick's more scientific approach, he would say, "My GMROI is 145 and my inventory turnover rate is 6.3."

Another of Philbrick's projects was to upgrade the display of products in the stores. Previously, that had been left to the dealers. They arranged their shelves to look good, but that wasn't necessarily the best way to prompt customers to buy. First, Philbrick ensured that the dealers had detailed information — much more than they had ever seen — about sales of various products. He used "velocity codes" to show the speed at which everything was selling, breaking all the items in an individual store down to A items, B items, and C items.

The idea was to put the fast-moving items in the customer's visual "strike zone," which meant no lower than knee level of a person of average height. This was meant to get the slow movers out of the strike zone and replace them with a large supply of fast movers. The system was tried out in some Ottawa stores that were suffering stagnant sales. The combined efforts of Philbrick, the dealers, and marketing staff resulted in a 15 per cent increase in sales in the Ottawa stores.

Another project during the 1970s was called Save the Small Stores. The corporation was expanding swiftly during this period, opening large new stores to serve a bourgeoning population. Canadian Tire's revenues were skyrocketing, rising from just under $100 million when Muncaster took over as CEO to $683 million in 1976, an average increase of 20 per cent a year. In this environment, it wasn't surprising that some of the smaller stores were neglected.

"The small stores were having a very hard time," recalls Philbrick. "Canadian Tire needed the small stores because that's where new dealers started. But guys were going to these stores and losing all the money they had. We needed to take some corporate money and fix them up. The dealer relations department picked the three worst stores and I gathered a group of people and we attacked these three stores."

One of the stores was old, dirty, and needed a paint job. Those things were done, and the selection of merchandise was overhauled. Another of the small stores was new but was doing poorly. It too needed to be "remerchandised," as Philbrick puts it. "But they all survived, they all came around. And that started the corporation going through and cleaning up the small stores."

One good reason for "cleaning up" the stores would be that it might help attract a few more female customers. Canadian Tire has not always been welcoming to women. In a 1974 interview, Dean Muncaster summed up the prevailing view at the time: "Internally we get into debates about how important it is that we have a male image. We wonder how much business we can do with women without distorting that image and how far we can stretch our product lines without undermining that fundamental strength in being a store in which a man feels very, very comfortable. Where he is, in effect, the leader."[20]

Muncaster's views changed over the years. "As we moved further into product lines that would typically be purchased by women, we ended up trying to make it a more receptive place," he said. "You didn't automatically think that when you went into a Canadian Tire store that the customer next to you would be some guy in an undershirt. It was part of an evolution."

The change in Canadian Tire reflected social change. The stores became among Canada's leading sellers of housewares, and many established large garden centres. Men could be found buying household items, while women thought nothing of venturing into the auto parts and hardware sections. As the 1960s progressed into the 1970s and 1980s, more women were living alone, postponing marriage and pursuing careers. Hardware dealers, including Canadian Tire, reported an increase in sales of electric drills and other tools to women.[21]

While it was focused on improving the displays of goods, Canadian Tire never lost sight of what had made it a success in the first place: low prices. Ron Down, a

▲ The Forest, Ontario, store before it relocated to a new and larger building, 1972.

retired Canadian Tire buyer, explains that whenever a buyer proposed selling a new product, a "marketing board" comprising the purchasing manager and the other buyers was summoned to decide whether to approve the product.

But before he could take it to the board, the buyer had to comparison shop to see what the competition's prices were. "You always had to come in with a better price than your competitor," Down explains. The scale of Canadian Tire made the buyer's job much easier in that respect. "In almost every case, Canadian Tire would get the best price from a supplier because we could order 10,000 of something where someone else may only be able to order 1,000 or 5,000."

The company continued to watch competitors' prices after it had put a product into its stores. Newspapers from all over Canada were scoured to find competitors that were underselling Canadian Tire. But newspapers did not provide information on enough products. In the late 1970s, Keith Pickering, as manager of marketing data, set up the shopping program. Employees were sent into competitors' stores to check the prices of selected items. Pickering's department collected the information and put it together into reports that went to the buyers.

The shoppers writing down prices were obvious and some of Canadian Tire's competitors would invite them to leave. "Some of the stores didn't bother too much, but others did," recalls Pickering. "The secret there was [to] have good-looking girls do it. We used girls a lot. They wouldn't hassle them so much."

▼

IN 1973, Canadian Tire continued its trek up Toronto's main street from downtown to uptown. In 1923 and 1924, the Billes brothers had opened, closed, and reopened their little store in several downtown Yonge Street locations, finally settling down for 12 years at Yonge and Isabella. In 1936, they moved a bit farther north, arriving at the Yonge Street and Davenport location that still houses a Canadian Tire store. The corporate office was above that store but, by the early 1970s, the space it occupied was no longer sufficient. Canadian Tire moved north again, leasing five floors in adjacent modern office towers on Yonge Street south of Eglinton Avenue.

Ron Down felt something important was lost when home office was moved to Yonge and Eglinton and the buyers no longer had a store at their disposal. At 837 Yonge, the buying offices overlooked the store. "We could always go out to the hallways and look down and see what was happening in the store. If a buyer needed

▶ The new uptown home office at 2180 Yonge Street, 1973.

to make any changes, he could just walk down to the store and ask permission to take a product out of the store and up to his office to examine it. So if we had a line of product where we thought the packaging should be changed or something like that, we could go down and actually get the product that was in the stores at that time and have a look at it and say, yeah, it is time it be updated. Then we would take it back to the store." After the move, buyers had to request to see items from the warehouse. It took more time and quite a bit of paperwork.

A.J. inhabited a small office at the new headquarters. His door was usually open to anyone who cared to drop by, just as it was when he was president. One day, an executive named John Canella encountered a long-haired young man in the corridor near A.J.'s office. "He didn't look very clean," recalls Canella, "and he was carrying a cobra."

"Do you know where I can find A.J. Billes?" the man asked Canella.

"He doesn't work on this floor," Canella lied, trying to protect A.J. from the stranger and his reptile.

The visitor left. But 20 minutes later, Canella happened to pass A.J.'s office. The door was open and he saw the same young man sitting in there, holding the cobra.

Afterward, Canella asked A.J., "Who is that fellow?"

A.J. said, "Oh, I met him in the subway and I thought he was interesting, so I told him, 'Come see me anytime.'"

"I was worried he would kill you."

"Oh no, we had a nice chat."

What they chatted about is not known, but perhaps it was profit-sharing, a topic that preoccupied A.J. during the years after he stepped down as president. He was especially focused on profit-sharing for employees of the dealerships. It was a sensitive issue, since the dealers were independent business owners and expected to make their own decisions about employee compensation. But for A.J., profit-sharing was an essential part of the Canadian Tire culture that should be implemented throughout the organization.

A.J. proposed a program administered from home office by him. He would collect 50 per cent of the stores' profits and distribute it to the employees. The dealers, not surprisingly, opposed this proposal, as did Muncaster and Hobbs.

"I had no trouble at all with the concept of profit-sharing," said Muncaster, "but I didn't think it should be layered onto the kind of organization that we had, where we're trying to develop an entrepreneurial spirit."

As home office tried to upgrade and modernize the stores, with Gary Philbrick and other outsiders pushing their own ideas about inventories and product placement, some dealers were wondering what was happening to the independence they were supposed to enjoy as business owners. This worried Muncaster. To then "tell the dealers they can't even determine how their employees are going to be motivated could well have been the thing that tipped it over the edge. Dealers would say, 'Well, what am I here for?' They probably wouldn't quit, but they probably wouldn't reinvest very much either."

The soft-spoken Muncaster preferred to avoid confrontation, so it was left to Hobbs to argue at board meetings with A.J. over his profit-sharing plans. "I really liked A.J.," Hobbs says. "We got along fine. I think he looked very favourably on me, but there were differences in opinions I had to express — that was my job."

Like Muncaster, Hobbs believed in profit-sharing and thought it an important part of Canadian Tire's success. But highly motivated dealers were also an important part of that success. Of course, dealers could not be allowed to abuse or underpay their employees, and the few instances of that were dealt with swiftly. On the other hand, A.J.'s profit-sharing plan should not be imposed on the dealers, Hobbs thought. Their participation, he argued, should be voluntary, and the board agreed.

Profit-sharing was eventually implemented across the full chain but not in the form that A.J. had wanted. It was left to the dealer to determine what percentage of his profits would be paid out to employees, above a minimum that was well below 50 per cent. Just as many corporate employees enlarged their bank accounts from profit-sharing, so did employees of the dealers. Jim Borland, a retired dealer who ran stores in the Ontario communities of Port Credit, Oakville, and Dundas, said that some of his long-term employees made as much as $250,000 from profit-sharing.

Today, many other lifelong Canadian Tire people feel as passionate about profit-sharing as A.J. did decades ago. "Profit-sharing, to me, is one of those holy grails that I would never, ever want to see touched," says Justin Young, a dealer in Waterloo, Ontario. "I came from a family that couldn't rub two nickels together, and I bought my first house when I was 19 years old because of profit-sharing."

In a 1997 interview, the late Arch Brown, dealer of the highly successful Barrie, Ontario, store, explained A.J.'s point of view. J.W., Brown recalled, had often said that everything Canadian Tire did had to benefit four groups: the supplier, the corporation, the dealer, and the customer. A.J. thought his brother had omitted one important group, the people who worked in the stores. Brown was keen on profit-sharing and his store — where Justin Young had his first Canadian Tire

▲ Alan Warren, c. 1960s.

job — was the first to implement it. In the 1980s, Brown was president of the profit-sharing committee at Canadian Tire and went on to chair the Profit Sharing Council of Canada.[22]

In the early years, the profit-sharing plans were invested only in Canadian Tire stock. Eventually, however, it became apparent that some diversification was needed, as it was too risky to have all one's retirement savings invested in just one company. "People were leaving with all their eggs in one basket," said Jeffrey Smith, who helped manage the profit-sharing program. "Any financial advisor will tell you not to do that. But nobody cared because the stock just kept going up and splitting."

But all shares fluctuate over time, and so retirees who retired during a stock market downturn suffered losses. As a result, diversification was introduced during the 1980s.[23] A minimum amount had to be held in Canadian Tire shares but after that, employees could choose from mutual funds invested in other stocks or in fixed-income securities such as bonds and treasury bills. Canadian Tire hired outside investment advisors to manage these funds. The annual profit-sharing awards, for both corporate and store employees, varied according to the company's profitability. In the early years it was usually around 20 per cent of an employee's salary. Later it dropped to around 15 per cent.[24]

Dom Fox, a Canadian Tire dealer at Lindsay, Ontario, and former director of profit-sharing for the dealers' association, recalls a disagreement with A.J. over the issue of the vesting of employees' holdings in the profit-sharing plan. If the money is vested, the employee can leave and take it with him. Fox wanted to reduce the vesting period for dealers' employees from 10 years to 5. A.J., recalls Fox, was adamantly against the idea, saying that if there were vesting after 5 years, half the employees would leave. "We got the 5-year vesting and nobody left," says Fox. There is now no waiting period for vesting. In addition to taking their money with them when they leave, staff can draw on the fund while still employed if the money is to be used to pay down mortgages or for education.

AS A NATIONAL RETAILER, Canadian Tire must also be a national distribution company. Moving thousands of products from manufacturers and importers to hundreds of stores across the vast geographical expanse of Canada is a massive undertaking. In the company's early days, goods were moved by independent truckers. To ensure

a sufficient supply of tractor-trailer units to move the goods, Canadian Tire helped the drivers finance their tractors by guaranteeing their bank loans.[25]

As expansion accelerated in the latter 1960s, it became obvious that Canadian Tire needed its own trucks. In 1971, Matt Mucciacito was hired to do parts purchasing and administration of the new transportation division. The company had leased some transport equipment and in 1971 it bought a trailer. By the time Mucciacito left 37 years later, it owned more than 10,000 trailers, each one a rolling advertisement for Canadian Tire with the red triangle emblazoned on the sides. The company discouraged the use of the word *warehouse*, with its connotation of goods gathering dust, preferring the term *distribution centre*, implying speedy delivery of goods from the source to the stores.

An important part of running an efficient distribution system is avoiding hauling empty trailers. That means a truck doesn't leave the warehouse until it has arranged a load of newly arrived goods to pick up from a manufacturer or distributor on the way back. Ideally, Canadian Tire would have a full truckload to deliver and a full truckload to bring back to the distribution centre. Sometimes, however, that didn't work out perfectly. If there were more goods to be picked up than delivered, an outside trucking company would be hired to accommodate the extra cargo.

▲ Canadian Tire's large fleet of trucks continue to provide mobile advertising.

▶▶ Cochrane, Alberta: a Canadian Tire store embedded in the local community and economy, 2012.

Owen Billes, the son of Martha Billes, worked in several areas for the corporation before becoming a dealer in Welland, Ontario. Distribution was his favourite. "It was just like a big game, a puzzle," he says. Billes was an "outbound planner" whose job was to organize the deliveries to the stores. The stores are divided into a five-day rotation, so certain stores receive their shipments on Monday, others on Tuesday, and so on. His job was to decide, for example, whether a store was getting a full trailer or whether product for two stores would be on that trailer. Sometimes he also helped with the actual loading. "You watch the really good guys do it, and it's like a game of Tetris. They load the stuff and pack it all in, but they're already deciding where the stuff is going seven steps ahead. You can't get a piece of paper between the boxes. It's really neat. The idea is to get as much inventory on a trailer as possible, because you save money that way."

Billes became friends with one of the best loaders, Richard van Hemert. They stayed in touch after Billes had moved on, and one day Billes said, "You know, Richard, why don't you try to become a Canadian Tire dealer? You've worked so hard for Canadian Tire, you'd be better off working for yourself."

Van Hemert said, "I wouldn't want my own store, but why don't you get a store, and one day I'll come work for you?" A few years later, Owen Billes did become a dealer and Van Hemert is his store manager. "He'd been around the corporate distribution centre so much, he probably knew more about warehouses than anybody," says Billes. "So he set up our warehouse, and he still works fourteen-hour days. He's unique."

Steve Bochen, as vice-president of distribution, worked closely with John Kron, who was in charge of the distribution operation while it was being rapidly expanded during the 1970s. Bochen's background in personnel was important — people are just as important as trucks in the distribution process. Canadian Tire's distribution arm was the biggest non-union operation of its kind in the country at the time and the company wanted to keep it that way.

The best way to keep unions at bay was to make sure that Canadian Tire was a good place to work. A neighbour of Bochen's at his cottage was a director of the Teamsters union. Bochen asked him, "Why haven't you taken a run at us?"

The man replied, "I'm not stupid. You guys are paying real good wages and you have a good benefits program. I would rather pick an easier target."

Muncaster, Kron, and Bochen represented management on a committee that met regularly with employees to ensure that any concerns were discussed and resolved. They understood the need to keep the drivers happy. Profit-sharing helped. "Once they became owners, we promoted the 'you're an owner' philosophy," Bochen says.

"Then they start to act like owners and they question you, which is healthy. But if you're a dogmatic person, it's not going to work very well. You have to have respect for the average worker.

"If the employee is getting screwed by management, the employee can screw you back, because he's not stupid. You won't even know what happened to you, especially in distribution. They could sabotage you or just not be motivated, or screw up and make errors. You're vulnerable because you've got millions of dollars worth of product. That's the big advantage of profit-sharing. If there's a lot of theft, which is going to affect the bottom line, it's going to reduce their profit-sharing reward. You can really work on that."

▼

THE BILLESES are not the only family with a strong attachment to Canadian Tire. So were the Muncasters, who produced five dealers and a president. And there have been many other, lesser-known Canadian Tire families. Three generations of the Hicks family, starting with Morley, an original shareholder in 1927, have worked for Canadian Tire. Dealer Larry McFadden boasts that his family has put in a collective total of 200 years working for Canadian Tire, including the careers of his wife, brother, and sister-in-law. "There were a lot of families," he said. "It was really something special. And it probably is today, but it was more so back then. It was really tight."

Dedicated Canadian Tire people like the McFaddens helped the company grow far beyond anything the founding Billes brothers could have imagined in 1922 when they put up their sign at the corner of Gerrard and Hamilton. Some companies succeed in a small way and never get bigger. J.W. Billes liked to say he would have preferred to run a single, small sporting goods store rather than a complex, endlessly expanding company like Canadian Tire. But growth is in Canadian Tire's nature.

So where to grow next? Canadian Tire had a retail formula that worked beautifully in Canada. Wouldn't it work in other countries just as well? The only way to answer that question was to try. In 1979, the company made a modest foray into foreign territory, buying 10 per cent, later increased to 36 per cent, of McEwans, an Australian hardware chain. At the same time, it began to contemplate the possibilities in the world's richest retail market south of the border.

But there was unfinished business to attend to first. In 1980, Canadian Tire entered British Columbia, thereby completing the company's coverage of Canada from coast to coast.

CHAPTER FOUR

New horizons

BRITISH COLUMBIA is not a foreign country, but sometimes it feels that way. It has the biggest mountains and, on the coast, the mildest climate in the country. Toronto and Montreal are distant places many British Columbians have never seen, whereas Seattle and San Francisco are easily accessible by car. The three-hour time difference between British Columbia and central Canada nourishes the province's sense of alienation.

It wasn't until 58 years after it was founded that Canadian Tire finally established a presence on the Pacific coast. One reason for the long hesitation was that freight rates were higher there than in central Canada. Another was that A.J. Billes didn't like unions and British Columbia had a tradition of militant trade unionism. Labour costs also tended to be higher in British Columbia. And land in the Greater Vancouver area, where most of the province's population resides, was so expensive that some questioned whether Canadian Tire stores could be profitable.

Nevertheless, Canadian Tire is a national company and British Columbia the third most populous province. Vancouver, growing and prosperous, is Canada's third largest city. In retrospect, said Dean Muncaster, "the idea of us not being in B.C. was crazy."

◀ The highly customized Cambie Street store in Vancouver, 2012.

▶ Press conference announcing the expansion of Canadian Tire into British Columbia, held at Hotel Vancouver, December 5, 1979: (from left) Vern Forster, Peter Edmonson, Dean Muncaster, and Don Graham.

When it finally came, Canadian Tire's entry into British Columbia was an initiative of a couple of eastern dealers. In 1979, Vern Forster was the dealer in Spryfield, Nova Scotia, where he had turned around the worst-performing store in the Canadian Tire chain. Previously he was a manager for a Scott Paper mill in New Westminster, near Vancouver, and was well acquainted with the west coast. The other dealer, Don Graham, a former IBM executive and a computer whiz, was running a store in Mississauga, Ontario.

One day in 1979, Forster was flying from Halifax to Toronto, where he was going with his horse-fancying young daughter to see the Royal Agricultural Winter Fair. He found himself thinking about why Canadian Tire had never ventured into British Columbia. He knew that expensive freight costs, real estate, and labour were all important issues. But he didn't think any of these problems were insurmountable. On arriving in Toronto, he called his friend Don Graham, who, six years before, had trained him in how to run a Canadian Tire store. He said, "Don, meet us at the airport. We're staying overnight at your house."

Graham said, "Why?"

"I'm not telling you why, just pick us up at the airport."

At Graham's house, the pair worked until 4 a.m. preparing a flip-chart presentation for Dean Muncaster. Their objective was to persuade Muncaster to award them the Canadian Tire franchise for Vancouver and surrounding area, known as the Lower Mainland. Canadian Tire had never before awarded a franchise for a whole region. But Forster and Graham argued that, given the high cost of real estate, the

stores they opened would be small, so they would need to have many outlets to create a viable business. Because each store would be only about 10,000 square feet, there would be no room for inventory, so the Vancouver outlets would need more frequent replenishment. Graham, who along with Reg Quinn had pioneered Canadian Tire's computerized cash registers, had the solution: a central warehouse combined with an in-store point-of-sale system that would ensure the stores were fully stocked. Deliveries would be made as often as twice daily. Another deviation from standard Canadian Tire procedure was that the B.C. pair would arrange for their own shipments from the east — at a lower rate, in fact, than they would have had to pay Canadian Tire's distribution arm. Also, they would charge higher prices — 2 per cent higher on average — than Canadian Tire stores in other regions. In this they would be following the example of Eaton's and other national retailers.

Their proposal was, in almost every way, a radical departure from the way the rest of the chain was run. Perhaps their imaginations were stimulated by the bottle of single malt Scotch they polished off while preparing the presentation in the small hours of the night.

Forster's policy when calling someone important for a meeting was never to ask for half an hour. "Ask for 40 minutes or 45 minutes or 50 minutes," he advises. "It sounds precise." So he called Muncaster and said, "Dean, I need 40 minutes of your time."

Muncaster wasn't sure he could spare 40 minutes. Graham said, "Look, this is something you're going to love. We'll see you or nobody."

Muncaster was curious, so he agreed to see them for 40 minutes. The meeting

Canadian Tire

NEWS

June 1980

OFF TO A ROARING START

B.C. STORE OUTPERFORMS SALES PREDICTIONS

The first Canadian Tire store in British Columbia opened May 1st in Langley. It's been a roaring success since the word go.

On the first day alone, over 16,000 *paying* customers (not counting the husbands, wives, friends and kids that accompanied them) gave the computerized point-of-sale cash registers a real work-out. And there's been a steady flow of customers ever since. All of which pleases Vern Forster and Don Graham (the two associate dealers involved in the B.C. entry) no end.

The Langley store is already operating at a volume which puts it up with established stores doing in excess of $3-million a year in sales. Initial sales predictions for the store went out the window within the first week of operation.

In Vern Forster's words, the reception by British Columbians has been "unreal".

Forty thousand Canadian Tire catalogues (a special B.C. edition) and 35,000 grand opening flyers were distributed in the immediate area of Langley. No major radio or television advertising was carried out since the store, with only 6,500 sq ft of retail space, would have been simply unable to cope with the crowds. As it was, with virtually no great opening razzle-dazzle, the store was such a success that an RCMP officer had to be called in to keep some semblance of order in the parking lot and on the street as cars jammed the 40-car parking lot adjacent to the store.

The seven automotive service bays also got a good work-out. Grand opening specials included a $6.99 oil change and a $29.99 brake job. In the first few days after opening, the seven full-time and four part-time garage employees had their work cut out for them coping with over 200 oil changes and 100 brake jobs. Needless to say, the service centre is already operating at maximum capacity!

Great care had been taken to create an image of Canadian Tire as the place to go for everything in hardware and automotive goods. Featured opening specials were geared to promoting this image, and consequently, there were no super-duper deals on Kleenex etc., to confuse the customer's initial impression of Canadian Tire.

The Langley store is open seven days and five nights a week and, in addition to the service centre employees, there are eight full-time and eight part-time store employees. The store has point-of-sale equipment linked to the feeder warehouse in Burnaby and although there were a few problems with the system during the first few days, fortunately it was nothing that caused any disruption to customer service.

Now that the first Canadian Tire store has proven to be such a hit with British Columbians, doubtless the succeeding stores will also be greeted with the same reception. As one former customer who relocated from Alberta wrote: "There are no other stores here that offer the price, service and range of goods that Canadian Tire does, so the sooner the stores open, the better."

Dean Muncaster was recently a guest on a Vancouver open-line radio talk show and he was buoyed by the feelings of goodwill felt towards Canadian Tire in British Columbia, even though we are but newcomers. For the duration of the show, the telephone lines were constantly lit up. It seems many residents of B.C. who have moved there from other provinces have positive memories of Canadian Tire.

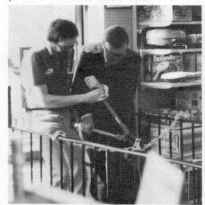

With assistance from store manager, Dave Worrell, Dean Muncaster cuts the chain on opening day.

As one avid customer calls it: "The great Canadian toy shop for grown-up boys." (His wife, however, isn't quite so enamoured; on their recent vacation to Paris, it seems hubby cloistered himself in the French equivalent of Canadian Tire and spent almost his whole vacation comparing products and prices.)

By the time this issue of Canadian Tire News reaches you, a new Canadian Tire store will have just opened in Chilliwack. B.C. Here's hoping it will enjoy the same overwhelming success...

The new Canadian Tire store in Langley, B.C.

The early success of the Langley store was celebrated in the June 1980 edition of the company newsletter.

lasted two hours. At one point, Muncaster objected, "In this plan, we're not making any money on the freight to Vancouver."

Forster replied, "Well, you're not making any money on the freight to Vancouver anyway because you haven't got any stores there."

Muncaster was keen to see Canadian Tire stores in British Columbia. And while the proposal at first glance seemed bizarre, it did have the merit of addressing important issues that until then had kept the company out of that province. He decided to throw his support behind Forster and Graham. "I had a lot of time for those two fellows," he said. "If somebody else had wandered in off the street and had the same idea, I might have said, 'Wait a minute now.'"

The Canadian Tire board wasn't persuaded so quickly. Some members of the founding Billes family resisted the dealers' novel ideas. "Freddy [Billes] was prepared to try anything, but the others were more conservative," said Muncaster. "They said, 'This thing's been working for the last 50 years, why do you want to change it?'" The other objection was the fear of unionization. Because of that, "there were some people who thought [Canadian Tire] should never go into B.C.," recalls Robin Law, the general counsel.

Muncaster prevailed and the expansion into British Columbia went ahead. The first store opened in the Fraser Valley town of Langley in April 1980. The doubters, however, were not soon won over: it would be seven years before the venture broke even. Canadian Tire built 21 stores for Forster and Graham, who had to stock them at a time when, as Forster puts it, "interest rates were at room temperature

▸ A North Vancouver store service team, early 1990s.
▲ Assistant service manager Rod Wenzel (left) with Tom Preckel, service manager of the Abbotsford, B.C., store. A sign advises customers of the new cheque-cashing policy.

The B.C. Distribution Centre
was an integral part of the
expansion into the province.

— 23 degrees." Learning how to manage 21 stores at once was a challenge. The two made their share of mistakes, such as ordering inventory that was wrong for the B.C. market, hiring the wrong people, and picking the wrong locations.[1]

Another problem was that Canadian Tire was set up for the four seasons in the other nine provinces. The west coast, however, has a mild winter with little snow and a spring that starts when the crocuses bloom in February. Bicycle accessories are big business year-round, and summer merchandise such as barbecues is needed earlier than Canadian Tire was used to shipping it.

In the rest of Canada, from the moment it opens its doors for the first time, a new store can count on attracting customers who already know Canadian Tire. In British Columbia, although a few people showed up with Canadian Tire money they had collected in other provinces, the business lacked name recognition and grew slowly. "At one point in 1984, we were $5 million in the hole," Forster recounts. "We owed so much money to the bank, the bank couldn't do anything about it. As Mark Twain said, 'You owe the bank $100, you worry. You owe the bank $10,000, they worry.' We were in deep doo-doo, but we hung in there. The only problem would be, if I had dropped dead anytime before 1986, my wife would've got nothing." When the loans were finally paid, the Toronto-Dominion Bank held a luncheon for the partners and returned their personal guarantees. Recalls Forster: "I burst into tears. That was one of the greatest moments of my life, a very emotional moment."

Graham's mandate was to make sure the stores were well stocked; Forster concentrated on merchandising and marketing. They hired managers to run each store, and it is a point of pride with Forster that, as of 2011, 22 of those former B.C. managers had become Canadian Tire dealers.

◀ Vern Forster and Don Graham at their newest Vancouver store,
the 35th to open in B.C. by 1987.

▲ Martha Billes and Roberta "Bobbie" Cochrane, Canadian Tire's top service manager at the time, opening the King Edward store, Coquitlam's second, in 1992.

The freight system they set up worked just as planned. Trailers carrying freight from Pacific ports to the east often came back empty or partially empty. Graham rented them and had them loaded with merchandise from Canadian Tire for his stores. "Our freight costs to Vancouver from Toronto were lower than Canadian Tire was charging from Toronto to Winnipeg," says Forster.

Forster had a knack for good relations with employees, which may explain why fears that militant unions would organize Canadian Tire's little stores turned out to be unfounded. One of the most innovative employee benefits was an education program, dubbed the "ignition program," that the partners initiated for their entry-level employees. They promised to pay for the employees' education after they had worked hours equivalent to three years of full employment. Once they were educated, Canadian Tire never wanted to see them again.

At the time, Forster and Graham between them had seven young children, and concern for their own children's future influenced their design of the ignition program. Graham said, "We wouldn't want one of our kids to start out as a cashier or a stock boy at Canadian Tire and, at age 25, still be in that entry-level job."

About 80 per cent of the 1,000 employees at the 21 stores were in their early 20s or late teens, most working as cashiers or as shippers and receivers.[2] "The problem when you have long-term employees in entry-level jobs," explains Forster, "is that there's nowhere for them to go because there are whole lot of people in entry-level jobs and very few up above. So what happens is you end up with Suzy, who joins you part time at 16, who works Friday night and Saturday and maybe Sunday, and then drifts into full-time employment, and now she's 25 years of age and she's still a cashier. And we can't pay her much more than we did when she was 19."

The ignition program worked like this: Before being hired, the applicant signed a letter of resignation that stated, "After 6,240 hours, I quit." That number of hours adds up to three years of full employment, although the hours could be accumulated over five or six years of part-time work. The rate of pay rose in increments of 25 cents an hour as the employee became more experienced. Once the employee reached the maximum number of hours and had to quit, the Canadian Tire franchise would pay for that person's tuition for two years at any institution of post-secondary education. Among the 500 ex–Canadian Tire employees who took advantage of the program are a dentist, a hairdresser, a baker, lawyers, and an airframe mechanic. Even after they had accumulated the 6,240 hours, the students could continue to work part time at Canadian Tire as long as they were enrolled in school.

The benefit to the company was that the program attracted motivated, bright

young people. When job applicants were interviewed, they were asked, "What do you want to be doing in five years?" If the answer was "I don't know," the applicant was unsuccessful. Another advantage was that, when an employee had reached the maximum hours and had to leave full-time employment, Forster could replace a $9-an-hour cashier with a $7-an-hour one who, in a few weeks, would be just as good. "We didn't do it for that reason," Forster hastens to say. "I know it's hard to believe that two money-grubbing bastards would actually put in a plan like that, without any idea of a payback, but we did." As it turned out, however, the savings on wages were more than the $3,500 average cost of each individual's tuition.

This innovative plan garnered considerable media attention, including an article on the front page of the Sunday *New York Times*. Having read the article, an industrialist from Kansas City came to Vancouver to find out how the program worked, with a view to implementing it in his own companies. Nevertheless, the program was not continued after Forster and Graham sold the business in 1994. Ross Saito, a manager under Forster and Graham and now the dealer of Canadian Tire's flagship store in central Vancouver, says it's no longer necessarily the case that retail is a mundane job that should only be a stepping stone to something better. "I look at retail as a lifelong job, something you want to aspire to," he says.

In 1994, Peter Ligé and John Pike bought out Graham and Forster and continued building up the B.C. business. (Ligé, a former vice-president of dealer relations, had joined them as a third partner five years earlier.[3]) Gradually, Canadian Tire in British Columbia began to resemble the company's operations in the rest of the country. Canadian Tire's transportation division found a way to reduce freight

▸ To celebrate the changeover of ownership of the B.C. stores to John Pike and Peter Ligé, three presidents (one past, one current, and one future) were present: (from left) Dean Muncaster, Don Graham, Wayne Sales, Peter Ligé, Steve Bachand, Vern Forster, and John Pike.

▲ Vern Forster, John Pike, Jim Ryan, Steve Bachand, Doug Waldie, and Peter Ligé at the very successful Kingsway store grand opening in Vancouver, October 18, 1995.

▲ Ross Saito at his Cambie Street store, 2012.

▶ Some of the Cambie Street store's unique features and Driving, Seasonal, and Living displays.

costs to British Columbia, so the B.C. operation no longer needed to rent its own trailers.⁴ As the years passed, several of the small stores were closed and replaced by larger ones.

Saito is one of the most prominent B.C. dealers. His new store, just south of downtown Vancouver, is in a densely populated area sprinkled with new condominium towers. Given the location, Saito must appeal to a young, cosmopolitan demographic. The store, built in 2005, has an Internet café and espresso bar, plasma TVs in the service centre waiting room, washrooms with granite counters and slate floors, and a Haida totem pole, one and a half storeys high, carved by a native artist. "We're striving for the 'wow factor,'" Saito says. "We want people to say, 'Oh, this Canadian Tire is different.'"

The store has a large furniture section to appeal to the condo dwellers. Unlike most Canadian Tire stores, it allows customers to call in and have an item put away for them. It also offers home delivery. Being able to respond to a distinctive local market is the major advantage of the dealer system, Saito believes. "I sit on the board of the dealers' association, and I always say our top dealers are going to define where we're going and what our stores should look like, not the corporation."

After working as a manager for Forster and Graham for several years, Saito moved east to work for the corporation. He started as a field merchandiser, which meant travelling around Canada helping out with expansions and new store openings. Then he moved to London, Ontario, as a district manager in 1987. Four and a half years later he landed in home office as a logistics manager, helping to manage the movement of goods through the supply chain.

In 1994, Saito became director of re-engineering, supervising various projects. A major one involved the same problem that had bedevilled A.J. Billes: returns of unwanted products. At the time, the company had a big adjusting department occupying a 130,000-square-foot warehouse. Defective goods were sent there from across the country to be returned to vendors or destroyed. Saito headed a team tasked with implementing a less cumbersome system. The warehouse was closed and defective goods are now destroyed or sold at a deep discount at the individual stores. The job of returning goods has been outsourced.

Saito's career path has been similar to that of many of the company's top dealers — work for the corporation first to gain a deep understanding of the business and then take over a store. Saito's first store, which he took over in 1998, was just about as far as one could get in Canada from his native British Columbia — in Stephenville, a town of 8,000 in Newfoundland.

CANADIAN TIRE IS PEOPLE...
PEOPLE ARE CANADIAN TIRE

Canada's Tire Expe

Having already managed a Canadian Tire store in Vancouver, he had to adjust to the demands of a different market. Newfoundlanders are more likely to be "do-it-yourselfers," he says, and so anything related to home repair, such as power tools, is a big seller. "And everybody deep-fries there, so when a deep fryer went on sale, I would sell 130 in that small store in Stephenville. If a deep fryer went on sale here in Vancouver, I'd sell six."

Stephenville was a bit of a culture shock for Saito, who is of Japanese descent and had lived in Vancouver and Toronto, both of which have large Asian populations. "When people saw me they knew I was either the guy who owned the Canadian Tire store or the other Asian, who owned the Chinese restaurant."

The store was losing money when Saito took it over. He made it profitable by upgrading the inventory and refocusing on Canadian Tire's core businesses of automotive and hardware. With only 7,000 square feet of space, there was no room for the seasonal products, such as patio furniture, found in larger stores. There was no room for housewares either. "We told customers, 'If you want housewares, go to Walmart. But if you want something to do with plumbing or electrical, you can find it here.'"

In 2000, Canadian Tire decided to break up the ownership of the B.C. stores. British Columbia now has large stores that can warehouse products, supplied from the distribution centres in Calgary and Toronto. There are now 47 dealers in the province, including Saito and his brother, Ward, who combined operate four stores. Ross Saito's store on Cambie Street, south of the downtown peninsula, replaced a smaller one. There was no room at the site for the typical Canadian Tire store with a large surface-parking area, so the parking is on top of the building, which also includes a Best Buy electronics store. As well, Canadian Tire put several separate pieces of real estate together to create a 58,000-square-foot shopping area, then sold the building to RioCan, a real estate investment trust, at a profit.

British Columbia is now a successful part of Canadian Tire's national operation. But the B.C. stores have to work harder than those in the rest of the country to get the attention of customers. One reason is the large proportion of immigrants in the province who had never heard of Canadian Tire before arriving in Canada. Another is the short history of the brand there. Explains Saito: "The customers don't have that history of 'I bought my first bike at Canadian Tire.'"

▼

▶ The green roof of the Port Coquitlam store, which opened in 2011 and debuted a modern building designed to reduce the store's carbon footprint.

Canadian Tire goes international

▲ McEwans' hardware and homeware storefronts, as shown in Canadian Tire's 1979 annual report.

BRITISH COLUMBIA was Canadian Tire's last frontier in Canada. Did that mean the company had to expand internationally or stop growing? According to Peter Edmonson, a corporate vice-president in the early 1980s, it did. "I went to the board and said, 'Look, we can't expand a whole lot in Canada and profit with the concept that we have, because we'd have to go into Humboldt, Saskatchewan, and build a little store, and it won't make any money.'"

In 2012, Canadian Tire does have a store in Humboldt, Saskatchewan, population 5,925. The dealer is Edmonson's stepson, Greg Velanoff, and the store is making money now that Canadian Tire has learned how to operate profitably in small markets. But in 1979, the big cities of Melbourne and Sydney seemed a lot more promising, even if Australia is 16,000 kilometres from the company's head office.

McEwans, with sales of about $160 million, was Australia's largest hardware chain. Its executive director, Tom Luxton, a member of the family that was majority owner, got in touch with Dean Muncaster to discuss whether the two companies might be able to work together in some fashion. The result was that Canadian Tire bought a minority share of McEwans on the understanding that it would eventually acquire a controlling interest.[5]

A.J. Billes was opposed to the venture because Australia was so distant and its unions had a reputation for militancy. "Anything that was very different from what had been done in the past was not something he embraced," commented Muncaster. But the chairman, Alex Barron, was supportive and the board approved the investment.

McEwans, an old-fashioned storefront hardware chain, was being challenged by new competitors with more modern formats. "McEwans' systems were archaic and the management team was very weak," says Gary Philbrick, who made several trips to Australia to work on upgrading McEwans. "But I thought we could make changes and make improvements very easily."

A.J. Billes remained skeptical. He wanted to see the McEwans stores for himself but hip problems prevented him from travelling.[6] Martha Billes, who was not yet on the board, and Fred Billes, who was, both made the trip. Neither was impressed. "The stores were a mess," Martha Billes recalls. "They were general hardware stores with some gardening products. There was a very shabby section for equestrian goods. I was riding horses at the time and when I saw the odd saddle and the odd brush, I thought our local co-op in Barrie, Ontario, was far better at presenting goods than what I saw at McEwans. I could not believe it."

▶ Rae Cowan, advertising and store planning director, shows off his farewell gifts from staff prior to his departure to Australia, 1982.

Muncaster believed Canadian Tire could have made a success of McEwans had it been able to acquire majority ownership. However, Australia's Foreign Investment Review Board ruled against a takeover. And so, in 1982, just three years after its initial investment, Canadian Tire sold its 36 per cent ownership of McEwans to Repco Corp., an Australian auto parts chain.[7]

The Australian foray was not a success for Canadian Tire but neither was it an expensive failure. According to Fred Sasaki, treasurer at the time, after all expenses, including travel costs, had been added up, the investment in McEwans cost the company only $24,000. Martha Billes, who joined the board in 1980 shortly after her visit to Australia, believes it was a huge waste of time and energy that could have been better utilized. Muncaster, though, thought it a worthwhile learning experience. The main lesson learned, he said, was that just because something works well in Canada doesn't mean it is easily transferable to another country. Ruefully, he added, "We probably forgot some of that by the time we went to the States."

▼

"U.S. ENTRY Opens Up Exciting Opportunities." So announced the *Canadian Tire News*, an in-house publication, in a banner headline in its January 1982 edition. The reasons for expanding to the United States were obvious. It was the richest country in the world, a vast market of 232 million people. The fastest-growing region, the Southwest, was just a three-hour flight from Toronto, and its big cities, with their sprawling suburbs and freeways, seemed a perfect fit for a company with decades of experience selling goods for the car, home, and suburban backyard. Exciting opportunities indeed.

Muncaster and Philbrick had been scouting for opportunities in the States. They had looked at several possibilities, including a California chain called Grand Auto, but it was bought out by an American company before Canadian Tire could act.[8] Then Household Merchandising, a finance company, approached Muncaster with an offer to sell White Stores, a hardware chain based in Wichita Falls, Texas. The chain consisted of some big stores, including 81 owned by the company, and more than 400 mostly small ones owned by franchisees. The stores were located across the Sunbelt, from New Mexico to the Carolinas. The business earned most of its revenues by collecting interest on goods sold on credit, with the financing supplied by Household Merchandising.[9]

Perhaps, Muncaster said later with an ironic laugh, "we shouldn't have been buying something somebody wanted to get rid of. But they could make a pretty logical argument that they were in the finance business, so what were they doing owning these stores?"

The White stores were rundown, and many of them were in locations that had seen better days. Nevertheless, Canadian Tire's board concluded that, at the low price of US$40.2 million,[10] it was a good deal. The idea was to impose the Canadian Tire formula, from the dealer system to profit-sharing, onto White Stores. Then, the deal's boosters assumed, the success already experienced in Canada would be repeated south of the border.

The board approved the deal unanimously,[11] but some of its members were skeptical and with good reason. Many Canadian retailers have tried and failed to capture the U.S. market, including Consumers Distributing, Peoples Jewellers, Reitmans, and Leon's. "Americans love to compete, and they're not as polite about it as Canadians are," observed Richard Currie, then president of Loblaw Companies, which operated, then sold, a chain of supermarkets in the States.[12]

As Martha Billes recalls the boardroom discussions leading to the White Stores venture, management presented it as a can't-miss opportunity. There were only three possible scenarios: good, better, or best. The possibility of failure was not considered.

A.J. Billes was opposed to the venture but he was no longer on the board, having given up his seat in favour of Martha. This was the only way he could get her on the board, as the family was entitled to three seats only and neither of the two Billes brothers was prepared to step aside.[13] As a newcomer, Martha did not feel qualified to debate management because she had no formal business training. "I did not know anything about retailing other than what I grew up with, and it was sort of by osmosis. I couldn't battle these guys — they knew it all." Her brother David deferred to management. As for her late brother, Fred, his attitude, she recalls, was "If they want to do it and they think they're so smart, then let them go and do it. God bless them if they get it right."

White Stores, which had been founded in the 1930s, appealed to Muncaster and his team; with more than 500 stores, it was big and it had a similar product mix to Canadian Tire's — hardware, sporting and automotive goods, housewares, and lawn and garden products. Just like Canadian Tire, it acted as wholesaler to independently owned retailers, whom it supplied from four warehouses. White Stores also had car service bays. But there the resemblance ended. The average White store had revenues about a third of those of a Canadian Tire store. And while

Twenty White stores, in larger Texas centres, were revitalized during the year with new signage, fixtures and in-store equipment. Merchandising taskforces followed close on the heels of construction crews to establish a new Whites image — inside and out. A red triangle, symbolic of Canadian Tire, was incorporated in Whites' redesigned logo.

An on-line cash register system is being installed in all converted White stores. The point-of-sale equipment captures complete data on customers' transactions to

the company-owned outlets were about the same size as a Canadian Tire, many of the franchised ones were small storefront operations. Yet another difference was that White Stores, unlike Canadian Tire, sold furniture and large appliances.

Management was not alone in considering White Stores a good opportunity for Canadian Tire. "Canadian Tire in the U.S.? It Sure Looks Good to Me" was the headline on an article by business analyst Tony Reid. "If Canadian Tire is able to achieve a modest equivalent of its Canadian success in the new U.S. operation, future earnings prospects could be potentially explosive," he wrote. White Stores were so promising, he continued, that Canadian Tire stock could double or triple in the next five years.[14]

Two retail investment analysts, Ron McTear and Martin Kaufman, praised Canadian Tire's strategy of positioning itself for U.S. growth at the same time as expansion opportunities in Canada were becoming exhausted. The White Stores purchase, they believed, was a clever deal that gave Canadian Tire a cheap entry to the U.S. market by acquiring an established position in a prosperous region. "There's no substantial difference in consumer patterns so the Canadian Tire concept should work," said Kaufman. "With this acquisition, Canadian Tire has paved the way for eventual dramatic improvement."

McTear said investors were slow to understand how good the White Stores deal was and consequently Canadian Tire stock was undervalued by $10. He pointed out that White stores were averaging sales of only $65 per square foot, while Canadian Tire's sales were $200 per square foot. "Given Canadian Tire's expertise in merchandising, I don't think it's unreasonable to at least double, if not triple, White's retail sales figure ... They're on their way to some fantastic growth in the U.S."[15]

Cynthia Rose, another investment analyst specializing in retail, pointed out in an interview that it would probably take three years — until 1985 — before the White stores would contribute to Canadian Tire's corporate earnings. Still, she liked the deal because it meant the company "has entered a virtually limitless market, where it faces little direct competition."[16]

These optimistic expectations reflected the thinking of management. Canadian Tire entered the U.S. market certain that White Stores was a perfect fit and would prove to be a great success.

Muncaster knew he needed a strong manager to turn White Stores around. One candidate was Bill Dawson, a former Sudbury dealer who had become the corporate vice-president of marketing, but he didn't want the job. Instead, John Kron took it on. Kron, a University of Western Ontario business graduate who had run

◀ The 1982 annual report coverage of White Stores highlighted how the new point-of-sale equipment captured and recorded sales transactions and sales history for computer-controlled inventory management.

▼

his family's trucking business in Kenora, Ontario, was an expert at distribution and had performed brilliantly as vice-president of that department for Canadian Tire. But he lacked a marketing background and had never had an assignment as difficult as that of transforming White Stores. It didn't make things any easier that his family did not want to move south. Kron had to commute, spending weekends at home in Toronto and flying back to Texas every Sunday night.

Kron believed it was White Stores' lack of direction that was causing it to lose money. "They've been taking a fragmented approach to the market," he said in an interview at the time. "They did not have a clear picture of what they wanted the store to be. As a result, consumers had an unclear image of the store. We'll change that. As with our stores in Canada, we plan to dominate in housewares, automotive goods, sporting goods, and hardware items."[17]

Rich Hobbs, who had more marketing experience than Kron, might also have been a candidate to run White Stores, but he had left Canadian Tire in 1979. Before leaving, he made a tour of the southern United States to try to find a chain of stores that might be a suitable acquisition. "I couldn't find anything there that made sense to us," he recalls. Hobbs believed in buying more land than was immediately necessary, so future expansion could easily be accomplished. The stores he saw did not have any extra land.

The decision to buy White Stores, he thinks, was wrong. "They were bad locations. The company had a bad reputation and it wasn't doing much business. They sent John [Kron] down to rescue it, and poor John had no experience running retail stores — he was a distribution guy, and he did that really well. But it was an impossible situation. Nobody was going to fix it."

Kron did his best. The 81 company-owned stores were remodelled to look like Canadian Tire stores. The number of products available in White Stores' four warehouses — three in Texas and one in Georgia — was doubled from 12,000 to 24,000 and a computerized inventory management system was introduced. Canadian Tire converted company-owned stores to dealer ownership. Many of the new dealers were Canadians with Canadian Tire experience.

Bob Hougham, who had been director of advertising at Canadian Tire, accompanied Kron to Texas as vice-president of marketing. Wichita Falls, where White Stores' head office was located, is a city of 100,000, located 200 kilometres north of Dallas, near the Oklahoma border. It is home to Sheppard Air Force Base, one of the largest in the States. Pilots from various NATO countries are trained there, giving Wichita Falls a cosmopolitan flavour. "I found it quite invigorating, says Hougham. "The people there are wonderful, and the

staff that we inherited were exceptional. Nobody could blame our problems on the quality of our talent, except for the vice-president of marketing, I guess." Hougham's job was complicated by the difference between the large stores and the smaller storefront operations. For example, to make the company-owned ones into Canadian Tire clones, the lines of furniture and appliances were removed. But the dealer-owned stores insisted on keeping those lines. "All the little mom-and-pop stores were quite interesting because each one was a new experience when you went in there," Hougham recalls. "They were run with a firm individual attitude."

It soon became apparent that Canadian Tire had overestimated the appeal its formula would have in a foreign country. "We thought we could just duplicate what we had done in Canada and if we produced 81 company stores that looked like Canadian Tire, everybody would come running in the door," says Hougham.

That didn't happen. One reason was that White Stores had powerful competitors. Another was that Canadian Tire had not fully understood why it had been able to buy the chain for a cut-rate price: the White outlets in big cities were situated in what Hougham calls "tired locations." The middle class had decamped for more affluent areas. The people left behind had less money to spend. Kron thought that

by upgrading the stores, he could attract more customers even if they had to come from farther away.[18] That turned out not to be the case.

"In hindsight, some of those stores should have been closed right off the bat," says Hougham. "We shouldn't have wasted any time on them. It probably would have stopped the bleeding we still had after we'd redone them and found out there was no customer base." Selling the stores in the worst areas would also have saved the cost of employing guards to prevent break-ins at night. "Some of those places in downtown Houston were like a war zone instead of a store," he recalls. Canadian Tire should have done a much more thorough analysis of the store locations, agreed Muncaster. It also should have appointed more Americans in top positions in the U.S. unit.

As White Stores continued to lose money, Kron kept promising that success was just around the corner. "We'll be operating at a profit before year's end," he told a trade magazine in March 1984.[19] But White Stores lost $55 million in 1984. Kron responded by predicting that 25 per cent of the 48 dealers White Stores had signed up to take over corporate stores would be in the black by the end of 1985. (The rest of the original corporate stores were still corporate-managed.)

Gary Philbrick thinks the White Stores purchase was a great deal and could have succeeded had it been better managed. The large stores that were converted to Canadian Tire clones badly needed a name change, he argues. "My suggestion was we call them 'The American Way.' The White Stores name had no value whatsoever, and the [revamped stores] were going to be so different that they needed a different name." If the name was changed, customers would not have a preconceived idea of what the store was all about. (Philbrick thinks the small franchised stores, which bore little resemblance to the big stores, could have kept the White Stores brand.)

Research revealed that people were indifferent to White Stores but they didn't hate it, and Kron believed the upgrades planned by Canadian Tire would bring them through the doors. And so the decision was made to save money by keeping the existing name.[20]

A name change probably wouldn't have been enough to save White Stores. None of the outlets converted to the Canadian Tire format ever made money. The dealers were losing an average of $300,000 a year. It was so bad that, in 1985, 22 of them sued Canadian Tire, saying they had sold their homes and invested their life savings and lost it all. The suit was settled out of court.

As of the spring of 1985, the total cost of the U.S. venture, including the cost of buying and upgrading stores and annual losses, was C$225 million, and Muncaster admitted that Canadian Tire was considering a retreat from the States. At the same time, Kron was making another attempt to turn things around by putting new emphasis on the auto side of the business, renaming the stores White's Autocenter Plus.

It wasn't enough. In June, Kron "relinquished" his job, a polite way of saying that the Canadian Tire board fired him. While the board searched for Kron's replacement, Fred Billes took over White Stores as acting chief executive and interim president, taking leave from his Canadian Tire store at the company's original location in downtown Toronto. The emphasis in the States now, based on the results of a board-ordered study from Arthur Andersen & Co., was on downsizing. Fred Billes proceeded to close 39 dealer and corporate-owned stores and a warehouse with a view to making White Stores profitable by 1986. "We're not going to let any grass grow under our feet," he promised.

Although he had supported the purchase of White Stores as a director, Fred claimed that he never liked it. "I would have preferred to see us expand to the U.K., or Ohio, or any market that is similar to our own — with the same climate, the same autos, and the same kind of products," he said in an interview.[21]

Martha was opposed to Fred taking over at White Stores. "I told him, 'Don't do it. You're not capable of doing it. You're not trained to do it. And it will just be bad news.' None of us were trained to run a big company like that. None of us had the experience. Therefore, why would he get involved? It would just bring heartache, and it did. It aged him quite a bit."

In October, Canadian Tire hired an American executive, Dean Groussman, to take over as president of White Stores. He had extensive experience at several major U.S. retailers, including Target, May Co., and, most recently, Zale Corp. By then, White Stores was losing $2 million a week and Canadian Tire wanted out. Groussman's job was to wind it up. In a deal completed in February 1986, Canadian Tire transferred the assets of White Stores to Western Auto Supply, a unit of Wesray Capital Corp. The deal was worth about $30 million to Canadian Tire,[22] which wound up losing a total of about $365[23] million because of its Texas adventure.

Hindsight offers several reasons Canadian Tire's American foray turned sour. One was that Kron, as he himself later admitted, was miscast. "I wasn't properly equipped to do the job, and I said that after the first six months. But we couldn't find anybody [to replace me]. I was taking on the corporate responsibilities that perhaps I shouldn't have, but I did try to do my best."[24]

Management was overconfident. "We had been so successful here in Canada, we probably had an overinflated view of our competence and capabilities," conceded Muncaster. "We turned out a beautiful-looking store that looked like a Canadian Tire store," adds Hougham, "and we made the same mistake 81 times before somebody said, 'Wait a minute, this isn't working.'"

By trying to revive a chain of 500 stores in an unfamiliar marketplace, Canadian Tire had taken on more than it could handle. Its outlets were too spread out for marketing to be effective. For example, there were just a handful of stores in the two biggest Texas cities, Dallas and Houston. It would have been better to have a large number of stores in both cities to justify major advertising campaigns. Hougham also wanted to go to a smaller city, such as San Antonio, put in a large number of stores, "and then experiment with our merchandising until we found something that worked. We were very good at automotive and hardware, because that was Canadian Tire's foundation. And I think we had a window of opportunity there."

But attempting to duplicate Canadian Tire's unique product mix in an alien market was a mistake. Unlike Canadians, Americans were not used to buying toasters and tea kettles at an automotive chain. They preferred to go to Walmart or Target, both of which had a bigger selection of toasters than White Stores.

Martha Billes says Canadian Tire developed and grew in response to the needs of the Canadian consumer. It is a product of the distinctive Canadian culture and so it was wrong to think a Canadian Tire clone could be plunked down in the U.S. Southwest and pull in customers the way a Canadian Tire can in Canada.

"The customer said, 'This is what we require,' and Canadian Tire always filled

Updated White stores, like Gary Manks's in Mesquite, Texas, applied decor elements and layouts similar to their Canadian Tire counterparts.

the niche. We worked for farmers. We provided the milking machines, tractor tires, and hand-cultivator equipment. And then the customer became more urbanized and Canadian Tire became more urbanized. The car took over from the tractor. Then the goodies associated with the car took over, and then more products for the home."

The problem with entering the United States was that every product category, from auto parts to housewares, was already well served. Canadian Tire knew the Canadian customer, but its U.S. competitors knew the customers in their neighbourhoods. Those customers had well-established shopping habits and White Stores, even after it was renovated to look like Canadian Tire, wasn't appealing enough to change those habits.

"I never understood why we had to go to the Sunbelt, to tell you the truth," says Martha Billes. Had the board not pulled the plug, "White's would have brought down Canadian Tire." As for A.J., he made no secret of his disdain for foreign adventures. "Three or more years were wasted in Australia, a labour-dominated country situated half way around the world from Canada," he wrote in a letter to a dealer, John Bourinot. "Then the plunge into Texas where five or more years and $300 million went into that sink hole, which all but brought a halt to the tried and proven progress here in Canada."[25]

WHEN THE CANADIAN TIRE BOARD met on June 6, 1985, Dean Muncaster had been president and CEO for 19 years. During that period sales had increased from $100 million to $2.1 billion, a remarkable achievement. True, Muncaster had enjoyed the advantage of presiding over Canadian Tire just when the massive baby boom population cohort was entering the workforce and needing the things Canadian Tire was selling. But to give Muncaster the credit he deserves, other stores had the same advantage and did not enjoy comparable growth. And it wasn't as if he just waited passively for customers to show up. He modernized and enlarged Canadian Tire's stores, speeded up the distribution system, introduced modern management systems, entered the banking business, and transformed the company from an eastern chain to a very profitable national one. But, in the wake of the White Stores disaster, the many achievements of his nearly two decades at the helm weren't enough to save his job.

The board had already made up its mind that he had to go and not just because of White Stores. Muncaster, in the view of some directors, had lost focus. He was spending too much time as chairman of Task Force Hydro, a commission established to reorganize Ontario's electric utility, and on outside boards such as those of Sara Lee and Black & Decker.

The criticism that he was distracted by non–Canadian Tire business is "fair comment," Muncaster conceded. But that wasn't the real reason he was fired — or, as the official announcement more delicately put it, why he decided to "relinquish his responsibilities."[26] In a letter to the directors a month earlier, he had made it clear that he and the "controlling shareholders" (the A.J. Billes family) were on a collision course.

Muncaster believed he acted on behalf of all 27,000 shareholders, including the vast majority who held non-voting shares. He pointed out that in a financial restructuring that took place in 1983, the controlling shareholders agreed that the board would have a majority of independent outside directors. "In this way, it was believed that the direction and supervision of the management of the corporation would occur in a manner similar to that of other major public corporations, and that the interests of all shareholders would be fully considered," he wrote.

In other words, management should be allowed to manage. However, between board meetings, the controlling shareholders were getting involved in day-to-day affairs, in some cases without notifying Muncaster. They made store evaluation trips; initiated an evaluation of the entire management group; and wrote to the vice-president of marketing, asking that a number of steps be taken to deal with what they saw as the company's "paint problem."

In his letter, Muncaster also complained about the Billeses' claim at a board meeting on April 3 that they "had the right to expect management to follow their dictates — to make things happen when they want them to happen. This opinion was reaffirmed during a meeting of two of the controlling shareholders and the president this week."

The two controlling shareholders he was referring to were Martha and Fred. Muncaster wasn't getting along with them. Nor was he getting along with their father, the man who had chosen him as his successor. In the same letter, he complained that A.J. was complicating the position of management by being "an active and aggressive participant" in trying to make the dealers implement his own version of profit-sharing. A.J. was still pushing for 50-50 profit-sharing in the stores and the dealers were having none of it. In a speech, he had harsh things to say about both the dealers and management, and Muncaster was offended. "It is counter-productive," Muncaster wrote, "to have dealers characterized as 'greedy' and management as 'spineless.'" A.J.'s statement that he would make 50-50 profit-sharing "a way of life for all Canadian Tire dealers" was seen by the dealer organization as a threat and a challenge to management, he continued.

Muncaster concluded this blunt missive by urging the board to "give consideration to the conditions under which the present management, or its successor, can be expected to function effectively and in the interest of all 27,000 shareholders." Twenty-six years later, Muncaster said that letter carried one simple message: "It's not working the way it is and there must be change."

Martha and Fred Billes believed there was no difference between their interests and those of the other shareholders. Both benefited if the company performed well. Martha analyzes the trajectory of Muncaster's career as president and CEO this way: "The first 10 years were great. The last 9 he slid away from operating the business. He was a wheeler-dealer more than a fellow that the dealers could talk to. He was unavailable to my father. Muncaster basically refused to see him because he was too busy doing other things. Muncaster changed character. Wheeler-dealer took over from conscientious, hardworking dealer's son that had come to Toronto to work for the company."

The hardworking dealer's son had never been close personally to any of the Billeses. "I was never invited into their homes. The only time I was ever there was very early on as part of a Dealer Convention. I was there as my father's son. I never saw the place at Shanty Bay."

Martha Billes has a different recollection. "Muncaster's family and my parents

were more than business associates," she says. "When Muncaster was married, I
wrapped the wedding present. My parents flew up to Sudbury for the wedding. His
first wife [Grace] was a sweetheart. My mother took her under her wing when she
came to Toronto from a small town. My mother and father were exceptionally kind
and considerate. In those days, I don't think very many business families did go to
each other's homes. They met at hotels and went out for the evening.

"Lots of people dropped in at Shanty Bay. Dean could have dropped in on the way
to Sudbury. When I was living in Mississauga in the mid-1970s, I had a Christmas

cocktail party and I invited senior management of Canadian Tire, the people that my father and brothers were talking about that I didn't get to know. And he would have been invited. I can't remember whether he came or not."

One thing Muncaster and the founding family agreed on in 1985 was that there needed to be a change. Muncaster's idea of change was that the controlling shareholders should stop interfering. The directors' idea of change was that Canadian Tire should get a new president.

And so, on June 6, "I *relinquished* my job," Muncaster said with an ironic laugh. "As I reflect on it more recently, I wonder why I didn't quit before they fired me."

Muncaster was not the only key figure to leave. Alex Barron, who had taken Canadian Tire public in 1944, was ousted as chairman of the board in 1984 because he had backed the wrong side in the struggle for control of the company a year earlier. He was replaced by Hugh Macaulay, a former General Motors dealer and member of a prominent Ontario Progressive Conservative family, who had spent four years as chairman of Ontario Hydro.

"I was not aware of the fact that Dean Muncaster would probably be going, and that was a very substantial disappointment to me," Macaulay says. The shareholders attending the meeting and staff elsewhere in the building were stunned when word of Muncaster's departure got out. "It was a black day at the office," recalls Larry McFadden, who was manager of dealer selection and training. "He was the only president most people had ever known. He was the guru who had taken the company so far. Everybody was walking around with their mouths open."

At the annual meeting, Muncaster delivered the last speech he would make to Canadian Tire's shareholders. He got through it, although it was obvious to the audience that he was shaken. He was in tears.[27] "I was kind of overwhelmed," Macaulay recalls. "I stood up after Dean sat down and I said, 'Now that's class.' And it was."

The Texas debacle was the end of the end for Dean Muncaster. The beginning of the end had occurred two years earlier, in 1983, when he had supported an attempt to take control of the company away from the A.J. Billes family.[28]

Tires

▲ Canadian Tire's wide selection of tires, all competitively priced, features predominantly in the 1928 catalogue.

▶ According to this 1934 ad, shoppers were increasingly choosing Canadian Tire's Super-Lastic tires over other brands.

▲ This small store manages to display its tires to full effect, c. 1950.

1922 When Hamilton Tire and Garage opens, the Billes brothers have no tires except the old ones they burn for heat. But they know tires will be a good business. With only 175 of the 27,000 miles of roadbed in Ontario paved, tires often blow out, and they seldom last more than 3,000 miles. Early car tires are as tall as 36 inches, yet only 3 inches wide. The typical air pressure is 70 to 80 pounds per square inch, compared with around 30 pounds in a modern tire.

1923 A.J. and J.W. Billes start selling tires. The first tires Canadian Tire promotes are Canadian-made Gutta Percha–brand tires with "gum-cushioned" tubes. The tubes have cushions of pure rubber inserted between the layers of cord to absorb the shocks of the road. Tire sizes range from 30 × 3½ inches to 37 × 5 inches. Canadian Tire advertises its tires as having "the longest run for your money."

1929 Super-Lastic, the original name of the Canadian Tire house brand of tires, is introduced as the "25,000 mile" tire with the "elastic stretch." By the late 1930s, Canadian Tire is selling one Super-Lastic tire for every four cars in Canada.

1931 Canadian Tire sells a 29 × 4.40 (4.40/21) tire for as little as $4.69. The highest quality available in the same size costs $8.60. Canadian Tire also offers the first unconditional guarantee for tires in Canada. Before this, the only guarantee available is for factory defects.

The corporation describes its guaranteed tires as "built of long staple Egyptian cords, woven especially to afford an elastic-like stretch that gives, instead of breaking, under excessive load or strain. Each cord is embedded into a Gum-Cushioned Pad. The long cure process of the 100% pure new rubber creates an extremely tough tread. These three developments combined into one tire place it far ahead of any competitor. All 'chance' in tire service is eliminated by such a tire and by the addition of our 'Bonded Guarantee' which is your positive protection."

DEPRESSION YEARS CTC sells tire reliners: "A complete relining for strengthening weakened and broken casings in both balloon and hi-pressure tires. Adds many miles of service to a tire that would otherwise be scrapped. No fitting necessary." Reliners are priced from $1.19 to $2.95. In comparison, a new tire starts at $4.60 and can cost as much as $27.30 for a heavy cord 10,000-mile, high-pressure model. Before the Depression, motorists usually replaced their tires with the original brand — if a car was equipped with Firestone tires, the owner replaced those tires with Firestones. But as money becomes scarce, motorists begin to shop for price and turn to Canadian Tire.

WORLD WAR II Synthetic rubber is introduced to tires as war in the Pacific cuts off supplies of Malayan rubber. Various reinforcing agents are used, including textiles such as cotton and rayon. Different tread additives, such as sawdust, carborundum, and ground glass, are tested. The use of synthetics changes the tire industry, since

▶ In the 1950s, the Sudbury store's tire department had space for 3,000 tires.

▼ The 1952 catalogue promotes Super-Lastic tires as a continuing top seller and "the safest tire on earth."

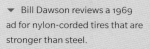

▼ Bill Dawson reviews a 1969 ad for nylon-corded tires that are stronger than steel.

▲ This photo of an employee with Canadian Tire's largest and smallest tires appeared in a 1953 *Toronto Star* feature article about the company.

▲ In the Sudbury store, all available space was used for merchandising — the tire department, for instance, was located in the basement.

▲ Barrie Rubber Company's informative tire display at the Products Parade during the 1967 Dealer Convention.

manufacturers can now tailor tires to specific uses. Nylon, Acrilan, vinyls, acetates, polyesters, and spun glass are used for cord casings. During the war, Canadian Tire has to cope with significant tire shortages and government restrictions on who can buy tires. J.W. Billes is able to obtain reliners for sale to customers at only $3 each.

1947–48 The first nylon cord tires are introduced. They are more durable and have a longer life than previous types. Tires are still hard to obtain, even though the war is over, especially once the company's main supplier, Dunlop, discontinues shipments of its quality products in 1948. Around the same time, Gutta Percha closes down. Goodyear, meanwhile, stops dealing with private distributors, including Canadian

Tire. At the same time, there is large consumer demand for replacement tires.

1949 Canadian Tire has virtually no tires in stock. A.J. Billes travels to the United States, where he makes an agreement to buy tires from Mansfield Tire and Rubber, based in Mansfield, Ohio. Canadian Tire is such a good customer that Mansfield builds a plant in Barrie, Ontario. This plant produces 5,000 Super-Lastic tires a day.

1955 Tubeless tires are now standard for cars. They are longer lasting and safer than previous types.

1961 Canadian Tire introduces a unique tire called Nytex. The cords in these tires are made of a combination of nylon and

rayon, both superior materials, to produce a tire that is strong and provides a smooth ride.

1965 Canadian Tire introduces the first four-ply polyester tire. Polyester offers the strength and safety of nylon and the better gas mileage of rayon.

1969 Canadian Tire becomes the first private brander to market belted tires in Canada. The catalogue describes the development this way:

"In every field great scientific accomplishments are occurring with overwhelming rapidity. Few, however, will be of greater significance to motorists than the Polyester tire reinforced with two Glass Belts. It gives lower cost per mile,

▼ This 1970s-era wall display made tire comparison easy.

▲ An eye-catching display in a London store, 1989.
◀ In the 1980 annual report, Canadian Tire proudly shares the success of the Odyssey 77 venture to break the Guinness world record, and the role that its Safety 99 Kevlar-belted radial tires played in the 74-day, 71-minute drive around the world.

improved safety. A great debt is owed research and development teams and their companies who, for more than a decade, labored to perfect two unlike fibers — Polyester and Fiberglass. While Polyester tires have proven their superiority over all others, a practical glass tire has yet to be produced. Combining imagination and research, 2 extra circumferential glass belts were added to the Polyester tire making it like 2 tires in one. Two combined tires with performance potential greatly exceeding their total individual performance. A new tire expected to give up to 1½ to 2 times normal wear, more than double the required strength, fast stopping and starting ability … and by some reports a gasoline savings of up to 1 gallon in 10."

1973 Canadian Tire is the first in the world to introduce Kevlar-belted tires. Kevlar is so new that there isn't yet a name for it; it is referred to simply as "Fibre B." A Fibre B tire is five times stronger than those made of steel, yet costs no more than a steel-belted tire. The revolutionary new tire belt is first introduced in the Safety 99 Multi Cord tire. Previously, fibres used in tire cord — cotton, rayon, nylon, and polyester — have all been adaptations of existing materials. Fibre B, on the other hand, is developed specifically for tires, the objective being to capture the virtues of all previous cords while avoiding their short-comings. The use of Kevlar, considered the most expensive man-made material in the world, produces a flexible and extremely strong tire — so strong that Canadian Tire's Safety 99 Kevlar-belted tires are selected by two Canadian drivers in their successful

attempt to break the Guinness world record by circumnavigating the globe in just over 74 days.

1986 Canadian Tire changes the name of its private brand of tires from Super-Lastic to MotoMaster.

1997 To address the complexity of tire sizes for newer vehicles and meet the needs of consumers, stores begin carrying national brand and dedicated brand tires, including Goodyear and Michelin.

2011 Canadian Tire continues to offer the latest in tire technology, such as Fuel Max Technology, which reduces rolling resistance, thereby improving a vehicle's fuel economy. It also launches an online tire store that offers over 5,000 tires, including its private-label brand, MotoMaster.

▼ Various tread designs meet Canada's wide-ranging road conditions.

▲ A more current (2009) "wall of tires" showcases the wide selection of tires available at Canadian Tire.

Endless tires

Over Canadian Tire's history, the tire department has handled huge volumes of tires in multiple sizes. At times during the 1970s, for instance, Canadian Tire had in stock more than 1.6 million cubic feet of tires, in more than 400 varieties.

The first carload of tires to arrive at the Yonge and Isabella store had to be manually hauled up two flights of narrow, enclosed stairs to a third-floor storage area. Some 40 year later, in 1973, the then new Brampton Distribution Centre began using the Towveyor, a completely automated system that moves merchandise from one level to the next, operating by means of a continuous moving chain embedded into a slot in the concrete floor. Independent four-wheeled cars are attached to the chain and moved to a pre-programmed destination, where they are loaded directly onto a waiting transport carrier.

Today, although the systems to move boxes, skids, and large quantities of merchandise are continually evolving, tires are still loaded by hand from trailers onto skids, ready to be moved by the distribution equipment.

▲ The efficient tire-handling operations at the new Sheppard Avenue Distribution Centre, 1961. *Executive* magazine ran a profile of the centre that same year.

▲ In 2012, tires continue to be off-loaded and palletized by hand; shown here, at the Brampton Distribution Centre.

CHAPTER FIVE

Who's in charge here?

WHEN J.W. BILLES DIED in November 1956, he left an estate of $6.2 million (about $52 million in 2011 dollars) and a will that disappointed everyone. A.J. had hoped to receive enough of his brother's Canadian Tire shares to assume a dominant control position. But there was nothing for A.J. in the will. J.W.'s immediate family had also expected to inherit a significant ownership stake, but they too were disappointed. Instead, J.W. left the bulk of his estate in trust for the benefit of 23 charitable and educational institutions.

J.W.'s will set in motion a struggle for control of Canadian Tire that would not finally be settled until 41 years later.

By the early 1960s, the A.J. Billes family held 29 per cent of the voting shares. A.J. could also count on the support of the corporate employee profit-sharing plan, which held 13 per cent. These two blocks were enough for A.J. to maintain control, but his position was shaky. What if the charities got permission to sell their 30 per cent stake to another company that might like to own Canadian Tire? What if that company then made an offer for the 28 per cent of common shares owned by the public? If those things happened, Canadian Tire would no longer be controlled by the A.J. Billes family.

◀ A.J. pitches the benefits of profit-sharing to dealers at the 1974 Dealer Convention.

▲ Fred, A.J., and David Billes, c. 1965.

▲ Martha Billes, 1981.

▲ Dick Billes, 1975.

Although it's not known for certain, J.W. Billes was probably planning to change his will before he died. He had wanted to speak to Dick about it but died suddenly before that discussion could take place.[1] "The family was horrified," recalls Martha Billes. "They had no idea what he'd done. It devastated them. Within five years, they had to go and beg the trust company for more money to live in the style they were used to."

Under the terms of the will, the trust would provide annuities of $25,000 (about $208,000 in 2011 dollars) for J.W.'s wife, Gladys, and $15,000 ($125,000 now) each for their three children, Gwen, John, and Dick. The rest of the dividend income from the shares in the trust went to, among other non-profit organizations, the University of Toronto, the Red Cross, Boy Scouts, the Salvation Army, and the Toronto Humane Society.

Ultimately, even these beneficiaries were dissatisfied. Canadian Tire was a growth stock, meaning that most of its profits were ploughed back into the company to finance expansion, rather than being paid out to shareholders as dividends. As a result, the charities received only modest amounts of income from their holdings. Some of them wanted the trust to sell the shares and put the money into mortgages and other securities providing more income.[2] But under the terms of the will, the trustees — National Trust, Gladys, and Dick — would have to agree to such a step. Gladys and Dick refused, as they did not want to see the shares dispersed. The Humane Society, the most outspoken of the discontented charities, tried unsuccessfully to have Dick removed as a trustee on the ground that, as a dealer and director, he had a conflict of interest.

In 1960, A.J. had decided that the share structure of the company needed to be revised in order to satisfy the needs of the charities while preserving the family's control. Alex Barron, the broker who had arranged Canadian Tire's first sale of shares to the public in 1944, was by then a director of the company. He and general counsel Robin Law devised a plan whereby each voting share was split into two voting shares and three Class A non-voting shares.[3] The J.W. Billes family and the charities could now sell their new non-voting stock without diluting the family's control.

At the time of this restructuring, A.J. was still the driving force of Canadian Tire, although he no longer owned any voting shares. Two years earlier, in order to avoid future estate taxes, he had turned over his common stock to Aldamar, a corporation named for and owned by his three children, Alfred, David, and Martha.

To further secure family control, a voting trust was set up in 1962. Under its

terms, the executors of J.W.'s estate and Aldamar agreed not to offer voting shares to a third party without first offering them to their partner in the trust. Only if the other party declined the shares could they be sold to somebody else.

To provide still more protection against takeover by an outsider, A.J. collaborated with Alan Warren, president of the dealers' association, on a plan by which the dealers would buy 20,000 of the voting shares held by the public and place them in a fund to be known as CTC Dealer Holdings. A rumour was circulating in the early 1960s that Gamble-Skogmo, a Minnesota-based retail conglomerate, might take a run at Canadian Tire. Major Canadian firms had also been rumoured as interested buyers. The dealers hated the idea of a takeover: an outside company might abandon the system of dealer ownership and turn the stores over to corporate managers. To help the dealers finance the share purchase, A.J. loaned them $1 million. The loan was repaid within a few months.[4] According to Warren, A.J. would have preferred that the shares be handed over to him as repayment, but Warren refused.[5]

The dealers' 20,000 shares comprised 9 per cent of the voting stock. Those shares, combined with the holdings of Aldamar and the employees, added up to 51 per cent. Canadian Tire, it seemed, was now safely under the control of A.J. Billes.

▲ A.J. thanks employees at the 1972 Pin Party after being presented with a gold Cadillac to celebrate his 50 years of service.

But the safety net had a couple of holes. One was the continued discontent of some of the charities, which had not given up hope of diversifying out of Canadian Tire stock. The other was Dick Billes. He had influence in the company as a director, trustee of his father's estate, and dealer at a large suburban Toronto store. But he had not abandoned his dream of a larger role, one denied him by his father's decision not to bequeath his shares to his family.

BY 1981, interest rates had climbed above 20 per cent, whereas the yield on Canadian Tire shares was a mere 2.14 per cent. The Toronto Humane Society had been complaining since 1979, and now other beneficiaries were voicing the same opinion. The Billes family was appalled at the ingratitude of the non-profit organizations J.W. had favoured at the expense of his own family. "My brother clearly intended that his shares would continue to earn dividends and benefit the charities," A.J. said.[6] Over the years, the shares had delivered the charities more than $11 million in dividends, in addition to the money they had received by selling their new non-voting shares. Moreover, as Dick Billes pointed out, the Class A shares had turned out to be good investments and the charities would have been better off if they had kept them rather than putting the proceeds from their sale into fixed-income securities.

Disappointment at the attitude of the charities was a rare instance of Dick and A.J. agreeing about something. Canadian Tire had long been a generous supporter of worthy causes. Now a group of charitable organizations that had received a lavish legacy from the company's co-founder had decided Canadian Tire shares weren't good enough for them. A.J. thought they were "greedy ingrates." But National Trust thought they had a point. In 1982, its chairman, J.L.A. Calhoun, wrote to Dick: "We have been concerned about the estate's holding of common shares of Canadian Tire ... because we feel that it would be prudent for the trustees to diversify." A report by Dominion Securities Ames also recommended that the estate sell the Canadian Tire stock. It pointed out that the estate's shares were worth more than the current market price because, although not a control block, they would give a purchaser a "springboard" toward achieving control that would justify the kind of premium associated with a takeover bid.[7]

In May 1983, National Trust, on behalf of 11 of the 23 beneficiaries, applied to the Ontario Supreme Court for permission to sell Canadian Tire shares held in the trust. On June 15, the court issued its ruling. "The trustees are ordered to sell common shares of Canadian Tire when the opportunity for an advantageous and beneficial sale of them arises," Mr. Justice John Holland stated in his judgment.

His decision triggered an all-out battle for control of Canadian Tire. The family was thrust into crisis mode, recalls Martha Billes. "Freddy was saying, 'Something's gonna happen, it's gonna explode.' And my father was quite beside himself."

Just three days after the court issued its ruling, A.J.'s fears were realized when Imasco, which was controlled by the British tobacco giant BAT Industries and was the owner of Shoppers Drug Mart and Imperial Tobacco, made an offer of $1.08 billion for all the voting shares and an equal amount of non-voting shares. Imasco would pay $72 a share — about $12 above the market price. Imasco said its offer was a friendly one and that it hoped to have the support of the major voting shareholders and management.

Typically in a takeover bid, the shareholders are interested in one thing only: how much money the bidder is offering. But Canadian Tire's shares were not widely held. Most of them resided in large blocks, the owners of which had strong emotional ties to the company. This made Imasco's task more difficult. As of 1983,

▲ A.J. chats with Chairman of the Board Alex Barron at the Yonge Street store. An organized visit to the store was part of the 1973 convention program.

▶ In 1969, reformed Sunday shopping laws, though highly controversial, were much anticipated by Canadian Tire stores.

"Our position has not changed one bit; we have lived for the company all our lives." — A.J. Billes

the Aldamar group consisting of A.J.'s sons and daughter held 30 per cent of the voting shares, as did the J.W. estate. The profit-sharing plan held 13 per cent, and the dealers had 9 per cent. That left only 19 per cent in the hands of the public.

The A.J. Billes family immediately rejected Imasco's offer, issuing a statement saying it planned to exercise its right of first refusal to buy the J.W. estate's shares. In a news release issued on June 20, 1983, the family said its decision was not strictly a business one; it was also about preserving Canadian Tire as a uniquely Canadian institution: "The 60-year-old Canadian Tire Corp. philosophy, the sharing of toil and profit, has evolved a unique Canadian corporate family from a small family store. Employees have become owners. First-, second-, and third-generation Canadian Tire Corp. 'family' members are working together within the corporate structure." In short, selling the company to an outsider would be, as Martha put it at the time in an interview with the *Globe and Mail*, against the philosophy that underpinned Canadian Tire.

In the face of the family's opposition, Imasco sweetened its bid, increasing the price it would pay to $75 a share, for a total of $1.11 billion. Shareholders would get $50 cash and 0.741 of an Imasco share for every Canadian Tire voting share tendered. If more than half but less than 66.6 per cent of the voting shares were tendered, Imasco would buy a matching number of non-voting shares. If more than 66.6 per cent of the voting shares were tende red, Imasco would buy all the non-voting shares that were tendered.[8]

The Billeses were unmoved. "Our position has not changed one bit," said A.J. "We have lived for the company all our lives." Added Martha Billes: "I'm not interested in money. I'm interested in the corporation. I'm afraid no outside takeover would make me happy in any way."

The Imasco offer and the family's adamant refusal to entertain it put Dean Muncaster in an awkward position. Months before the court decision and Imasco's bid, he had gone to Montreal, where he met with Paul Paré, Imasco's chairman and CEO. He said later that he would have been happy to see Imasco buy Canadian Tire, which is what he told Paré at the time. Not only did Muncaster admire Imasco

▲ Dealers present A.J. with an oil painting at the 1984 convention. Those dealers with 25 years of service also received paintings.

▼ Fred Sasaki, c. 1980s.

and its management, he knew that the probable alternative to an Imasco takeover would be acquisition of the estate's shares by the Aldamar group, and that didn't sit well with him.

"I was very concerned about the prospect of having absolute control vested in one side of the Billes family," he said. "In my mind, things had worked very well with a balance of control. In terms of thinking about alternatives, the Imasco folks, I thought, had done a fine job with Shoppers Drug Mart."

With Shoppers, Imasco's policy was to let management manage. Muncaster assumed it would treat Canadian Tire the same way, a prospect that appealed to him. Purdy Crawford, an Imasco director in 1983 who later became president, has since confirmed that Imasco would have followed a hands-off policy: "We would have left it exactly as it was," he said.

Imasco had two other appealing attributes: deep pockets and patience. At the time of the Imasco offer, Canadian Tire's struggling U.S. unit, White Stores, was losing money steadily. Pondering what might have been had the Imasco bid been successful, Muncaster said, "I think the U.S. would have been a very different thing. There would have been a different attitude towards the fact that these things don't happen overnight."

As president and CEO, Muncaster felt it his duty to recommend the Imasco bid as being in the best interests of the majority of shareholders. But both sides of the Billes family were against it, and the dealers supported A.J. That left one significant block of shares, the 13 per cent owned by the profit-sharing plan. Muncaster and Fred Sasaki were trustees of the plan, along with an employee representative. Sasaki decided he could not oppose A.J., who had welcomed him into Canadian Tire when many others would not hire someone of Japanese descent. If Sasaki had agreed to support the takeover bid, Muncaster said, the profit-sharing plan's shares would have been tendered to Imasco. But given Sasaki's position, Muncaster saw no point in taking a public stance in favour of the Imasco bid.

"When it was clear that [an Imasco takeover] wasn't going to happen, I wanted to maintain a publicly neutral position. And then to be able to do the things that would be right to keep the organization intact," said Muncaster.

In a letter to employee shareholders, he said that the senior management team was "not unmindful of the fact that Imasco is a very fine, well financed company, managed by a dedicated group of Canadian executives." Nevertheless, the managers preferred "to maintain the corporation as a truly independent Canadian organization with its unique emphasis on profit-sharing for employees, and ownership of

▲ A primary objective of the 1979 "We Can Do It" employee campaign was to unite the company through improved awareness of each department's activities.

shares by employees of the corporation, the associate dealers and employees of the dealers." The letter went on to say that maintaining Canadian Tire's status quo was most likely to happen if the company continued to be a partnership among the founding family, employees, and dealers and their employees.[9]

Imasco called off its takeover attempt on June 25.[10] Many of the shareholders, including the charities and owners of non-voting shares, could not have been happy at missing out on the windfall they would have reaped from selling their shares at a premium price. In response to the news, the common shares dropped $10, to $62.50. But Muncaster pronounced himself "relieved" that Imasco had dropped out. He said Canadian Tire employees would not have been comfortable in the embrace of "that big an entity."[11]

With the Imasco offer dead, attention was now focused on the future of the J.W. estate's 30 per cent block of voting shares that the court had ordered be sold. Two days before Imasco abandoned its offer, the trustees had invited interested parties to submit tenders. Their purpose was to find out if there were interested buyers other than Aldamar and how much they would be willing to pay. Aldamar would still have first right of refusal.

There were several bidders and one of them was Dick Billes, who had lined up financing in a complicated arrangement with the Toronto-Dominion Bank and the investment house Burns Fry. The bank agreed to lend Dick $67.2 million at the prime rate and another $4 million to cover the interest cost to April 1984. TD would keep $700,000 of the loan as its fee and pay $140,000 to Burns Fry, which would get the right to sell the shares. In return, Burns Fry agreed to cover up to 20 per cent of any loss to the bank.

Dick was handicapped in his attempt to acquire the estate's shares by a legal constraint on how much he could bid. The Ontario Securities Commission ruled that he was not personally a party to the voting trust but rather an executor of the estate that was a member of the trust. Therefore, he could not offer more than a 15 per cent premium without also offering the same price for all the shares, both voting and non-voting. The profit-sharing plan, which was also a bidder, was under the same constraint, but Aldamar, as a party to the voting trust, was not.[12]

The auction took place at a Toronto law office on October 3, 1983. In addition to members of the Billes family, Dean Muncaster and Fred Sasaki were present as representatives of the profit-sharing plan. Aldamar started the bidding at $63, Dick countered with $64, and the profit-sharing plan offered $65. When the dust had settled, Aldamar claimed victory with a bid of $73, for a total of $76.7 million.

The result was a blow to Dick Billes; he had lost his last-ditch attempt to regain a place of importance in Canadian Tire, a place his father's will had denied him. The charities, on the other hand, were winners because they got the cash they wanted. But the biggest winner of all was the A.J. Billes family. Control of Canadian Tire was now firmly in its hands.

▲ The Canadian Tire board of directors in 1983: (from left) Robin Law, David Billes, Fred Billes, A.J. Billes (seated), Martha Billes, A.L. Sherling, Dean Muncaster (seated), Alex Barron, John Kron, and A.H.D. Crooks.

▼

THE UNITY FORGED among Fred, Martha, and David in 1983 did not last. The basic problem was that Fred and Martha simply couldn't get along. And so hostilities in the battle for Canadian Tire resumed in 1986. The battle would last three years and would involve the offspring of A.J., as well as the dealers, non-voting shareholders, and the Ontario Securities Commission.

Fred owned 20 per cent of the voting shares and, in April 1986, Roderick McInnes, president of Carling O'Keefe, one of Canada's largest brewing companies, asked if he was interested in selling them. Carling proposed to offer to buy 50 per cent of Canadian Tire's non-voting shares at a 20 per cent premium over the market price. It would then buy the Billes siblings' shares at a big premium. This

would give the beer maker a majority of the total equity. Although discussions with Carling O'Keefe went nowhere, Fred made up his mind that he did want to sell. His lawyer, Biff Matthews, later recalled that he advised Fred to "get some kind of auction going for the shares." David agreed to sell his as well and, on October 15, they announced their intentions.

Why? According to Fred, Martha was "a loose cannon. She's not controllable and it's not worth the fight." David said, "I decided it was time for the family to get out. I think other people can now run it better, given the size it's grown to." David had never shared his siblings' passion for the company and, unlike them, was usually silent during board meetings. He preferred to concentrate his attention on his mechanical engineering business in Barrie, Ontario.

Fred and Martha got on each other's nerves. As an example, Martha recalls an incident in the 1960s when she voiced an opinion about the displays in Fred's store at Yonge and Davenport, in Toronto. She objected to the tables and bins filled with pots, pans, teapots, and other housewares. The items were in the stores at the insistence of the corporation, not the dealers. "It was like Kresge's or Woolworth's. The thing that really got me was the apple corer because I bought one and it broke. My brother said, 'Take it up with corporate. They're supplying it.' And I said, 'You've got all this trash. Why have you got it at the front of your store? It doesn't belong in our stores.'

"He said, 'Martha, my dear, this is the way it's going to be.' He'd always say, 'Martha, my dear.'"

Still, Martha was taken aback when Fred announced he wanted out of Canadian Tire. "I didn't know that Freddy was so disillusioned with me that he wanted to sell until he started talking about evaluations [of his stock]," she said. "I had no idea."[13] As A.J. explained it in a 1987 interview, the problem between the two siblings was rooted in Fred's belief that his opinions should carry more weight since he knew more about the business, having worked both in the corporation and as a dealer. But lack of similar experience did not deter Martha from having, and expressing, her own strongly held ideas about how Canadian Tire should be run.

The news that the brothers wanted to unload 40 per cent of the control block naturally fuelled takeover speculation. Their common shares plus their non-voting shares were worth a total of $92 million. Merrill Lynch Canada, on behalf of Fred and David, began soliciting bids from major corporations in Canada, the United States, Britain, and Australia.

The sale of Canadian Tire shares was complicated by the existence of a "coat-tail" provision that was put in place in 1983 when the Aldamar group acquired the shares of the J.W. Billes estate. It provided that, should a majority of the voting shares be tendered in response to a takeover bid, owners of the non-voting shares would automatically get voting rights. The intent was that a corporate buyer, wanting full control, would have to make a follow-up bid for the non-voting shares, thereby ensuring that all shareholders, not just the few who owned voting stock, would share in the takeover premium.

The coattail was enacted as part of a capital restructuring that resulted in each voting share being split into one voting share and four non-voting shares, while each non-voting share was split into five non-voting shares. The purpose of the split was to let the Aldamar group sell about $56 million worth of non-voting shares to help them cover the cost of purchasing the estate's shares.

The enactment of the coattail provision was a successful effort by the company's directors to make the non-voting shares attractive to investors. Many of the new non-voting shares created at the time were purchased in large blocks by sophisticated institutional investors who were satisfied with the coattail provision.[14]

The first name to surface as a suitor was Cara Operations, operators of the Swiss Chalet and Harvey's chains, airport restaurants, and flight kitchens. The proposal, made public on November 20, was for a merger of the two companies, rather than a takeover. Details of the merger idea were not made public. Cara may have suggested a merger rather than a takeover because its chances of gaining control were slim even if it obtained the brothers' 40 per cent. Martha had not put her shares up for sale, nor had the profit-sharing plan, nor the dealers. And even if it did obtain a majority of the common (voting) stock, Cara would have had to follow up with an offer for the 78 million non-voting shares, an expensive proposition. The non-voting shares, the day after the brothers' announcement of their intent to sell, were valued at $14.50, while the voting shares cost $35.75.

Martha had not made a public statement as to her intentions, and they were unclear. She had taken part in discussions with Carling O'Keefe but only to obtain a valuation of her shares.[15]

As for A.J., he was adamantly against his children selling their stock. He wanted Canadian Tire to continue being run as it was, with him influencing the direction of the company through Aldamar's control block. To try to dissuade his children from selling, in the fall of 1986 he called a meeting at his penthouse condominium in north Toronto. The three siblings were present, as well as several other family members. So was Fred Sasaki, A.J.'s close associate and friend. "A.J. asked me to speak first," Sasaki recalls. "I spoke about how the brothers, A.J. and J.W., had worked so hard and that the children owed it to their father to get together and continue the work."

A.J. spoke from prepared notes, which were later typed as a one-page letter entitled "Message to My Children." He recalled how, in 1945, he was told incorrectly that he would die within 10 years. "I willed all that I owned ... to my mother and sisters with the understanding that they in turn would will them to you, my children. There was nothing legally binding to that transaction, just a moral obligation on their part ... I entertained no doubt that my mother and sisters would carry out my wishes. Nor did I entertain any doubt about my children carrying out my wishes to perpetuate the standards and direction of Canadian Tire ... Obviously that was wrong because each of you have gone your own way without giving the slightest thought as to your father's wishes."

The meeting degenerated into a shouting match and ended quickly. "I just couldn't understand it," says Sasaki. "They all wanted to sell it, Martha too. A.J. was very disappointed." In an interview with *Maclean's* magazine a few weeks later, A.J. said, "I expected more of them."[16]

Martha Billes says Sasaki was mistaken. "There was no way that I wanted to sell," she says. A.J., however, had been convinced that she did. One day, in the midst of

Canadian Tire's iconic "Albert" commercial, first aired in 1984, featured a child overlooked for his hockey talents only to grow up to be one of Canada's greatest hockey heroes.

TRACTION

A monthly publication for and about the people of Canadian Tire Corporation

Corporation declares:
"Our employees are People in the News"

CANADIAN TIRE HONORS 24,263 YEARS OF SERVICE!

At Pin Parties to be held across Canada, Canadian Tire Corporation honors every employee with five or more years of service with the Company. Two thousand and forty-one employees are eligible to attend. Between them they have a remarkable 24,263 years of service!

It is expected that about 1,200 employees and guests will attend each of the Pin Parties to be held at the new Metro Toronto Convention Centre. At the April 26th Pin Party, employees from the Sheppard and Brampton Distribution Centres, Transportation, Adjusting, Central Supply & Services, Internal Audit and Personnel will be honoured.

Employees from Home Office, Cantire Products, Auto Parts Depots in Ontario (except Ottawa), and employees of Petroleum Retail will be honored May 3rd.

Two regional Pin Parties will also be held. The Montreal Pin Party will be held May 24th and will honor those employees from the Montreal, Ottawa, Halifax, and Moncton Auto Parts Depots, Petroleum Retail employees in Quebec and Dealer Relations staff and eastern field representatives working out of the Montreal office. The fourth Pin Party will be held May 31st in Edmonton and will bring together employees from the Edmonton Distribution Centre, Auto Parts Depots in Vancouver, Edmonton and Winnipeg as well as Petroleum Retail employees in Alberta and Thunder Bay, and the western field reps.

"People in the News", the theme of our 1986 Service Awards presentation dinners seeks to show that every one of you is a celebrity. This is the company's opportunity to express its appreciation for the outstanding effort put forth by all of you across the country. We hope you all enjoy your evening...and that special feeling of pride that comes with being a "news maker".

▼

Message from the President

Tonight we are here to honor all of you who have distinguished yourselves by the duration and excellence of your service to Canadian Tire. Perhaps it is best summed up by these words from our founder, A. J. Billes in the 1961 Pin Party program: "Simply staying with a company for many years is no great achievement, and age in itself possesses few virtues. What we have in this room tonight is not simply a record of longevity, but a striking example of our common purpose to a single cause — The Canadian Tire Way of Life."

That, ladies and gentlemen, is what this evening is all about: every single person here has played an important part in helping build Canadian Tire Corporation into what I see as the most successful merchandising organization in Canada.

Without you, it could never have happened. So tonight we honor you, our Canadian Tire celebrities... our "People in the News".

Although I myself have been with Canadian Tire Corporation for only a few brief months, I cannot help but be impressed by the strong sense of purpose, commitment and pride in your company that I see everywhere I go.

On behalf of the Corporation, I thank you for the part you have played in making Canadian Tire "the best".

I take this opportunity to offer my personal congratulations to every one of you here tonight... especially those of you who are attending your very first Pin Party and are receiving your five year pin... those of you who have retired after years of distinguished service... and of course, our honored VIPs tonight, our 25 year people.

Yours is a very special achievement, one of which you can be justly proud.

Dean Groussman

▼

Special Pin Party Edition

Features:

* A listing of all Service Pin recipients
* Employees' years of service
* Our recently retired employees
* A special section devoted to our V.I.P.s — all 25 year pin recipients.

the turmoil, A.J. and Martha had a discussion in his office in which he suggested that the family should sell all its shares and start over, building a new company. It was an impractical idea but indicative of his state of mind, Martha says; "He was so heartbroken."

Meanwhile, the investment community was trying to figure out the significance of the For Sale sign on Fred and David's shares. Would Martha try to buy them, thereby taking full control herself? Or might she combine her shares with those held by the employees and dealers to prevent control from slipping away to an outsider? The dealers had made it clear in 1983 that they weren't interested in an outside takeover that might threaten the lucrative system by which they owned their stores. What would the dealers do now?

That question was answered on November 28 when CTC Dealer Holdings, which was owned by 348 store dealers and held 17.5 per cent of Canadian Tire common shares, made an announcement. The dealers were bidding for an additional 49 per cent of the common stock. Since 49 per cent was less than a majority, the dealers would not need to make an offer for the non-voting shares. Thus, they could grab control of Canadian Tire without the coattail provision coming into play. The holders of 96 per cent of the equity in Canadian Tire were being left out in the cold.

The dealers offered the astonishing sum of $160 for shares that were by then selling for just $41.50. The offer represented 140 times annual earnings per share; a typical takeover price was about 15 times earnings. The total payout by the dealers would be about $270 million. The bid was financed by the Canadian Imperial Bank of Commerce.

The dealers' offer caught Martha's attention. On December 3, she announced that she would sell them her 20 per cent of the voting shares. She felt she had no choice — if she couldn't win control it was time to get out. "I would have been left out in the cold," she says, meaning that her 20 per cent by itself would leave her with no influence. Fred felt the same way. As his lawyer, Biff Matthews, explains it, "They [the three siblings] weren't going to control it unless they could get along, and clearly they couldn't get along. So the next step was to sell it."

The reaction in the investment community was furious. Stephen Jarislowsky, a prominent Montreal investment counsellor, said the deal was wrong in every possible way. In addition to being unfair to the non-voting shareholders, the takeover would leave the dealers in a "blatant conflict of interest" because, as Canadian Tire Corporation's only customers, they would be both seller (wholesaler) and buyer of the company's products. Jarislowsky, whose clients owned 5 million non-voting

▲ Dean Muncaster and A.J. Billes present Elva Desmarchais with her 45-year service pin.

◀ In 1986, 30 years after the first Pin Party was held, honouring long years of service continued to be an integral part of the company's culture.

▲ Canadian Tire was the official retailer of Expo '86, held in Vancouver. It sponsored the Swiss-built "Canadian Tire Express" monorail, which crossed the Expo grounds from one end to the other, providing great brand awareness for the company.

shares, was so provoked that he claimed he would ask the courts to liquidate the company unless the takeover bid was stopped.

Jack McArthur, the *Toronto Star*'s veteran business columnist, wrote that the dealers could afford to make such a high bid because they did not have to offer anything to the non-voting shareholders, who owned most of the equity. Despite the high price offered for the Billeses' shares, it was a great deal for the dealers — for $270 million they would get control of a company with annual sales of around $2 billion. Many companies issue non-voting shares, McArthur wrote, but the disparity between the number of voting and non-voting shares was unusually great in Canadian Tire. "No system should countenance the possibility that arises at Canadian Tire — that so little needs to be invested to control an organization of such size that has other owners with many times more at stake ... No wonder capitalism has a bad name in some quarters."[17]

A.J. Billes was also outspoken in his opposition to the proposed dealer takeover. "I can't help but feel we're sort of like a drunk who has reached the bottom of the barrel," he told the *Globe and Mail*. "We have no place to go, except back up. I honestly hope that somehow or other, this thing will turn around ... It's not the way things were meant to be."[18]

In the midst of the furor, Cara elaborated on its proposal: it would pay $345 million for all of Canadian Tire's voting shares. It would not buy the non-voting shares, but the holders of those shares could stay on as owners of the newly merged company. Cara's bid was a non-starter: the Billes siblings could not sell to Cara, as they had each accepted deposits from the dealers — Fred and David pocketed $7.5 million each and Martha received $15 million. (She got more, Martha says, because her shares were the "key" to control for the dealers.) A proposal by the board of Canadian Tire to buy out the Billeses and restructure the company also failed to gain any traction.

The only offer under serious consideration was the dealers', and they seemed surprised at the negative reaction. Alan Warren, former president of the dealers' association, was reluctant to discuss the takeover offer in an interview in October 2010, two months before his death. He did suggest, however, that at the time it seemed a straightforward business transaction: "We wanted the dealers to own rather than an outsider. I talked to Fred and Fred said, 'No problem.'"

Actually, there was a problem and it was called the Ontario Securities Commission. The OSC was inundated with complaints from owners of non-voting shares. Even the Toronto Stock Exchange had issued a statement saying it "does not regard it to be in the public interest" for the dealers' bid "to proceed as presently structured."[19] Was the evasion of the coattail provision legal? The OSC decided to find out. On December 10, it announced that it would hold hearings into the matter.

On the face of it, the deal appeared to be legal. But to its critics it was a devious way of circumventing the intent of the coattail provision. Buyers of non-voting shares had purchased them in the expectation that they would be protected in the event of a takeover. Now they were being left out.

The voting shares closed at $64.50 on December 18, whereas the non-voting shares were valued at only $13.50. Yet just seven months previously, both were trading in the $16 range. The non-voting shareholders were so angry about this state of affairs that some of them formed a group, the Canadian Tire Class A Shareholders Protection Association. Bill Allen, a broker and spokesman for the group, warned that legal action was being contemplated. "You cannot make commitments to shareholders ... and then simply turf those out when some legal loophole has found a way around it," he said.[20]

The advocates of the deal could not plausibly argue that the non-voting shareholders should have known that their shares would be less valuable in a takeover. When the coattail provision was adopted in 1983, Dean Muncaster had written in a letter to shareholders that its intent was to put owners of non-voting shares "in a position similar in effect to the minority holders of common shares in the event of a change of control of the corporation pursuant to a takeover bid."

The hearing was conducted jointly by the OSC and the Quebec Securities Commission. Alex Barron, who had been removed as chairman of Canadian Tire in 1984, testified that it was his clear understanding that non-voting shareholders would be protected in a takeover. "I would have been embarrassed voting for something that could be turned over so easily," he said. Barron told the hearing that he would have voted against the restructuring that took place at the time the A.J. Billes siblings acquired the J.W. estate's shares had there been no protection for non-voting shareholders. He also said that he had expected that the A.J. Billes siblings would hold their interest in the company indefinitely. "It never crossed our minds that in a few years they would want to sell their shares."

Fred Billes's lawyer at the hearing, Thomas Heintzman, argued that the coattail provision said nothing about a change of control. It simply referred to a majority of shares. The dealers were proposing to take only 49 per cent of the shares, he said, and 49 per cent is not a majority. "The bid was designed after careful reading of the terms of the coattail to be sure the non-voting shareholders would not be affected," explained lawyer Peter Dey, acting for the dealers. "The dealers simply did what any investor would do." David Billes's lawyer, Donald Wright, attacked the OSC hearing as "a combination between a fishing expedition and a witch hunt" in which the commission's lawyers were trying to subvert "a perfectly legal and proper transaction." And Fred Billes testified that, by selling his shares to the dealers, he was protecting the owners of non-voting shares by ensuring that some "fast-buck artist" didn't get his hands on the company. He did not indicate whether he considered Carling O'Keefe or Cara to be fast-buck artists.

Martha Billes's lawyer, Sidney Lederman, told the commission that his client was a "victim" who was forced to "strike the best deal she could" after her brothers decided to sell. She had never wanted to sell and "was doing everything in her power to have them change their minds."

On January 15, 1987, the Ontario Securities Commission announced its decision. It blocked the dealers' takeover bid, describing it as "grossly abusive" and "not in the public interest," and issued a cease-trade order against the three siblings who had agreed to sell most of their controlling interest in Canadian Tire. The unexpected decision was hailed as victory for the rights of non-voting shareholders. Bill Allen, spokesman for the non-voting shareholders, said the decision would "add to the

INSIDE: THE SAVAGE BATTLE FOR THE GULF

Maclean's

JANUARY 26, 1987   *CANADA'S WEEKLY NEWSMAGAZINE* $1.75

THE EPIC STRUGGLE FOR CANADIAN TIRE

A PATRIARCH'S REVENGE

Co-founder A.J. Billes

A.J. appeared on the cover of several magazines over the years. In 1987, *Maclean's* ran a detailed story about the Ontario Securities Commission's decision on the dealers' takeover bid.

integrity of the capital markets." Immediately after the decision was announced, the non-voting shares rose by $1 while the voting stock plunged by $28.

The decision was greeted as a good thing for investors in non-voting shares in all companies, and it was also applauded as a good thing for Canadian Tire. "I'm glad, absolutely, that they've stopped it," said A.J. Billes. "And I'm glad for one reason only: because it could bring the idea of real profit-sharing back. If the deal had gone through that couldn't have happened. But now it's still possible because perhaps there's more money that can be left aside."

Asked 23 years after the OSC decision to describe her reaction to it, Martha Billes mimics a hockey fan cheering after her team has just scored the winning goal. There is a huge difference between operating a retail store and a $10 billion corporation, she argues, and the dealers would not have operated the corporation successfully. Many dealers agree with her.

A dealer takeover would have changed the dynamic of the organization. Would a dealer-controlled corporation have bargained for the best prices from its customers, the dealers? Would it have insisted that dealers pay their fair share of advertising expenses? Terry Connoy, who was executive director of the dealers' association for 20 years, believes the "creative tension" between dealers and the corporation is a good thing. "It forces both sides to analyze what they're doing, which is a real strength because the corporation can't go off on a frolic of its own and do something because the dealers will push back aggressively and vice versa. So it forces a thorough analysis of each step. They don't make that many mistakes."

That creative tension would have been gone had the dealers taken over the company. Still, the dealers who had led the initiative to buy the control block were not happy with the outcome. "To this day I don't understand [the OSC decision], but it's not important that I do," said Alan Warren, a trace of bitterness in his voice, in 2010.

The dealers, blocked in their takeover attempt, had another reason to be unhappy. They had paid a total of $30 million in non-refundable deposits — $15 million to the brothers and another $15 million to Martha. In exchange, the Billeses had agreed not to consider any offers except from the dealers until the end of March. After that date, they could keep the money and consider new offers. Rumours circulated on Bay Street that Sears Canada, Seagram, and Wal-Mart Stores were among companies interested in buying Canadian Tire, but no new offers materialized.

The dealers appealed the OSC decision to the Ontario Supreme Court which, on March 12, 1987, upheld it. A further attempt to overturn the ruling also failed in April when the Court of Appeal for Ontario refused to hear the dealers' case. Also in

April, Martha Billes launched a lawsuit in the Ontario Supreme Court against her brothers, accusing them of breaching an agreement they had made in 1983. Under the agreement, if any of the three A.J. Billes offspring wished to sell their shares, they were to notify the others and offer them the right of first refusal. Martha's suit alleged that the notice given her was defective because it was a joint offer from both of her brothers, thereby creating "significant economic hardship" for her by depriving her of the right to purchase from only Fred or David. The suit asked the court to order Fred and David to sell their voting shares to Martha for $12.25 each and pay her $2 million in damages. At that time, the voting shares were selling for around $46. As an alternative to selling the shares, the suit asked for $125 million in damages.

The lawsuit silenced any takeover talks that the brothers may have been engaged in, as they would not be able to produce the shares if the ownership of them was in dispute. It was believed that it might be two years before court proceedings would even begin. David and Fred responded to Martha's suit with one of their own, arguing that she had breached the agreement and they were therefore entitled to buy her shares for $15 each.

At the annual meeting in Toronto in June 1987, Fred and David sat in the front row with the other directors. Martha, however, preferred to sit off to the side in another section of seats. If reporters were expecting fireworks from the feuding siblings, they were disappointed. Speaking to reporters after the meeting, Martha said she wanted to preserve the status quo at Canadian Tire by buying out her brothers. David replied that he would be happy to sell but that the offer so far had been too low.

Martha said she still hoped that the family could resolve its differences, but, she added, "Family is family. Business is business." She also said that, though not seeking a day-to-day role in the company, she had always wanted to remain as a shareholder and director.

In October, one year after Fred and David put their shares up for sale, a shareholders meeting was held to consider a proposal to strengthen the coattail provision by making non-voting shares convertible to voting shares on a one-for-one basis in the event of a takeover offer to owners of the voting shares. The company's board opposed the move, since it would damage the value of the common shares. The Billeses and dealers were also against the proposal, which was supported by large institutional holders of non-voting stock. The proposal needed the support of two-thirds of voting shareholders, but only 14 per cent supported it.

By January 1988, the ownership structure of Canadian Tire was still unsettled. David and Fred still wanted out and Martha wanted to stay in. The owners of voting shares wanted to preserve their value, while the owners of non-voting shares wanted to be assured of participating in any future takeover. That wasn't just a theoretical proposition. Canadian Tire had U.S. tax losses of $140 million on its books as a result of the White Stores experiment. These would be valuable to a U.S. buyer, and Sears, Roebuck & Co. was rumoured to be interested.

The Canadian Tire directors came up with a plan to settle the ownership dispute. Fred and David could convert each of their voting shares into 2.75 non-voting shares and sell them. Martha would stay on as a voting shareholder, as would the dealers. The dealers and Martha would elect one-third of the board. The non-voting shares would then get full voting rights and, therefore, control of the board of directors. But the institutional holders of large blocks of non-voting shares opposed allowing the Billes brothers to get 2.75 non-voting shares for one voting share. The only fair conversion, said the institutions, was one for one. But the special committee of the board that drew up the plan said it was the best way to settle the impasse between the owners of the two classes of shares.

In February, the shareholders rejected the plan, with owners of voting shares overwhelmingly in favour but only 45.5 per cent of owners of the non-voting shares — short of the necessary two-thirds — in favour.

So the long battle for control of Canadian Tire still had no winner. The Billes brothers still had the 40 per cent of Canadian Tire voting stock they had been trying to unload since the fall of 1986, and their lawsuit and their sister's would now resume. (They had promised to drop the legal actions if the proposal had been accepted.) The dealers were still out the $30 million in deposits they had paid the Billes siblings (under the proposed restructuring they would have recovered $13 million of it). The non-voting shareholders, who would have nominated a majority of the directors under the proposal they rejected, continued to have little influence over company policy.

A new voting trust had been planned to take effect in the event the restructuring was not approved. It provided that the three Billeses and the dealers group could each nominate 3 of the 15 board directors for a two-year period. Martha decided to remain as a director, but her brothers stepped down.

It took several months of negotiations and large amounts spent on legal fees but, finally, in October 1989, the three Billes siblings arrived at a truce. Their agreement extended their voting-trust arrangement for 10 years. The deal specified that as

◀ Martha presents her brother Fred with a gift of an album containing 75 years' worth of Canadian Tire pictures at the 1998 board of directors dinner to mark Martha's acquisition of her brothers' shares.

long as the three of them owned at least 50.1 per cent of the voting shares, they would have the right to nominate the majority of the board of directors. They continued to have right of first refusal on each other's shares. If the Billeses offered shares to an outside party, the dealers would have the right to match any bid. The dealers promised not to hold more than 33 per cent of the voting stock — a nod to the strong feelings of Martha and her father that the dealers must never gain control of the company.

And so, after three years of fighting over control, Canadian Tire was back where it began — the three children of A.J. Billes, although not the best of friends, were still the controlling shareholders. The owners of 85 million non-voting shares still lacked the takeover protection they wanted.

But the non-voting shareholders weren't entirely dissatisfied. It seemed that people needing auto accessories, housewares, fishing gear, and all the other products on Canadian Tire's shelves didn't much care about who ruled in the boardroom. They just wanted quality at a fair price. And so, despite the battle for control, Canadian Tire was raking in profits and implementing an aggressive expansion program. In 1987, while the newspapers were full of stories about the battle for control, Canadian Tire quietly enjoyed a 6.8 per cent increase in revenues, to $2.48 billion. "The interests of the (non-voting) shareholders," conceded Bill Allen of the Class A Shareholders Protection Association in a newspaper interview, "are certainly being served in that regard."

The Canadian Tire Dealers' Association

IN OCTOBER 1952, Canadian Tire dealers from around northern Ontario assembled in North Bay. The basic purpose of the meeting, North Bay dealer Sandy MacDonald wrote later, was "to make us better [Canadian Tire] dealers and to better understand our mutual problems."* Issues discussed at that meeting included staffing requirements, appropriate retail square footage, and service department management.

Other regional dealer groups were formed in the aftermath of that first meeting. In 1968 they were all brought together as the Canadian Tire Dealers' Association (CTDA). Based in Mississauga, Ontario, the association deals with the same sorts of problems as those discussed at that first meeting in North Bay. It has an executive director and 20 staff members — plus a president, elected from among the dealers every two years — tackling such issues as human resources, the environment, and loss prevention. The association's most important activity, however, is negotiating a contract with the corporation covering every aspect of the relationship between Canadian Tire and its dealers.

Some 13 regional groups continue to operate under the umbrella of the national association, dealing with issues peculiar to their areas. In addition, 33 committees of dealers work on every aspect of the business, including supply chain, inventory best practices, and automotive operations.

It's the nature of Canadian Tire that there will always be a degree of conflict between the corporation and the independent entrepreneurs who operate the retail stores. "There are issues of control, issues of independence," says Terry Connoy, former executive director of the CTDA. "The dealers want to be more independent, while the corporation wants them to be less independent. That's pretty standard stuff. The relationship today is actually quite good."

"What benefits one of us benefits all of us," wrote Sandy MacDonald after the first dealers meeting back in 1952. "We had no secrets from one another." The same holds true today.

▲ An early meeting of dealers, most from northern Ontario, c. 1954: (clockwise from foreground) Derek Foreman (Huntsville), Clare Binkley (New Liskeard), Victor Muncaster (Sault Ste. Marie), Hing Young (Espanola), Howard Greenfield (Cochrane), Bob Irvine (Huntsville), Sandy MacDonald (North Bay), Walter Muncaster (Sudbury), Bernie Johnston (Timmins) (partially obscured), Harry Roy (Rouyn, Que.), and Frank Butorac (Kirkland Lake).

▲ Dealers enjoy a good laugh during a business session at the 1953 Dealer Convention. A.J. Billes is seated in the back row on the far right.

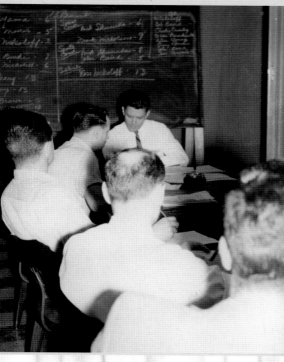

◄ A meeting of the newly formed Canadian Tire Dealers' Association, 1950s.

▼ Walker Anderson, the first associate dealer, and A.J. Billes admire a bronze bust of J.W. Billes gifted by the Canadian Tire Dealers' Association. The presentation ceremony was held at the Yonge and Davenport store on April 27, 1959.

▲ Alan Warren, 1979. Warren was an active member of the dealers' association for many years.

◄ The Mouthpiece, a monthly newsletter produced by home office employees, dedicated a section to reporting the latest associate store news and events.

▲ A 1983 dealer training session.

Retail

CANADIAN TIRE
FINANCIAL SERVICES

GAS⁺

CHAPTER SIX

The new world of retail

IT'S DIFFICULT to attract a top-flight CEO to Canadian Tire because most of those qualified to lead such a large, complex organization don't relish the prospect of working with several hundred independent-minded dealers.

The top job at Canadian Tire is a tough sell. "It's one of the most political jobs you could possibly think of short of being elected to Parliament," said Dean Muncaster. "I felt I had to balance the interests of the shareholders, all 27,000 of them, and the interests of the controlling shareholders and the interests of the dealers and the interests of the employees and the interests of the consumers."

Canadian Tire did not find the job easy to fill after Muncaster left it in 1985. The news release issued stating that Muncaster would "relinquish" the presidency of Canadian Tire also said that he would assist in the selection of his successor.[1] But he declined to do that, choosing instead to cruise Georgian Bay on his boat. Hugh Macaulay, the chairman, filled in as CEO for the next 10 months while the company tried to find a permanent replacement for Muncaster.

Macaulay agreed that the dealer system is a disincentive for some CEO candidates. "You would rather be a general of an army where everybody had to take your orders than put them to a vote," he said. "It's hard to fight a war when you've got

◀ This 2007 signage reflects the extent of
Canadian Tire's businesses at the time.

to have a ballot box on the front lines. But that's the way Canadian Tire has to be run." A former Pontiac Buick dealer, Macaulay adds: "That's also the way all of the automobile companies sell their cars in North America." As it turned out, the new CEO the company hired was an American, Dean Groussman, who disliked the dealer system and, not surprisingly, didn't get along with the dealers.

Groussman, 47 years old when he replaced Macaulay in the CEO's chair, grew up in the world of retailing. At the age of 10, he was selling newspapers on a street corner in Los Angeles and at 14 he was cleaning floors and emptying garbage at his father's discount store in Utah. After obtaining a degree in business administration, he worked for Target and two department stores before taking over as president of Zale Corp., a large U.S. jewellery retailer. Canadian Tire hired him in 1985 to make one last try at turning White Stores around; instead he presided over the sale of the unsuccessful chain. After four months at White Stores, he moved to Toronto to occupy the CEO's chair.

Dean Groussman's six years at Canadian Tire were turbulent but not unproductive. The belief that had prompted the Australian and American ventures — that Canadian Tire had exhausted growth opportunities in Canada — had been discarded by the time he arrived. Suddenly it seemed there were plenty of growth opportunities in Canada. New suburbs were expanding around Toronto and other major cities, which meant that Canadian Tire could build new stores without poaching on the territory of existing ones. In 1986, the company implemented 13 projects to add, expand, or replace stores. In 1987, there were 21 such projects. Between 1986 and 1990, Canadian Tire added 75 gas stations and 17 retail stores, pushing sales past $3 billion.

Macaulay recalls Groussman as an expert retailer. "He could walk down an aisle in a store and tell you what should sell with what, how high it should be off the floor, what shelf it should be on, what price range it should be in. It takes some experience to be able to do those things."

"Dean had some very fine qualities," recalls Robin Law, the former general counsel and board member. He enhanced the company's human resources department, paying particular attention to services for employees having personal difficulties. He also led the way in making the corporation and its employees major contributors to the United Way.

Groussman's wife, Maria, quickly made a splash on the Toronto social scene as an organizer of the Brazilian Carnival Ball and other glamorous events and as a member of the Toronto Symphony Orchestra board, among others. A native

▲ Hugh Macaulay, chairman of the board, 1988.

Texan, she had a perky personality and lots of energy, but her rapid rise in the Toronto social scene aroused jealousy in some quarters. In *The Glitter Girls*, a book about Toronto high society, Maria rated a chapter all to herself, entitled "The Upstart."[2]

Macaulay thinks the dealers as a group were distrustful of Groussman because of his background. The dealers could relate to Dean Muncaster, who came from a small Canadian city, where he worked in his father's Canadian Tire store. Groussman, in contrast, came from Texas and had no experience in a franchised operation. "A CEO of Canadian Tire *has* to be able to relate to the dealers," Macaulay says. Groussman had difficulty doing that.

Soon after he was appointed, he hit the road to meet some of them. In Vancouver, he had dinner with Vern Forster and Don Graham, operators of several B.C. stores. Recalls Forster: "He blurted out to me that he didn't like the dealer organization, he didn't see any reason for it, and he thought the stores should all be run by the company. I said, 'I am sure you and every other person in the corporation has thought that at some time. But if you make it obvious to Dealerland that that is how you think, you're sunk because they'll get you.' And they did."

▲ A Retail Planning display at the 1990 Dealer Convention.

▲ The grand opening of an Auto Source store was a great opportunity to attract customers to the eye-catching in-store hoist.

The major issue was the division of the gross margin between the dealers and the corporation. The dealers contended that the corporation was not calculating it fairly. Gil Bennett, a dealer nominee on the board of directors, was involved in meetings with management to try to resolve the issue. He concluded that the dealers were right. As a result of this conflict, the relevant section of the contract between the dealers and the corporation was clarified to avoid future disagreements.[3]

The dealers also quarrelled with Groussman over the issue of rent. The dealers own the inventory of their stores and the fixtures inside. The corporation owns or leases the building itself and the land it sits on. The dealers rent these from the corporation. Groussman wanted to raise the rent. The dealers didn't think that was a good idea. The issue, debated for three years, was resolved when the dealers accepted a rent surcharge based on the corporation's capital expenditures. However, the surcharge was scrapped by Groussman's successor, Steve Bachand.

The dispute between Groussman and the dealers went on for years. Surprisingly, the business reporters who follow Canadian Tire never knew about it. Given that Canadian Tire is a public company followed closely by the media, "it's amazing how [the issue] never became public," observes Robin Law.

Encouraged by growing sales at home and undeterred by the White Stores failure, Groussman decided in 1991 to have another run at the U.S. market. This time, rather than buying an existing operation, Canadian Tire launched a new store of its own, Auto Source, specializing in auto parts. Three stores were opened — two in Indianapolis, Indiana, and one in Dayton, Ohio.

Influenced by the growing trend toward superstores, the biggest Auto Source outlets had 24 service bays and 30,000 square feet of retail space. Canadian Tire had ambitious plans for this new venture — there were to be 100 or more outlets eventually, with annual sales of $1 billion. Unhappily, the second try to win over American consumers was not any more successful than the first. Auto Source was a money-loser from the start, partly because the American economy was experiencing a downturn and partly because of growing competition from other auto parts superstores and from discounters such as Walmart. By 1994, the chain had 10 stores and losses totalling $109 million. Bachand closed it down.

White Stores and Auto Source both failed for the same reason. "We tried to draw customers in," explains Martha Billes, "but customers had habits. You can't change their habits unless you are giving them something that is absolutely spectacular."

By 1992, relations between Groussman and the dealers were so acrimonious that members of the board were considering whether a change was in order. Gil Bennett, who would become chairman of the board in 1996, says that, in his opinion, Groussman would likely have been fired had he not decided to accept an offer from his former employer, Zale Corp., to return as chairman and CEO.

▼

IN 1991, Canadian Tire honoured A.J. Billes by naming its brand new, $200 million distribution centre in Brampton, north of Toronto, after him. The A.J. Billes Distribution Centre was state of the art in warehouse technology, an automated operation in which driverless vehicles could quickly pluck boxes of products ordered by stores and efficiently convey them onto waiting trucks for speedy delivery.

▲ The A.J. Billes Distribution Centre.

There was, however, one big problem: the A.J. Billes Distribution Centre didn't work. The software operating the machinery that was supposed to bring products to the loading dock was not up to the job. The warehouse accommodated 75,000 pallets containing inventory, but much of that inventory could not be located. And by the time the lost inventory was found, the sale that Canadian Tire had advertised in its flyers was over, the advertised items still in the warehouse.

With business continuing to grow — total sales reaching the $3 billion mark by the early 1990s — Canadian Tire needed the new distribution centre. But the facility had massive start-up problems. Ray McDonald arrived from Hudson's Bay Co. in May 1992 to take charge of the distribution system, with the A.J. Billes centre at the top of his priority list.

"It was a total disaster," recalls McDonald, who is now a Canadian Tire dealer in Niagara Falls. "The dealers were all mad as hell because they weren't getting product for their sale events and they weren't getting their regular weekly replenishment orders. There were something like 2,500 trucks in the yard when I arrived, full of product. So you have to decide, which truck do I take in first? Do I take in the one that's for last week's sale event that we missed? Or the one for next week's sale event? Or do we take in all those thousands of products that have been on back order for a month?

"I know, being on the dealer side now, we take such a beating when we don't have a product. And [the dealers] would have hundreds of products that they would be out of stock on at the start of the sale event. It was just staggering."

In normal circumstances, a store would get supplies every week or so. But because of the chaos at the A.J. Billes centre, those supplies stopped coming except on rare occasions. Many dealers tried to compensate by ordering extra large amounts. As

▼

▲ (Top row, left and centre) The A.J. Billes Distribution Centre under construction, aerial view, August 1989; northwest view, July 1990;
(top right) northwest aerial view of the nearly completed distribution centre, October 1990; (bottom) conveyor system at the A.J. Billes Distribution Centre.

a result, instead of getting an order for 1,000 copper elbows for a group of stores, the corporation would get an order for 100,000 — an astronomical amount. This caused problems at the supply end, since the vendor would need extra time to assemble so large an order. And it would add to the difficulties at the distribution centre, which didn't have room for 100,000 copper elbows.

"Everything was out of control," recalls McDonald. "The place was ready to implode. People couldn't work any harder, and they couldn't figure out what was wrong."

McDonald sent his family to France for six weeks so he could focus on the task at hand, fired certain people, and hired new ones with special expertise in applying information technology to distribution issues. He set up a "war room" where his team worked from 7 a.m. to 9 p.m. seven days a week for six weeks. It took a month to identify the major problems and another few weeks to fix them. "By September, the dealers were starting to feel confident that when they placed normal-sized orders, we could actually replenish the product," he recalls.

By the end of 1992, the A.J. Billes centre was operating smoothly, but work remained to be done redesigning both the software and the building. Among those who were instrumental in rewriting the warehouse management systems (WMS) software were Bruce Johnson, Doug Rapien, Peter Puglia, and Paul Jovian.

Johnson, who had been working for Hudson's Bay Co. running distribution for the Zellers stores, arrived in September 1992 to work for McDonald as senior director of distribution. A week later, Martha Billes called and arranged to meet him for lunch in the cafeteria at the A.J. Billes centre. She asked Johnson what he thought of the modern, new warehouse. Johnson replied, "It never should have been built."

What Johnson meant was that a less complex structure would have worked better. "The problem with highly automated buildings of that particular type is you pay the price in flexibility. It's a very inflexible building, and it requires a high level of operating discipline, which was not part of [Canadian Tire's] environment at that time in distribution. They had other distribution centres with limited automation, but this building was a totally different cat."

Canadian Tire's distribution system today, with the A.J. Billes centre at its heart, is superbly efficient. It *had* to improve because, just as the centre was opening, new competition was on the verge of arriving in Canada. That competition included the world's largest retailer.

"Walmart is a distribution company more than a retailer," says Johnson. "That's its strength. Its supply chain, its ability to land the product at the store at the lowest cost, is what has allowed them to maintain low prices and still achieve significant profits."

Distribution

DISTRIBUTION — getting products from the manufacturer to the distribution centres to the shelves of the stores — is a critical function in any large retail operation. When Steve Bachand took the reins of Canadian Tire in 1993, he inherited a distribution system in disarray. Stephen Wetmore was more fortunate: he inherited a system that, while more complex than ever, was running smoothly.

Many people think that the most important aspects of a supply chain are the handling and movement of the products. That's not true, says Pat Sinnott, former executive vice-president of information technology and supply chain, and now strategic advisor. The key, he says, is the flow of information about what products are needed from the stores to the corporation to the suppliers. "This information enables suppliers and every supply-chain partner to work together to provide stores and consumers with the products they need in a timely, efficient manner."

In 1997, the company implemented new planning systems using the most advanced software available. Sinnott explains: "If we need a certain number of units because that's what the supply chain forecasts, how do we convert that information into something the suppliers can use, the ocean carriers can use, the railway can use, the truckers can use, and the distribution centres can use?

"The supplier is interested in how many items he has to make. For each product, the supplier needs a week-by-week demand forecast for many weeks to procure raw materials and manufacture the product. The ocean carrier needs to know how many containers are going to be needed every week so that we can say to them, 'Seven weeks from now we need 150 containers to be sent to a bicycle manufacturer and then to the Port of Shanghai for shipment to Vancouver and Halifax.' And if we can't give the ocean carriers that information today, then we're going to pay more, and we may not get the 150 containers when we need them. Railways and trucking companies need similar information.

"Finally, the distribution centres need to know weeks in advance how many containers they must unload and how many cubic feet of product they must process, so that they can manage the labour force. The planning systems provide all this."

As a result, the company has never had to lay off distribution centre workers. Canadian Tire has about 1,300 full-time production employees in its two distribution centres in the Toronto region. It avoids layoffs because it employs only as many workers as needed during periods of normal demand. The heaviest demand occurs in spring when patio sets and barbecues are shipped and in fall when Christmas trees, shovels, and snow blowers are sent to the stores. During those times, 200 to 500 part-time workers are added.

Another 600 people are employed in Calgary and Montreal by Genco Distribution System of Canada, a separate company that runs the centres in those cities. Canadian Tire decided to employ the services of Genco when it opened

▲ (Clockwise from left) One of two delivery vans in use in the 1930s, providing both speedy service and mobile advertising; the small store in Yarmouth, Nova Scotia, finds a creative way to off-load shipments of goods into its second-floor storage area; Charlie McGrath at work in the Pears Avenue warehouse, 1955.

its Calgary Distribution Centre in 2002 for two reasons: Genco's expertise and the fact it was already running Canadian Tire's returns facility.

When the Calgary Distribution Centre was built, Canadian Tire negotiated with the city for the right to build it at the railhead, which has big advantages. Canadian Tire has a private entrance to the CP rail yard, where containers arriving from Asia or Toronto can be moved into the distribution centre without shunting over public roads. The Calgary facility, which opened in 2002, has 500,000 square feet and serves 135 stores in western Canada. In 2006, the facility was expanded to 940,000 square feet to handle increased volumes and a higher proportion of product from Asia.

An important change for the better was the implementation of a system known as time-phased replenishment (TPR), which gets products from the manufacturer to the shelves of the stores faster than was previously possible. TPR was implemented in 1996 by Sinnott,

who was then vice-president of logistics. Before TPR, Canadian Tire would give a supplier an annual forecast of how much product would be needed. Then, when Canadian Tire needed a supply, it would issue a purchase order. After that supply was exhausted, another purchase order would be issued. Since the manufacturer did not know when Canadian Tire would order more or how much product it would need, the lead time to fill the order was long and the supplier might not have the capacity to fill it.

With the TPR system, the projected weekly requirement of a product for each of the next 26 weeks is sent to the supplier. Each week, the projected requirement is updated and communicated to the supplier. This allows the supplier to have the necessary raw materials on hand and to schedule production to meet Canadian Tire's needs.

Some modest improvements were implemented from 1993 to 1996, but it was the introduction of TPR in 1996 that had the greatest impact on service levels

to stores and inventory costs. In a speech to the Strategic Leadership Forum in November 1997, Steve Bachand said that, since 1993, service levels had improved by more than 12 per cent. Most of the improvement was due to TPR. Orders were arriving complete and on time. The result for Canadian Tire was higher sales off lower inventory.

The second major improvement came in 2002 and 2003 with the opening of the Calgary centre and introduction of new distribution channels, just in time to support the rapidly accelerating increase in imports from Asia. The Calgary building can process products from Asia destined for stores in western Canada, rather than sending the products to Ontario and then back west again.

The addition of new distribution channels increased the capacity of every facility and reduced costs. In 1993, the only distribution channel working well was storage in the distribution centres. That is the most expensive way to distribute product. The cheapest is "direct to

▲ (Top left) Trailers inside the Brampton Distribution Centre, c. 1973; (bottom) truck cab, 1980s; (right) inside the newly completed A.J. Billes Distribution Centre, 1991. This cutting-edge 1.2 million-square-foot facility has 20 kilometres of conveyor belts and 1.5 kilometres of storage aisles, and what was likely the world's largest double-deep automated storage and retrieval systems when it opened.

▲▲ Canadian Tire Retail's new Montreal Distribution Centre in Coteau-du-Lac, Quebec, was officially opened on June 16, 2009, by Quebec premier Jean Charest; Stephen Wetmore, president and CEO, Canadian Tire Corporation; and Herb Shear, president and CEO, Genco Distribution System.

▲ The Montreal Distribution Centre, equipped with state-of-the-practice, automated equipment. With an area of 1.5 million square feet and capacity for 250 dock doors, it can accommodate 20 kilometres of conveyor equipment and handle some 14,000 SKUs.

◀ A 500,000-square-foot distribution centre and transportation hub was opened in southeast Calgary in January 2002. Serving 140 Canadian Tire stores in western Canada, and with links to Canadian Pacific Railway's intermodal lines, the facility is integral to the company's supply chain expansion strategy.

the store," as it cuts down on transport costs and eliminates storage costs. "Let's say we have 400 container loads of lawn and garden furniture coming in from Asia," explains Sinnott. "And we have 487 stores. We're not going to bring 400 container loads of lawn furniture into our distribution centre. We're going to wait until we get the stores' orders, and we're going to send those containers straight from the supplier or the port of entry to the stores."

Another distribution channel is called "cross-dock." Take, for example, orders of fishing lures from many stores, each order different. The vendor packages the individual orders in little boxes, then sends a big box full of these little boxes to the distribution centre. Each little box goes onto the next truck destined to the dealer who ordered it, without ever being placed in the storage area. The package contains only fishing lures, so it can be sent directly from the receiving dock to the retail shelf without any sorting.

Sinnott took over as executive vice-president of information technology and supply chain in 1997. At that time, approximately 12 per cent of the product volume was sourced directly outside North America. But manufacturing was in decline in North America. As a result, Canadian Tire employed only about 30 drivers and did not hire new ones to replace retirees. Prior to 2001, a truck might drive from a Toronto distribution centre to Quebec, unload goods at stores there, and then pick up a load from a manufacturer in Montreal to be taken to a Toronto distribution centre for storage

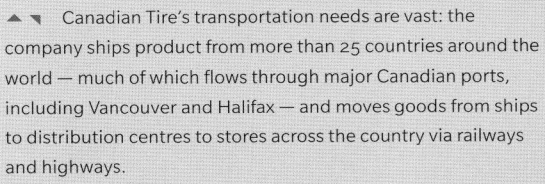

Canadian Tire's transportation needs are vast: the company ships product from more than 25 countries around the world — much of which flows through major Canadian ports, including Vancouver and Halifax — and moves goods from ships to distribution centres to stores across the country via railways and highways.

and order fulfilment. But if the manufacturing is happening in Asia instead of Montreal, that system doesn't work. "Unless you can stay at least 80 per cent full on the way back, it's uneconomic to have your own drivers," says Sinnott.

The solution was to use independent trucking companies that had multiple sources of freight and were thus better able to avoid running empty trucks. By 2001, the flight of manufacturing from Canada had become so pronounced that Canadian Tire laid off its remaining drivers. However, it still owns domestic containers (which can be transported either by rail or road) and trailers. As of 2012, Canadian Tire owned 2,301 trailers, most of which were emblazoned with

the red triangle, and 5,500 domestic containers.

Today, about 70 per cent of everything Canadian Tire sells is made in Asia. About 40 per cent of that is purchased directly from Asian manufacturers, and the remaining 30 per cent ordered from suppliers of global brands that are based in North America, or from agents or consolidators. The company almost always takes possession of the goods at the Asian ports. Once they arrive in Canada, most of the goods travel to their destinations by rail. Canadian Tire is the largest user of trains of any Canadian retailer.

Because of the huge volumes of product, the vast distances involved, and the need for timely delivery, maintaining an

efficient distribution system is one of the most difficult aspects of the business. By implementing state-of-the-art planning processes and adding distribution channels and distribution centres, Canadian Tire has improved service to the stores substantially. Less inventory sits in storage and more is on the shelves of the stores, and it is getting from factory to store on time. In today's ultra-competitive retail environment, first-rate distribution isn't a luxury — it's essential because Canadian Tire's competitors are very good at it. If Canadian Tire had failed to upgrade its distribution channels and systems, says Sinnott matter-of-factly, "we wouldn't be here today."

The arrival of Walmart and Home Depot was a "hugely challenging" time for Canadian Tire, says Maureen Sabia, the current chairman who was then a board member. "Everyone started counting us out. They said it was the end of Canadian Tire. Once Groussman had departed, we looked for someone who could take us to meet the competition successfully."

▼

STEVE BACHAND worked for three decades at Hechinger, a home improvement chain based in Maryland that was similar to Canadian Tire in three important ways. First, its history was one of steady, rapid growth, from $9.5 million in annual sales when Bachand joined to $2 billion in 1993, when he left to become president and CEO of Canadian Tire, taking over the reins from Hugh Macaulay, who was serving as interim CEO. Second, like Canadian Tire, Hechinger was a public yet family-controlled company.

The third similarity was a troubling one. Canadian Tire, like Hechinger, was vulnerable to powerful new competitors. Bachand had seen up close the phenomenal growth of Walmart and Home Depot during the 1980s, and he knew what those big box stores could do to a competitor that didn't react effectively. Hechinger did react. It built bigger stores, but it did not have the financial resources to build warehouse stores. The company became a money-loser and, in 1999, it declared bankruptcy.

"I think a lot of people don't appreciate how vulnerable companies are," Bachand says. "Even if you're doing $3 billion [in sales], it only takes a little bit of lack of success and everything starts to unravel: you can't replace things that need replacing, you can't grow, you can't take care of your people properly. It doesn't take much to turn you from success to failure.

"Walmart and Home Depot revolutionized retailing. There's a graveyard full of companies that were unable to adjust, for whatever reasons. Hechinger was a company that was founded in 1911 and suddenly it was gone, leaving 30,000 people out of work."

Bachand had visited some Canadian Tire stores when Hechinger was considering expanding into Canada. He was unimpressed by the product assortment, as well as the size, layout, and design of the stores. "I remember thinking, 'This is no competition. They may be big and have a lot of stores, but this is a business that's in trouble.'"

◀ Ray McDonald, Steve Bachand, and Bruce Johnson, 1994.

That sounds like a good reason for not taking the job, Bachand admits, but there were four reasons he agreed when asked to be a candidate to lead Canadian Tire. One was that he had been passed over for the CEO's job he had coveted at Hechinger. Also, the major U.S. players had not yet announced any plans to move into Canada; it was anticipated that they would come, but there was time to fix the business before they did. Third, Canadian Tire was still profitable and had very deep pockets. "Hechinger couldn't afford to fix itself, and I thought that Canadian Tire would be able to."

Finally, Canadian Tire's brand was a powerful asset. "Canadians liked it," Bachand found. "I remember getting a letter from a customer, saying, 'When are you going to fix my Canadian Tire store?' Most companies would die to have a customer say 'my store.' People thought of Canadian Tire as an important Canadian institution."

What bothered him most was that the people in the company seemed to lack a sense of urgency. In the United States, the competitor is the enemy. Canadians felt that way at a hockey game but not, Bachand thought, when they came to work. "That was a challenge — to re-energize the place, give it a sense of urgency, and give people a feeling that we're going to win this game, we're going to put the puck in the net."

▶ Matt Mucciacito, general manager of Canadian Tire's transportation department; John McBoyle of CP Rail; and Clyde Vieira, of the transportation department, help hold up a Canadian Tire container at the CP rail yard, c. 1990.

Canadian Tire had enjoyed decades of steady, profitable growth, and Bachand believed its people were taking too much of the credit for that success. Some of the credit was also due to good fortune in the form of population growth and lack of competition. "It was just organic growth on top of organic growth," says Bachand. "Keep opening the stores, you're doing well, just keep opening them."

It didn't take long before a sense of urgency was felt throughout Canadian Tire. Just months after Bachand's arrival, Walmart acquired Woolco, and Home Depot acquired Aikenhead's Hardware. "That was not good news," he observes. "But sometimes there's nothing better to get an organization focused and in high gear than a burning platform."

The big issue was cost. Such competitors as already existed — department stores and small hardware stores — did not challenge Canadian Tire on price, but there was no doubt the invading giants would. So the most urgent order of business was to get costs down and to get lower prices from vendors. That didn't necessarily mean being cheaper than Walmart on everything. "But you've got to be close," says Bachand, "you've got to be within 5 per cent."

The poor relationship that had developed between the corporation and the

dealers had to be addressed because "you can't run a franchise operation when you're at war with your franchisees ... The question was, how do we get the dealers to invest? Because they're responsible for the fixtures and the equipment in their stores, and this can add up to a lot of money, whether it's cash registers or forklifts. You've got to get a dealer who is an independent businessman to buy into what you want to do and to commit his own money to it."

One of Bachand's first moves was to identify a dozen of the most respected and successful dealers. He brought them together to talk about Canadian Tire's problems and what needed to be done to solve them. "We weren't going to announce the new strategy; we were going to create the new strategy together. Which we did."

The dealers became Bachand fans. "He was responsible for bringing us into the retailing of the new age," says Adam Bucci, a Quebec dealer who became president of the dealers' association after Bachand took over as CEO. Toronto dealer Eric Sellors goes further: "Steve Bachand saved this company," he says.

But some dealers could not adapt to the new reality. Canadian Tire would pay for increasing the size of the store, but it was up to the dealer to rebuild the interior and put more money into inventory. It was a big risk that some of the older

▲ Bancroft, Ontario, store, 1995.

dealers were not prepared to take. Jim Ryan, who headed dealer relations at the time, recalls that "you had guys who were saying, 'I know it's the right thing to do but I'm 60 years old and I don't want to take this on.' We had to work through those situations. Plus there's always the naysayer group who say you don't need to build the stores this big, they won't be successful, it will drive up our operating costs because we need more staff per hour and so on."

Bachand then asked the most basic question: What do we want to be? To answer it, a committee of dealers and corporate executives looked at every category in the store. There were three approaches to each category: dominant, which meant better than any other store; competitive, which meant as good as most; and convenient, meaning that the basics are covered. The committee decided Canadian Tire should be dominant in every category relating to automotive. In the sporting goods area, it would be dominant in hockey but just convenient in golf. That meant Canadian Tire would be the place to buy a 12-year-old's first set of clubs, but the serious golfer who wanted the latest in golf technology would have to go elsewhere.

This kind of analysis has far-reaching implications, Bachand points out. "Once you decide where you want to be in each category, you can quickly figure out how

many linear feet of space it takes. And when you've done that, you can figure out what your aisle widths are and then what the store size needs to be.

"So you don't start with a box and jam stuff in there. You start with what you want the store to look like and how you want to present your assortment of goods, and then you put a wall around it."

Another American who played an important part in preparing Canadian Tire for the American invasion was Wayne Sales, who came aboard in 1990 as senior vice-president of marketing. He was hired away from Kmart, where he had spent 25 years. Like Bachand, who arrived three years later, Sales was seen as someone with valuable experience competing with the big box stores.

Arriving in the midst of the difficult Groussman years, Sales was not impressed with what he found — discord between the dealers and home office and between management and directors. Not only had he not been told that the dealers had boycotted the most recent convention that annually brings together dealers and home office, but the company "had just spent an enormous amount of money on a brand new distribution centre, and I hadn't been informed of how poorly it was performing. I found absolutely no growth strategy whatsoever. So [Canadian Tire] was, in my view, completely rudderless. It was, frankly, a mess."

But, despite the problems, Sales saw great potential. He thought it was good that he had trouble describing the Canadian chain to puzzled friends and relatives in the States.

"Do they manufacture tires?" his father wanted to know.

"No."

"Do they sell tires?"

"Yes, but much more than that."

"Is it like Home Depot?"

"No."

"Is it like Walmart?"

"No."

People inside the corporation were worried about the lack of a clear image but Sales told them that it was a good thing because it meant Canadian Tire was different and, to be successful, a retailer has to differentiate itself from its competitors. "If you say you are like Walmart and you're trying to beat Walmart at their game, I don't think you're going to be successful."

Sales travelled the country to meet dealers and to talk to customers about what Canadian Tire meant to them. It was critical to have the cooperation of the dealers; "it was very clear that we needed re-focusing. The company needed to change its behaviour in the marketplace in anticipation of what I knew was headed our way."

He reeled off the names — Walmart, Home Depot, Sports Authority, AutoZone, Target, Lowe's. All of them, if they came, would compete with Canadian Tire in some category. Was Canadian Tire ready for them? No. What should it do to get ready?

Brainstorming sessions produced plenty of ideas. One was to transform Canadian Tire into a Home Depot–type warehouse store. Another was to pattern it after Walmart. Yet another notion that had support within the company was to spin off Canadian Tire's major categories into separate stores — an automotive store, a sporting goods store, and a hardware store.

Sales didn't agree with any of those ideas. He thought Canadian Tire should build on its advantages: its long history as part of the Canadian retail landscape, its famous Canadian Tire money, its dealer network. Canadian Tire, said Sales, should focus on its auto, home, and leisure categories and provide better assortments at lower prices than the competition. "We are three specialty stores under one roof," he said at the time.[4] In short, don't try to emulate Walmart or Home Depot; instead, become "a different and much better Canadian Tire store."

There needed to be more consistency, both in the appearance of the stores and in

▲ Wayne Sales receiving the Distinguished Canadian Retailer of the Year Award, June 7, 2004.

the assortment of products they offered their customers. "The shopping experience that we were delivering was very inconsistent," said Sales. "You really didn't know, if you had a shopping list and you set out on a Saturday morning, whether the store that you normally visit would have everything on the list or not."[5]

A key part of the strategy that evolved under Bachand and Sales was to upgrade the appearance of Canadian Tire's stores and increase their size without trying to be as big as Home Depot or Walmart and without reducing the number of stores. "It's always important in retail: you've got to play your own game, don't play their game. And part of our game was convenience." Convenience is critical to Canadian Tire."

Most Canadians are within 15 minutes of their nearest Canadian Tire store; Walmart and Home Depot can't make that claim. On the other hand, Canadian Tire isn't easier to get to in smaller markets that have only one Canadian Tire store. In those cases, it had to rely on its dominant position in key categories to keep customers choosing Canadian Tire over its competitors.

Canadian Tire had outgrown its stores. Too large an assortment of products and too many customers were crammed into too small a space, resulting in congested aisles and lineups at the checkout counter. In addition, whereas most chain operations strive to make each store the same so that customers feel at home in every location, the design and layouts of Canadian Tire stores varied widely from place to place.[6]

Under Bachand, four sizes of stores, with standardized layouts, were introduced. The largest was 53,000 square feet of retail space. The interiors of the stores were completely redesigned. The main departments were colour-coded — red for automotive, blue for household products, and green for sports and leisure. The aisles were widened and clearly labelled, and softer lighting was installed.

The new store formats were known as the "Class Of" stores, as in "Class of 1994," "Class of 1995," and so on, based on the year each format was introduced. The stores had essentially the same layouts, decor, and signage, but refinements were added in each year. For example, in the Class of 1997 store, a door was moved 20 feet to make it easier for a shopper seeking car parts to find the right counter.

Even the triangle was enlarged and given a more modern look. The words *Canadian Tire* were removed from the triangle; customers in focus groups said it wasn't needed — everybody knew what the inverted red triangle with the maple leaf on top meant.

In October 1994, Walmart began to change the signage on the Woolco stores it now owned to that of Walmart. Within weeks, the first 10 "Class Of" Canadian Tire prototypes opened. They were the biggest, shiniest Canadian Tire stores

▲ Elwin Derbyshire's new
Kingston store, 1990.

anybody had ever seen. It was one of the most crucial strategic moves the company had ever made. If it had not been made, Sales and many others believe, Canadian Tire might not exist today.

Redesigning the stores was only part of meeting the U.S. challenge. The other big piece was getting prices down. Canadian Tire's acquisition costs (the amount it pays to suppliers) were competitive by Canadian standards but not by those of the United States. Throughout 1992 and 1993, the company had been telling its suppliers that Canadian Tire henceforth would require "North American acquisition costs."[7]

The savings that resulted were passed along to customers. At the same time, the larger stores resulted in higher labour costs, higher electricity bills, and higher rents. The changes made some dealers nervous and quite a few bailed out. But all the dealers who owned the 10 prototype stores made money and their enthusiasm for the new Canadian Tire spread to other dealers, who bought in when they saw that the new store formats were working. They would call Bachand and ask, "When am I going to get my store? You guys are only doing 40 or 50 a year; it's going to take forever to get to me."

The impatience of the dealers to take part in the transformation of Canadian Tire was a nice problem to have. The board, too, was onside. It was an expensive undertaking that was changing the public face of the company. Meanwhile, the less

visible parts of the business, including its computer systems, were also undergoing modernization. Bachand would not have been surprised if the board had backed off. "I know it was scary for them," he recalls. "But they were very supportive."

Decisions were made on the assumption that Canadian Tire was going to be around for a long time. The rebuilding of the store in Kingston, Ontario, is one example of such a decision. It was slated for expansion to 53,000 square feet, but that created a problem, a shortage of parking. There was no obvious way to solve the problem, as the store was hemmed in by a road. But the dealer, Elwin Derbyshire, convinced Bachand that more parking was essential. As it happened, there was some empty land across the road from the store. So Canadian Tire bought it and then traded it to the city for the land occupied by the road. The city closed the road and the land it had occupied was used for parking. Later, when the store was expanded to 90,000 square feet, the land that had been traded to the city was repurchased by Canadian Tire.[8]

"I have so much respect for Steve Bachand," says Derbyshire. "He could see what I was saying, even though our real estate department was saying no. If we hadn't bought that land and had expanded on our original lot, we probably would have been doing $20 million in sales now instead of $40 million. If you restrict your parking, there's just no way you can grow."

Bachand allocated a total of $1 billion for renovating, expanding, or replacing 250 stores by 2000. It would have been disastrous for Canadian Tire if so huge an investment had not had an equally huge payoff. But it did. The average increase in sales was about 50 per cent. "Without that kind of a sales lift, we would have had to scrap the program and [go] to Plan B," says Bachand. "But there was no Plan B, and I don't know if I could have thought of one."

Why did sales increase? Because customers made more visits to the revamped stores and spent more money per visit. "That was always Walmart's success, when compared to Kmart," says Sales, drawing on his U.S. experience. "Walmart had twice the number of visits per customer as Kmart."

If Walmart thought Canadian Tire would roll over before the world's largest retailer, it was soon disappointed. One Walmart strategy was to put a shopping cart of Walmart merchandise in front of its store, with the total price posted, along with the same merchandise from Canadian Tire, to demonstrate how much money the customer could save by choosing Walmart. The Canadian Tire dealers responded by promoting products they were selling at prices lower than Walmart.

Walmart sent employees to Canadian Tire stores to check the prices. One dealer responded by going on his public address system to announce, "Canadian Tire customers, we have some special guests in our store today. They are from Walmart and they are here to see how low our prices are so they can lower theirs to match ours."[9]

Canadian Tire never adopted a defensive posture toward its new rivals. An example was the internal debate over whether to build a Canadian Tire store across the street from a huge new Home Depot in the Stockyards area on the west side of Toronto. One argument was that the location was too close to the Home Depot. The other was that Canadian Tire needed to learn how to live next door to Home Depot. The more confident argument won the day. The store was built and is doing well.[10]

Over Bachand's objections, Jim Ryan brought in a retired senior Walmart executive to speak at the annual Canadian Tire Dealer Convention. A dealer asked him, "If you were the president of Canadian Tire, what advice would you give us?" The Walmart executive had four pieces of advice: (1) have your products in stock, (2) never let there be more than three people in the checkout line, (3) keep the aisles wide, and (4) never be out of advertised specials. "They were the same points that Steve Bachand was trying to get across to our dealers," Ryan says.

▼

▶ The Midland, Ontario, PartSource store was one of eight to open in Ontario and Manitoba in 2007.

▲ PartSource grand opening in Midland, Ontario, April 20, 2007.

DESPITE THE FAILURE of Auto Source in the United States, Canadian Tire did not abandon the concept of a specialized auto parts store. In August 1999, in a project spearheaded by Sales, it launched PartSource, a national retail chain designed to appeal to do-it-yourself customers and professional automotive installers.

Bachand described the initiative as "an opportunity to fulfill customer needs in an underserved part of the automotive parts business." Plans called for spending up to $400 million to open 200 stores. The company began with five test stores located in southern Ontario and two in Calgary. When they were successful, it announced that PartSource would become a national chain. As of 2012, 87 stores were open in five provinces, including 59 in Ontario. There are three store formats, carrying 12,000, 24,000, and 50,000 auto parts respectively. The 50,000-part stores, known as "hubs," also function as mini–distribution centres to the smaller outlets. In addition, PartSource can quickly obtain any of the roughly 300,000 items in the universe of auto parts when they are needed.

In 2000, the board of directors decided Canadian Tire needed a strategic plan to ensure that it would maintain its place in the top quartile of North American retailers. Bachand in turn decided he did not want to work on a new strategic plan. His feelings at the time, he recalls, were "It's been a good run, the company's in good shape, and it's time to give somebody else a shot at it."

The monster truck was an added attraction at the Midland PartSource opening.

Bachand's run at Canadian Tire was a success, although it wasn't all smooth sailing, partly because of his quick temper, which he wasn't at all afraid to display in the boardroom. "He acted like a brat in front of the board but he did the right thing for the company," says one director. "He used to lose his temper and throw his books on the floor when he got mad in the boardroom."

Maureen Sabia, who was on the board during Bachand's tenure, says that if he displayed a temper during board meetings it was in part because the relationship between management and the board wasn't yet working as it should. "In those days, management controlled all the information. Unless you were a very knowledgeable director, you sometimes didn't ask the right questions. Management dispensed information grudgingly, and that doesn't work in today's world; it's too complicated. In the last 10 years, that has all changed. If management is confident in the relationship, it is eager to share good news and bad news with the board, and welcomes board input. But it takes a very secure CEO and management team to do that."

"[Bachand] was an impressive kind of a guy," says Martha Billes. "He'd get really gung-ho on stuff. But he had one hell of a temper. He showed it in the boardroom more than once to me, but on a regular basis he would tell Maureen Sabia to either sit down and shut up or to get the hell out of the boardroom."

"We got on fine" is how Bachand describes his relationship with Martha, who was preoccupied with matters relating to the struggle for control during Bachand's time as CEO. "Probably the best way I would describe our relationship is that we were respectful to each other."

Bachand picked a good time to leave. In February, the stock price plunged to $19.50 thanks to a write-down in the book value of the shares caused by weaker-than-expected results and large one-time costs. These included building an e-commerce site, preparing computer systems for the year 2000, and Bachand's $6.5 million retirement package.

The board did not look far for a successor. After a six-month search, Wayne Sales was appointed president and CEO. His background was similar to Bachand's. He was also an American with extensive experience in U.S. retail. Like Bachand, he enjoyed going to the stores and he was popular with the dealers. And like Bachand, who spearheaded the redesign and rebuild of the Canadian Tire chain, Sales wanted to see Canadian Tire grow.

Eric Sellors, a dealer at a large Toronto store, recalls meeting the new CEO after Sales had moved to Acton, a rural community west of Toronto. Acton was the site of a small Canadian Tire store that had been Sellors's first.

Sales said, "What would you think about putting a 50,000-square-foot store in Acton?"

Sellors replied, "I think you'd be out of your mind to do that."

Sellors was right: Acton, with a population of about 8,500, cannot support a large store. "But," Sellors says, "I liked that he was thinking big and asking, 'What do we have to do to compete and grow this thing?'"

An example of thinking big was the acquisition, in 2001, of Mark's Work Wearhouse, a Calgary-based chain of 320 stores[11] specializing in work and casual clothing. The acquisition of Mark's was more proof, if any were needed, that the notion Canadian Tire had nowhere to grow in Canada never made sense. In 2001, there were 454 Canadian Tire stores and not much need for more. Why not grow by expanding into a related product line, thereby selling different things to the same customers who already shop at Canadian Tire? Mark's sells the clothes people wear when they use what they buy at Canadian Tire. That's why there is a Mark's connected to Sellors's store on Sheppard Avenue, in suburban Toronto. The store is one of a handful that has a Mark's Work Wearhouse outlet adjacent to it in the same building.

Like Canadian Tire, Mark's Work Wearhouse started small. Its founder, Mark

▸ Mark's exterior branding, Ottawa Innes Centre, 2010.

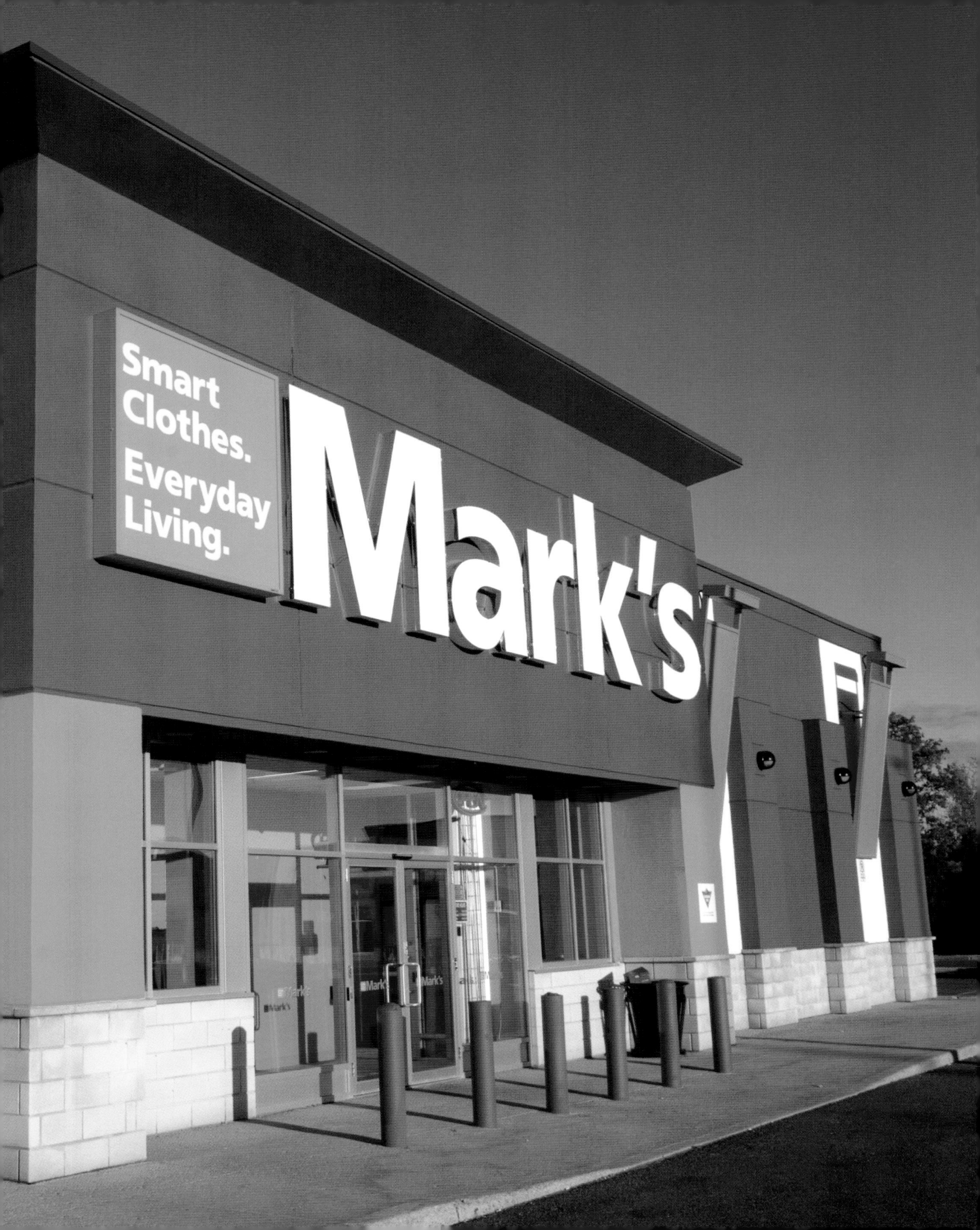
Smart
Clothes.
Everyday
Living.
Mark's

▲ The look of Mark's Work Wearhouse at the time of acquisition, Calgary, 2002.

Blumes, received $27,000 in severance pay when he was fired from a managerial position with Hudson's Bay Co. in 1977. He decided to use the money to go into business for himself. There was a steady demand, he knew, for blue-collar apparel, but most of it was sold in dimly lit, unattractive department store basements. Why not sell work wear in bright, attractive surroundings instead?

His timing was just right. In the late 1970s, workers were flooding into Alberta from all over the country for jobs in the booming oil and gas industry. Blumes sold $20,000 worth of work shirts, boots, and gloves the first day his Calgary store opened.[12] When Canadian Tire paid $116 million to buy the business, Blumes was long gone and Mark's Work Wearhouse was a national chain.

The takeover was known within Canadian Tire by the code name Project Steeltoe while it was being negotiated. Sales explained that Mark's Work Wearhouse was a good fit with Canadian Tire because the demographic profile of the clientele of the two stores was the same. In addition to blue-collar workwear, Mark's also sells casual wear, which appealed to Canadian Tire as a way to benefit from the trend to less formal dress.

Investment analysts hated the Mark's Work Wearhouse deal and, when it closed, Canadian Tire stock plunged. "They were surprised," recalls Michael Medline, who, as senior vice-president of business development, negotiated the acquisition. "They

didn't see how it fit. They said, 'It's soft goods. You don't know soft goods. You are a hard goods retailer, so why are you buying this?'"

It required quick action on Medline's part to make the deal happen. He was watching his son play in a basketball game when a banker called to say that Mark's was about to be sold. Through intermediaries, he let Mark's know the same day that Canadian Tire was interested and asked for time to consider offering a deal.

When Medline and his team began to look at Mark's, it quickly became clear that the deal made sense. Mark's was a public company, with all the expenses that entails. By absorbing it into Canadian Tire, those expenses could be eliminated. Also, Canadian Tire could provide Mark's with the cash it needed to build more stores and do the marketing required to increase its business. "We freed up Mark's to be able to grow," says Medline.

With memories of the White Stores debacle still lingering in the corporation's executive suite, the deal was a confidence builder for Canadian Tire, as it proved the company could grow successfully through acquisition. Within five years, Mark's was worth $1 billion,[13] almost 10 times what Canadian Tire had paid for it. As of 2012, there are 380 Mark's stores across the country.

▼

▲ ◥ Construction of the first Canadian Tire gas bar, at Yonge and Davenport in Toronto, 1958.

▲ Originally called Mor-Power Super Service Station, the Yonge Street gas bar was rebranded as a Pit Stop in 1970.

CANADIAN TIRE'S retail gas business, launched by A.J. Billes in 1958, had grown to 118 stations by the time Dean Groussman took over as president and CEO in 1986. Two years later, Jim Ryan replaced Arch Malcolm as president of the petroleum company. Although most gas bars at that time were located on the same property as a Canadian Tire store, they were managed as separate businesses, and their managers and employees were corporate employees rather than employees of the store dealer.

When Ryan took over, he discovered that some dealers didn't understand the benefits of having a gas bar on the property. Rather than seeing the gas bar as a driver of business, they complained about lost parking spaces. Ryan spent his first year educating the dealers about the benefits. He explained to them that, since the Canadian Tire money wasn't redeemable at the gas bars, all the benefits of it flowed to the stores. His analysis showed that this extra business was worth $250,000 a year to the average store. "So you could argue that the Canadian Tire gas bar was the single biggest customer of every store," Ryan said.

In the 1950s, gas customers received coupons that could be redeemed in the gas bar for mugs and other small rewards. The Canadian Tire stores, which were

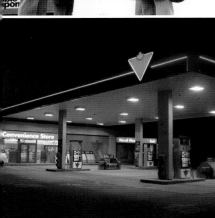

The evolution of gas bars: (from left, top row) Kitchener, Ont., *c.* 1962; Yonge and Davenport gas bar, 1977; Kitchener, Ont., gas bar, late 1960s; (second row) Rosemont, Montreal, 2007; Mississauga Southdown "lubritorium," 1960s; vintage gas bar, 1960s; (third row) Orillia, Ont., gas bar with swooping canopy, 1961; Willowdale, Ont., 1960; Amos, Que., gas bar, with updated signage, 1980s; (fourth row) Arnprior, Ont., gas bar opening, January 1981; Pit Stop promotion in Calgary, 1982; Winnipeg, *c.* 2001; (fifth row) Swift Current, Sask., 2006; prototype Highway 400 series Concept 20/20 gas bar near Trenton, Ont., 2010; (bottom row) Nanaimo, B.C., 2004; Torbay, Nfld., *c.* 2012; O'Connor Drive, Toronto, 2011.

Pay at the
Pump Only

EXPRESS
Debit and Credit Cards ONLY

→

THIS LANE

selling their own line of housewares, objected.[14] Eventually, the gas bars stopped handing out rewards. Instead, customers get coupons that entitle them to great deals on products in the stores. "One time we did hammers and I think we sold something like 600,000 hammers in a week," Ryan recalls.

Just as in A.J.'s day, Canadian Tire Petroleum never advertised lower prices than the major oil retailers. Its price was about the same, but the customers got a better deal because they collected Canadian Tire money as well as the special sale coupons. An important restriction was placed on the gas bars: they could not even think of adding car repairs and service to their offering. That was the preserve of the dealers.

The other major subsidiary business, financial services, also continued to grow during the 1990s. In 1988, Jos Wintermans replaced the president, Bruce Wilson, who had founded the business in Welland, Ontario, in 1961. Wintermans's previous employers had included American Express, so he was well versed in the credit card business, which had become an important profit centre for Canadian Tire.

Canadian Tire's card business was riskier than some, since cards were issued to people who wouldn't qualify for Visa, MasterCard, or American Express. To compensate for the added risk, the interest rate was higher. About 40 per cent of cardholders did not pay off their balance in full, and the interest they paid was an important income stream. The dealers contributed to Canadian Tire Acceptance's revenues by paying a fee every time the card was used.

The issue of whether Canadian Tire should accept Visa and MasterCard had been a source of controversy within the company as far back as Dean Muncaster's time. Until 1980, the only credit card accepted at Canadian Tire stores was the company's own. Consistent with A.J. Billes's belief that customers should be rewarded for using cash, no Canadian Tire money was awarded to customers who used the card.

It seemed obvious that if customers who didn't have Canadian Tire cards could use their Visa or MasterCard, they would spend more money. The dealers were lobbying for letting the bank-issued cards in, but Canadian Tire Acceptance was opposed.[15] A customer survey was done and, surprisingly, it revealed that customers said they wouldn't spend more if they could use Visa or MasterCard. But a closer reading of the study showed that most of those surveyed already had Canadian Tire cards; those that didn't said they would spend more if they could use the cards they already had.[16] When Visa and MasterCard were finally introduced in 1980, Canadian Tire Acceptance compensated for the lost revenues by charging a fee to the banks for processing transactions on the bank cards.[17]

◄◄ When this Mississauga Gas+ service station was renovated in 2011, the original 1968 swooping canopy was preserved. Only three Canadian Tire gas bars with this specific Googie architectural design have survived.

CTAL 1966

20 EMPLOYEES   2.6 MILLION
Annual Credit Sales
SERVICING
20 CANADIAN TIRE STORES

The president of Canadian Tire Acceptance at the time, Bruce Wilson, insisted that Canadian Tire must retain its own card and not cede Canadian Tire's entire credit business to the banks. In the United States, he said in a speech, the federal government had decided to restrict consumer credit. Among the methods being used were limiting the number of cards issued, increasing fees charged to cardholders, and adding service charges. "You can imagine the consequences if we were to place our fate solely in the hands of the banks," Wilson warned. "Should such bank restrictions occur in this country, our credit sales would drop in very big hurry — resulting in lower profits because of sales that we just would not make."

Another worry was that the banks could decide to increase the discounts they charge retailers on credit sales. Without its own card, said Wilson, Canadian Tire "would be at the mercy of any decision made by the banks."

Moreover, the 1.6 million Canadian Tire cardholders were a valuable asset for the company. They spent twice as much as bank card customers and they were a market for other products, such as the Canadian Tire Auto Club.

It didn't happen for another 15 years, but Canadian Tire found a way to combine the appeal of a card that can be used anywhere with the advantages to the company of operating a proprietary card. In 1995, it became the first non-bank in the world

▸ The new headquarters of Canadian Tire Acceptance Limited (now Canadian Tire Financial Services) in Welland, Ontario, 1976.

▲▲ A close-up look at the Welland office reveals that the triangle is an integral part of the company's identity.

▲ A 1966 poster proudly marks the achievements of Canadian Tire Acceptance Limited (CTAL) at the time Canadian Tire acquired a majority interest.

▲ Tom Gauld, past president of Canadian Tire Financial Services, succeeded Wayne Sales as president and chief executive officer of Canadian Tire in 2006.

to issue its own MasterCard.[18] Under the leadership of Tom Gauld, who replaced Wintermans, 8 million Canadian Tire cardholders were gradually switched over to the Canadian Tire Options MasterCard. In a final blow to the Billes brothers' policy of favouring cash sales, shoppers were rewarded for using the card in the form of a new kind of Canadian Tire money. The money was "on the card" rather than in paper bills and could be redeemed only when using the card. Yet another advantage the new card had over the old Canadian Tire card was an interest rate about 10 per cent lower.[19]

The Options card was an immediate hit. By the time the conversion program was completed in 2004, 4 million customers carried the card, which had become the second largest MasterCard franchise in Canada, after the Bank of Montreal.[20]

Canadian Tire Acceptance changed its name to Canadian Tire Financial Services and established the Canadian Tire Bank. The advantage of being a bank was that Canadian Tire's credit operations could follow a single set of federal rules rather than 10 sets of provincial regulations.

Cash was no longer king, a transition that might have dismayed A.J. and J.W., but one part of A.J.'s legacy — profit-sharing — lived on. A.J. spent his last years working on ensuring that profit-sharing, which initially was offered only to corporate employees, was available also to employees of the dealer-owned stores across the country. A.J. and the dealers did not always agree on how the profit-sharing plan should work. One dealer, Alan Warren, refused to implement it, although his North Bay, Ontario, store was highly profitable.[21] But by the turn of the 20th century, profit-sharing was securely in place across the chain. "It's solved," says Terry Connoy, former executive director of the Canadian Tire Dealers' Association. "It's not really an issue any more. There's a minimum dealers have to contribute, and if they want, they can contribute over that." Connoy's years managing the dealers' association, from 1991 to 2011, provided him with a good vantage point to observe Canadian Tire during a time of rapid change. "When I first got there, the relationship was bad," Connoy recalls. "[The dealers and management] weren't even talking to each other. They were divided over rent, strategy, management, sharing of the margins, profits, just everything. The dealers were not happy with where Canadian Tire was going or with the management team."

Things improved in 1993 when Steve Bachand replaced Dean Groussman as president and CEO. "The key thing he did was to get the corporation to think of itself as a retailer instead of a wholesaler," said Connoy, who worked in the grocery

PACIFIC ASSOCIATE STORES LIMITED
4150 McCONNELL DRIVE
BURNABY, B.C. V5A 3Y9
PHONE 421-9300

000001

FEB. 9 19 91

PAY
TO

THE SUM 31079 DOLS 00 CTS $ 31,079.00

PROFIT SHARING PLAN

PACIFIC ASSOCIATE STORES LIMITED

THE TORONTO-DOMINION BANK
TORONTO-DOMINION TOWER BRANCH
700 W. GEORGIA ST., PACIFIC CENTRE
VANCOUVER, B.C. V7Y 1A2

"000001" ":90040"004":   "9369"

◀ Burnaby, B.C., store staff with a cheque in the amount of their share of the store's annual profits, February 9, 1991.

industry before joining the dealers' association. When the corporation thought of itself as primarily a wholesaler, it didn't pay sufficient attention to what happened once the goods reached the stores. As a retailer it adopted more of a leadership role in store design and product display. When the dealers saw sales rising as a result, they dropped any objection they might have had to the more intrusive corporate role in store management.

However, the tension between the corporation wanting more uniformity and the dealers guarding their independence persists. This is a good thing, says Connoy. "I think it was best described to me by a person from Walmart who said that, of all the competitors they face, they found Canadian Tire the most difficult to confront because there was no normal. In any other enterprise the head office dictates what gets done. That doesn't work at Canadian Tire, where the franchisees have a lot of freedom in pricing their goods. The maximum price is set by the corporation, but the dealer can sell for less than that. And that confused Walmart."

If you are manager of a corporate-owned store, "you don't do anything creative, you don't drop prices; you wait for direction and follow the rules and the policy." Connoy and many others wonder whether Canadian Tire would have survived the

▶ In 1976, A.J. Billes was invested by Governor General Jules Léger as a Member of the Order of Canada for, as the employee newsletter noted, "his contribution to the community of business, his concern for his employees and the sharing with them of his successes right from the very start."

onslaught of the powerful new competitors that arrived during the 1990s without the determined defence of their territory by the dealers, many of whose life savings were on the line. The stores of Eaton's, Woolco, Kmart, Zellers, Simpsons, and Woodwards were all corporately owned and run by salaried managers. All are gone. The dealer-owned stores of Canadian Tire survive.

▼

DEAN SIMONTON, a psychologist at the University of California, says a genius is a person who puts together a vast number of ideas, insights, observations, and theories and comes up with something great. The genius has more good ideas than the average person but, because the genius has so many ideas, there are lots of non-starters as well. Quality is "a probabilistic function," he writes. "The more successes there are the more failures there are too."[22]

Simonton's profile of a genius sounds a lot like A.J. Billes, who died in 1995 at the age of 92. "He believed you had to try a lot of things before you get one thing right," says Maureen Sabia. "You've got to have a thousand ideas, and if one or two of those work out, you've succeeded."

"You've got to have a thousand ideas, and if one or two of those work out, you've succeeded." — Maureen Sabia quoting A.J. Billes

Yet A.J. did not fit the stereotype of the egocentric genius. On the contrary, he was humble enough to know when it was time to step down as president and take a lesser role. And he worked tirelessly for profit-sharing, convinced that the success of Canadian Tire was a collective effort. In April 1976, Governor General Jules Léger presented A.J. with the Order of Canada in a ceremony at Rideau Hall in Ottawa. "I felt as though just by being there that I was the representative of everyone connected with Canadian Tire; employees, associate store owners and their employees, management, and even our many suppliers," A.J. commented afterward.[23]

A.J.'s respect for his employees was part of the management style that made him, and Canadian Tire, so successful. An effective CEO needs the best possible information, and A.J. knew that sometimes the most accurate information doesn't come just from senior management. "He would come into your office to find out what was happening," recalls retired buyer Ron Down.

Pat Stephenson worked for Canadian Tire for 35 years, 10 of them as A.J.'s secretary. If a customer called with a complaint, A.J. wanted to hear about it, and so Stephenson would put the customer through. A.J. wanted everyone, secretaries included, to take an interest in the business, and he was delighted when Stephenson said she wanted to know more about tires. "I checked with some other girls who were also interested and A.J. arranged for a little group of us to have a tour of a big tire manufacturing plant," she recalls.

Like Fred Sasaki, Art Arai was a Japanese Canadian evacuated from the west coast during World War II. A.J. hired him in 1949. First he worked in the small order department. Then he worked as a computer programmer and became manager of data processing. After 25 years in that job, he decided to retire, but A.J. dissuaded him. He became A.J.'s right-hand man, helping with the profit-sharing program and driving when the boss could no longer take the wheel.

"A.J. led a fairly structured life," recalls Arai, who is now retired. "He had his routine. Most of it involved work. Even the weekends were workdays for him. I picked him up at 7:30 in the morning and he was all ready to go … He talked about business, about his ideas, things he was proposing to do."

A.J. embodied the work ethic that built Canada. His devotion to profit-sharing, unique among major Canadian companies, illustrated his generosity. Yet at the same time, he was frugal. "He wasn't mean, but he made a penny work," is how Tommy Rye, a retired buyer from the early days puts it. Art Arai recalls the time A.J. got in the car and said, "I had a terrific evening last night." He had gone out with his second wife, Marjorie, to dinner and a performance by the singer Tom Jones. Arai expected to hear an account of the show. "Instead he just talked about how cheap it was. He had a hamburger and boiled potato, just $1.25. Then he talked about how cheap the senior's ticket for the show was. That's all he had to say about the evening out. Nothing about Tom Jones."

But wanting a good deal didn't mean not living well. When he discovered that one of his executives, Mayne Plowman, had a better car than he did, A.J. decided that wouldn't do. "I bought my first Lincoln in 1972," recalls Plowman. "It was a beautiful car. Alf was in my office talking to me one day and he said, 'What about this car you're driving?' I said, 'It's lovely.' Then he said, 'I think I'll get one.' So he did. J.W. kept driving his Oldsmobile."

Larry McFadden worked with A.J. in the tire department in the early 1970s. A.J. could have lunched in any of Toronto's luxurious private clubs that catered to the business elite. But, McFadden recalls, he preferred to eat with his staff at Mount Pleasant Lunch, a small family restaurant, or Swiss Chalet. "It was kind of neat because here I am, a 23-year-old guy, rubbing shoulders with A.J. He was just a down-to-earth, intelligent, great manager." The topics of conversation were A.J.'s dogs and business. For McFadden, now a dealer, it was an invaluable business education.

The least self-important of men, A.J. would not have felt at home in a plush club. His grandson, Welland dealer Owen Billes, puts it this way: "If you didn't know who he was, you wouldn't know he was who he was, that's for sure."

His idea of relaxation was to putter in his vegetable garden at his country home at Shanty Bay. "He would set me up on an old tractor at the cottage," recalls Owen, "and I'd just sort of race around the driveway all weekend. He had this amazing watering system that he had designed. He was a tinkerer. I never had the impression he did things for the money. I guess once you do well and have lots of money you don't have to do things for the money anymore. You can do stuff for the passion of it. And that's probably why he ended up doing profit-sharing, just because he believed in it so much."

Ten years after his death, A.J. Billes was inducted into the Sales Hall of Fame in a ceremony in Toronto. "The secret to A.J.'s great success was simple," said Martha

Billes in accepting the award on behalf of her late father. "Treat every employee as your equal. My dad would never ask anyone to do anything that he would not do himself … My dad and my uncle knew what extensive research has proven today — that when employees are treated fairly, customers benefit."[24]

▼

SINCE THE EARLY 1990S, Maureen Sabia, Martha Billes's good friend and colleague on the Canadian Tire board, had been urging Martha to make an offer for the voting shares owned by her two brothers, Fred and David. Martha was the natural successor to her father, Sabia says, because "she is just like him. She is the one with the Billes DNA and smarts and understanding and long-term commitment to this enterprise. She is passionate about Canadian Tire.

▲ Maureen Sabia and Martha Billes, 2012.

"She knew she was smarter than her brothers were about this company. David is a very smart engineer. Fred didn't articulate things well and put people off, but in hindsight a lot of what he said was right. But the three could never function as one."

Moreover, Canadian Tire would benefit if Martha could buy out her brothers, Sabia argued; with three controlling shareholders, the board was "siloed." It was difficult to get the appointees of Martha, Fred, David, and the dealers "to think as a whole, rather than furthering someone's agenda." Having only one controlling shareholder would fix that problem.

By 1997, Fred had moved to the Cayman Islands and he wanted to sell his stake in Canadian Tire. David did not want to sell. Several proposals were discussed. Some involved converting voting shares to non-voting shares and then selling them, leaving just enough voting shares in the hands of Martha and David to retain control. But Martha was determined not to have any repeat of what had happened 10 years earlier when a deal between the Billes family and the dealers ran afoul of securities regulators. In the end, she and David could not agree on how to structure a deal for the two of them to buy Fred's share. David then decided to sell. As part of the buyout deal, the $30 million paid to the Billles siblings in 1986 (see page 164) was equalized among the three of them.

Martha paid a total of $45.4 million for both brothers' voting shares, giving her control of 61 per cent of the voting shares and thus control of the company. "I ran around and collected all the money I could and bought the brothers out," she says. The price per share was less than 15 per cent above the market price, so she was not required to make an offer to the non-voting shareholders.

The struggle for control of Canadian Tire, triggered 41 years earlier by J.W. Billes's problematic will, was finally over.

▼

IN 2007, an eight-year-old girl named Jennifer registered for a soccer league. The fees and equipment were paid for by Jumpstart, Canadian Tire's program to help kids take part in sports and recreation. One in three Canadian families can't afford to pay for sports participation for their children, and Jumpstart is there to make sure kids like Jennifer get to play.

Jennifer was shy and afflicted with behavioural problems that left her unable to function in the regular classroom setting. In her first season as part of a soccer team, she gained skill and confidence. During the next two seasons, she continued to improve. At the age of 11, she qualified for the provincial soccer team. At 13, she was playing in two premier leagues. With her improved behaviour and self-confidence, she was able to enrol in a regular grade 7 class.

"Her love of and passion for the game is evident," said Martha Billes, speaking at the 2011 Dealer Convention. "Jennifer has grown from a shy little girl into a confident and capable young woman with achievable goals and a plan for the future."

All it took was a gift of registration fees, equipment, and transportation expenses to make a huge difference in one child's life.

Canadian Tire, both at the dealer and corporate levels, has always supported good causes. "The spirit of helpfulness ... is the moral fibre of Canadian Tire — the very essence of this far-flung organization," A.J. said in a speech to dealers in 1959.

In the early days, this spirit was often expressed informally. J.W. and A.J. would take money from their pockets or the cash drawer to help people, including the occasional person in need who wandered in off the street. On a regular basis, they gave a substantial portion of their retail markup to members of the clergy to aid the disadvantaged.

The corporation made frequent donations to hospitals and schools. As for J.W., his belief in the importance of supporting community causes was such that, when he died in 1956, his estate of $6.2 million was left in trust to 23 charitable organizations.

In 1983, the Canadian Tire board created a Social Responsibility Committee, which became a special interest of Fred and Martha Billes. The philanthropic budget was expanded with a renewed emphasis on charities benefiting children.

In 1989, Canadian Tire announced it would help fund and organize a national program to support charities devoted to the health, safety, and welfare of children. The first recipient of funds under this initiative was Stay Alert Stay Safe, a national street-proofing organization, which received $700,000.

In 1993, the company established the Canadian Tire Child Protection Foundation. It continued to fund Stay Alert Stay Safe and also provided financial support to Canadian Tire Cycle Safe, Learn Not to Burn, the KIDestrians traffic safety program, and AquaQuest, a Canadian Red Cross water-safety program.

Six years later, Martha Billes was the driving force behind the creation of the

▲ Wayne Sales (far left) shares a toast at a Foundation for Families event.

▼ Foundation for Families volunteers unload much-needed supplies for a community in crisis.

▶ In response to an escalating flood crisis in Manitoba in 2011, teams from Canadian Tire, Mark's, and Jumpstart moved quickly to provide assistance to thousands of affected residents. Canadian Tire loaded 53-foot-long tractor-trailers with emergency supplies, Jumpstart activated its Community Crisis Response program, and Mark's provided footwear and clothing: (from left) Ken MacAuliffe, Corporate Affairs, Canadian Tire; Dan Thompson, president of Jumpstart; Prime Minster Stephen Harper; Grant Wallace, dealer; Glenn McLean of Jumpstart; and Adrienne Alexander, Corporate Affairs, Canadian Tire.

▲ Martha Billes, chairman of the Canadian Tire Foundation for Families, and Wayne Sales, president and CEO of Canadian Tire, are joined by skaters and Canadian Tire employees at a skating event to launch Jumpstart. The Great Skate event took place on February 20, 2005, in Ottawa and at ponds, rinks, and arenas across the country.

Canadian Tire Foundation for Families, of which she served as chairman. Its mission: To provide a helping hand to families in crisis, ensuring that life's basic needs are met — food, shelter, clothing, and essential goods. Through the Community Initiatives program, the dealers support local food banks and shelters. Through the Community Crisis Response program, they provide families with basic needs in crises such as the Quebec Ice Storm and the Manitoba floods.

Jumpstart was launched in 2005. It is national in scope but local in focus, working with 314 chapters representing 1,800 community partners, including police, schools, community centres, and other organizations serving children. Among these are Big Brothers Big Sisters of Canada, which identified Jennifer as a child needing help. She is one of more than 479,000 children who, as of June 2012, had become involved in organized sports thanks to Jumpstart. Because of the phenomenal success of Jumpstart, Canadian Tire decided in 2009 to group all of its charitable activities, including the Foundation for Families, under the name Canadian Tire Jumpstart Charities.

Jumpstart's Quebec branch, La Fondation Bon départ de Canadian Tire, created in 1990, raises $1.5 million a year to help underprivileged young people and facilitate sports participation. It operates an outdoor camp, Base de plein air Bon départ, in the Laurentians, that welcomes 500 youngsters every summer. A total of 6,500 kids each year, of whom 2,500 are handicapped, use the camp, which is open year round.

Children from many backgrounds across Canada take part in a variety of sports through the Jumpstart program. Everyone should know how to swim, and Jumpstart has helped 59,000 children to do just that. There were no programs available to teach swimming to children living in St. James Town, a low-income district of central Toronto with a large immigrant population. Working with local community groups, Jumpstart developed a plan. It obtained a

volunteer from the Toronto Swim Club to help set up the program. Speedo Canada donated swimsuits, goggles, kickboards, and flippers. The result was that children who might have grown to adulthood without this basic life skill learned swimming and water safety.

Canadian Tire provides the greatest portion of Jumpstart's funds. Other donors include Sport Canada, a federal agency that provided $1 million in 2011. Donations also come from the governments of Newfoundland, New Brunswick, Ontario, and Manitoba; corporations; and the general public. Dealers hold fundraising events and the corporation often contributes a percentage of the revenues from certain products

advertised in the flyer. A highlight every year is Jumpstart Day, when Canadian Tire stores across the country host special events, games, and fundraising activities. In 2011, Jumpstart Day raised more than $3 million, including $200,000 from customers. The annual Canadian Tire Jumpstart Invitational Golf Tournament is another major fundraiser. In 2011, it collected $1.1 million.

Total revenues for the year were $13.2 million, an increase of $1 million over 2010. Canadian Tire Corporation and its suppliers take care of all the administrative expenses, so that 100 per cent of the money raised goes directly to help needy children take part in sports and recreation.

One of the most enthusiastic supporters

is former Newfoundland and Labrador premier Danny Williams. He was looking for a cause to support, a charity that helps at-risk kids and has very low administrative costs. Finding just the cause he was looking for, he donated $250,000 to Jumpstart.

Jumpstart is an innovative tool to combat what has been called an "epidemic" of inactivity among young Canadians. Inactivity is associated with increased risk of type 2 diabetes, depression, and drug use. "Together with our partners," says Martha Billes, "we are effectively helping children to stand up and exchange sedentary TV and computer time for physical activity."

CHAPTER SEVEN

Adventures in dealerland

THE EXPERTS told the Billes brothers they were crazy. Why would you let independent dealers own Canadian Tire stores? You invented Canadian Tire; therefore, the profits belong to you. Let the corporation own the stores and hire managers to run them.

That was the advice J.W. and A.J. Billes were given in the 1930s when Canadian Tire stores were beginning to appear in towns and cities across central and eastern Canada. Despite the disapproval of the financial advisors, the new stores were owned and operated by independent dealers, with Canadian Tire Corporation acting as the wholesaler, providing everything for sale in the stores. Why did A.J. and J.W. reject the advice of the experts? "Because the two brothers saw something more than numbers," A.J. explained in a letter to a dealer 50 years later. "They saw what the experts failed to comprehend — the power of fully dedicated people outperforming the experts' mathematical expectations."[1] From its earliest beginnings, the entrepreneurial spirit has pervaded the company.

But the system has always had its doubters, including two of the six presidents and CEOs who have run the company since A.J. Billes stepped down from that role.

◀ The first store in Sussex, New Brunswick, May 1936.

"To have a smooth-running, forward-looking Canadian Tire, you have to have the corporation and the dealers working together." — Maureen Sabia

Dean Groussman was one, and Tom Gauld, president and CEO from May 2006 to December 2008, was the other. Gauld wanted the corporation to assign salaried managers to new stores and to existing ones when a dealer retired. Having 20 or 30 profitable corporate-managed stores, he maintained, would improve the corporation's bargaining position in contract negotiations with the dealers. The corporation would be able to argue that it didn't really need dealers — salaried personnel could do the job just as well.

It bothered Gauld that when the corporation made a big investment to enlarge a store, the dealer reaped most of the increased profits. According to Gauld, the corporation was making a smaller return on capital from the stores than the dealers. The average dealer was making significantly more than he would doing the same job that a Walmart store manager does for $200,000 a year. Partly due to the financial imbalance, the profits of Canadian Tire Retail — the division responsible for the Canadian Tire stores — were modest. Growth in earnings per share was being fuelled by Canadian Tire Financial Services and Mark's Work Wearhouse, while growth in the earnings delivered by Canadian Tire Retail remained slow.

Gauld challenged the idea that the dealer model is superior by pointing to the success of two competitors, Walmart and Home Depot, both of which operate only corporate-owned stores. Moreover, Canadian Tire Corporation does possess expertise in operating corporate-owned stores, since most of its Mark's Work Wearhouse outlets, obtained in a 2001 acquisition before Gauld became CEO, are run by salaried managers.

Gauld made the dealers nervous, and that made the board nervous. "To have a smooth-running, forward-looking Canadian Tire, you have to have the corporation and the dealers working together," says Maureen Sabia, who recalls the discussions around the board table at the time. "[Gauld] didn't know how to relate to them. He never reached out to them because he thought they made too much money."

Martha Billes acknowledges that the dealer system is not perfect. Nepotism "still exists, no matter how hard you try to enforce the rules," she says. Then there are

CANADIAN TIRE CORPORATION

ASSOCIATE STORE   HAROLD THOMPSON

SPORTS

HARDWARE

absentee dealers who leave their stores in the hands of hired managers, a practice that is inconsistent with the Canadian Tire philosophy of dealer-operated stores. And there are dealers who try to keep labour costs down by hiring mostly part-time staff; this is not ideal, as part-timers are less knowledgeable than full-time employees.

Despite such problems, management is convinced the dealer system is the best one for Canadian Tire. The company operated two corporate branch stores between 1927 and 1929 and both flopped. A.J. Billes said later that he and his brother didn't know how to run a branch store. It's hard to know for sure whether that would still be the case; although some board members found Gauld's arguments interesting, Gauld didn't stay long enough to push his plan for corporate stores to the implementation stage. It never amounted to anything more than just talk around the board table. "It was just pie in the sky," says his successor, Stephen Wetmore, who dismisses the idea. He believes the dealer system is an essential aspect of Canadian Tire's business model.

Franchising developed early in the 19th century when brewers in Germany and England began providing financial aid to tavern owners in return for their agreement to stock the brewers' beer. North American franchising started in 1851 after Isaac Singer invented the first sewing machine that used an up-and-down motion. Singer soon discovered he had a problem: he could make sewing machines, but he lacked a way to get them into the hands of customers. A potential customer needed training in how to operate a sewing machine and that meant she needed direct contact with a retailer. Singer knew he needed a sales force but he lacked the capital to set one up. So he came up with the idea of licensing local entrepreneurs to sell the machines and teach new customers to use them.[2]

This new business model was suited to the burgeoning capitalist economy of North America in which innovators like Singer and Henry Ford were inventing new products but needed help to distribute them across a vast continent. As the Billes brothers realized some 80 years ago, franchising is a way of growing by using other people's money. The franchisor gets increased revenues; in return, the franchisee gets a proven system, the buying power of a powerful chain, and most valuable of all, a name that customers already know. A new independent store will not establish a steady clientele for months or years, if ever. A new Canadian Tire dealer has loyal customers from the moment the doors open for the first time.

Canadian Tire differs from other franchisors in an important way. In most franchised chains, the prospective franchisee applies for the right to operate a store in

◀ Rouyn, Quebec, store staff arrive at the 1973 Products Parade, held in the Automotive Building on Toronto's CNE grounds.

a particular area. In the Canadian Tire system, new dealers have to be ready to pull up stakes and go where they are told. Generally, they are at first assigned small stores, usually in small towns. Only when they have proven that they can operate the small store efficiently do they get a chance to move to a bigger, more profitable store. However, once installed in that first store, the dealer has the right to refuse another move.

In some chains, the new operator has to have, or be able to borrow, a large amount of money because he or she must buy the land and finance the building of the store. But in the Canadian Tire system, the corporation owns or leases the land and the building, whereas the dealer owns the inventory as well as the shelves and all the rest of the inside fixtures.

About 120 people (mostly men; there are only 12 female dealers) apply to be dealers each year. The process starts with an interview, online or by telephone, followed by an in-person interview at the corporate office. Candidates who get past that stage meet with a panel consisting of corporate executives and dealers. The panel is looking for people with an aptitude for business, strong leadership and interpersonal skills, and a commitment to customer service and to Canadian Tire.

Those who pass this stage enter a six-month training program, conducted partly in the classroom and partly in-store. The trainees absorb the knowledge of established dealers and then go back to home office for testing every few weeks.

This system is in stark contrast to that used by a typical franchised operation, points out Wetmore. "They interview you and check your background and, if you can write them a cheque, you get the franchise and you're off and running. Here at Canadian Tire you have to quit your job, go through six months of training, and get ready to move, but you don't know where. And you may not make it through dealer training. Or a store may not become available. That's a huge commitment to make. Probably no other company in the world does it this way. And it's worked that way for years and years."

Canadian Tire's unique mobility system for dealers, says Wetmore, "allows privates to become generals — provided you follow the rules." Dealers are supposed to spend at least two years at each store. They have a chance to move up to higher-volume stores based on their performance as determined by a number of factors, including financial results. However, there may be good reasons why a small store in a remote community is not profitable and the new dealer may be moved along from there after two years regardless of his audit scores. Mobility also depends on the availability of stores — it could be several years before a larger one becomes available.

It's the dealer's job to hire and manage sales staff and manage the store's finances. The corporation is responsible for advertising, sales promotions, ongoing dealer training, and central purchasing. Some franchised chains have books full of rules that franchisees must follow in their retail operations; uniformity is required. That's not the Canadian Tire way; rather, dealers have considerable autonomy on how to run the business and on product selection from the array offered by the corporation. However, there is less autonomy on that score today than in the past. Dealers must support all major merchandising and marketing programs and demonstrate their best effort to make those programs a success. And they must offer all the basic Canadian Tire lines, such as sporting goods and minor appliances.

Most dealers aspire to graduate to a very large store, which can earn them more than $1 million a year. But some form strong ties to their communities and are content making a good living operating a smaller store.

A new dealer is required to put up a smaller amount of money than are franchisees in most other major chains and, if he doesn't have it, Canadian Tire helps to arrange a bank loan. The relatively small entrance fee gives Canadian Tire access to a wide pool of talented potential dealers. The possibility of earning a very high income lures highly capable people. And the farm system method — bringing dealers up progressively from small stores to big ones — ensures that only experienced ones make it to the biggest stores.

▼

ARCH BROWN left a good job as General Motors' youngest-ever district manager in 1958 to join Canadian Tire. Brown was determined to be his own boss. Dick Billes, an old high school friend, had promised him that the company would finance his first store if he worked for the corporation for five years first.[3]

Brown started out on roller skates at the Sheppard Avenue Distribution Centre and worked in several other departments before becoming dealer sales manager. His job involved inspecting every store in the chain at least once a year and analyzing the market to see where new stores should go. He also interviewed the finalists of the 1,200 applicants a year in that era who wanted to become dealers.

Brown took a much different attitude to new applicants than competing companies such as Imperial Oil and Western Tire, he recalled in a 1997 interview. "They rolled out the red carpet to new applicants. I went the opposite way and I gave every applicant a really bad time. That threw a lot of them off their guard. In my office, I put a sign up that was on the inside of the entrance door. You would read it only as you were going out. Most people, with their body language, gave away how it affected them. The sign said: 'Measure a person by the amount it takes to discourage them.'

"Most of the applicants, when I peppered them with difficult questions, just gave up. So the sign told the story. I believe that tenacity is one of the major ingredients of a dealer's success." In 1963, just as he had been promised, Brown got his store. It was located in downtown Barrie, on Lake Simcoe, about 80 kilometres north of Toronto. At the time, Barrie had a population of about 22,000; it is now one of the fastest-growing cities in Canada, with a population of 145,000. Three dealers had preceded Brown in Barrie. Canadian Tire had placed one of its earliest associate dealerships there in 1938, probably, Brown thought, because A.J. Billes's country retreat was located nearby, at Shanty Bay.

"I had the advantage of being a field man, and knowing what the weaknesses and strengths were of all stores. When this store came up, I realized its potential." Realizing that potential required a personnel shakeup, and so he fired the underperformers and hiked the wages of the rest by 50 per cent. He used the money he had accumulated through profit-sharing during his five years working for the corporation toward buying the store and also decided he should return the favour; he thus became the first dealer to implement profit-sharing for his employees. "I said to myself, when I first opened the store, I would treat my employees in the same way Canadian Tire had treated me, so I was the first dealer to have a profit-sharing plan," Brown said.

▲ Arch Brown, newly a dealer, delivers a presentation at the 1963 Dealer Convention.

▶▶ Arch Brown's first store in Barrie, on Dunlop Street West. He bought and demolished surrounding houses to allow for more parking.

He set an example for his employees. "For the first few years I purposely stayed out of any extracurricular work," he said. "All my energies went to the store. That meant not taking holidays, and working seven days a week."

Brown spent heavily on advertising and promotion, and he made a point of talking to his customers. On busy Saturdays he liked to stand in the parking lot and ask departing shoppers if they had found what they came for.

Brown's early career had been marked by wanderlust. As a teenager, he hitchhiked across the country. Later, he did radio interviews about his trip to England via horse boat. At the age of 21, he landed a job with Trans-Canada Air Lines, the predecessor of Air Canada, eventually spending six months at the airline's office in Nassau, in the Bahamas, before joining General Motors.

But once he landed in Barrie, his travelling days were over. He liked the town and decided to stay, building his business as the city grew. His store was bigger than most downtown Canadian Tire stores and, with one of the highest market penetrations in the Canadian Tire chain, it was profitable. But Brown wasn't satisfied. In 1967, a three-storey, 50,000-square-foot building adjacent to Highway 400 on the outskirts of Barrie became available and Brown decided to move.

No other Canadian Tire store was nearly as big, and Brown's would remain the largest in the chain for 17 years. Some Canadian Tire people, thinking Barrie couldn't support such a large store, called it "Brown's Folly." That it was a three-storey building created logistical problems. "It wasn't because I was smart, it's because I had a vision that I went with a large store," Brown said. "That first year was an anxious one because I was gambling."

But the gamble paid off. The store became a roaring success and Brown became a rich man. From 1963, when he bought the downtown store, until 1995, when he retired, his annual sales grew from $300,000 to more than $25 million. By then, he was much more than a prominent businessman — he was a pillar of the community.

No one was more deeply involved in supporting a wide variety of local causes than Brown and his wife, Helen. He fostered close relations between the community and the nearby Canadian Forces Base Borden, birthplace of the Royal Canadian Air Force, and helped to establish a museum at the base. He proudly wore the uniform of honorary colonel. And Base Borden became one of his biggest customers.

When he died in 2009, flags were lowered at Georgian College, which had lost its staunchest supporter. He was involved with the college for 35 years and served as chairman of its board of governors. In 2004, Brown donated $1 million to the college, the largest single donation it had ever received. To mark a previous donation of $500,000 in 1997, the art building was named the Helen and Arch Brown Centre for Visual Arts.

"He was the most involved unelected member of the community," said former Barrie mayor Janice Laking. "Anything that the city was doing he wanted to be involved in. He just liked to be at the forefront of things." After retirement, Brown supervised construction of a 10,000-square-foot house. "Arch just wanted the project," Helen explained. "He always wanted a project."[4]

The career of Arch Brown exemplifies the Canadian Tire dealer system at its best. A talented entrepreneur becomes a Canadian Tire dealer because he wants to be his own boss and make a lot of money. A salaried manager could have done a good job, but he could never have earned enough to donate $1.5 million to a college. Nor would he have been likely to stay long enough to earn the name that was bestowed on Arch Brown by the local press: "Mr. Barrie."

▼

DEALERS and company executives often talk about the "creative tension" between dealers and corporation that, over the long run, tends to make Canadian Tire stronger. But sometimes it gets a bit too creative. Justin Young, a dealer in Waterloo, Ontario, whose first job was at Arch Brown's second Barrie store, previously worked for the corporation as retail support manager, which meant acting as a liaison between dealers and home office. In this position, one of his duties was an annual assessment of the 28 stores in his territory, from Dryden, in western Ontario, to Lloydminster, a small city that straddles the Alberta-Saskatchewan border. These reports were important to the dealers, as they determined whether they would get substantial bonuses. (Such bonuses have since been discontinued.)

When a house goes up for sale, sometimes the real estate agent will encourage the seller to "stage" it to impress potential buyers by clearing away the clutter, perhaps painting the living room, and even bringing in better furniture. Young's problem was that sometimes dealers would stage their stores to get a better mark.

An extreme example occurred in 1999. Young got off a plane at Thompson, Manitoba, at 10 p.m. He noticed a man loitering in the terminal. He thought he had seen the man before but wasn't sure where.

Young was planning to visit the Canadian Tire store unannounced the next morning but decided to drive by it in his rented car on the way to the hotel. The store was closed and the retail area was dark, but he noticed a few cars in the parking lot.

He stopped for dinner, and then, at 11 p.m., drove by the store again. Now it was brightly lit and more cars were in the lot. He peeked through a window and saw a crew of workers sweeping and organizing. The service bays were also being cleaned.

Young realized that the man in the terminal had been a spy for the dealer who, knowing a report was due imminently, would have been expecting Young to show up any day. Young climbed back in his car and found a spot to park in a nearby alley that afforded a good view of the store. Three hours later, at 2 a.m., the store was still brightly lit and the work continued.

"I said, 'Screw this, I'm going to grab a couple of hours of shut eye,'" Young recalls. He returned at 6:30 a.m. to find the staging project still going full blast. He drove to the airport and caught the next plane for Winnipeg without ever entering the store.

"The dealer called me a week later and said, 'I hear you might have been in town.' I said, 'Yeah, I was.' He said, 'Why didn't you say something?' I said, 'I was afraid of what I would've said to you.'"

Two years later, Young obtained his dream job: he became a Canadian Tire dealer. His first store? The same one in Thompson, Manitoba, that he had spent the small hours of a morning spying on from a parked rental car.

Young has never worked anywhere except Canadian Tire. His career began in 1980, at the age of 12 in his hometown of Barrie, when he got a job as a bagger. "My father was an avid Canadian Tire customer, and he talked to the manager and I got the job." Bagging was just the beginning. Young, it seems, was born to work at Canadian Tire. "I loved what I was doing. I would go to the store right after school from 4 to 6 p.m. Then I would go home, have dinner, and do my homework. I would be back at the store at eight and I would work until nine, collecting all the carts. On Saturdays, I did carry-outs for customers and deliveries." His pay was $2.15 an hour.

Young suffered from osteosarcoma, the same bone cancer that killed Terry Fox. When he was 16, he spent a year in chemotherapy treatment at Toronto's Hospital for Sick Children. During that year, he lost his left leg. His boss, Arch Brown, came to the hospital and presented him with a VCR — an expensive item at the time — on behalf of all the staff.

Shortly after finishing his chemotherapy treatments he was presented with a five-year pin at a Christmas party by Arch Brown and A.J. Billes. A photo of the event is among his proud possessions.

Losing a leg didn't mean losing his desire to work at Canadian Tire. After high

▲ Justin Young with A.J. Billes and Arch Brown in 1985, being awarded his five-year service pin.

school, he studied economics at the University of Western Ontario, working at Auto Centre Plus, an all-automotive Canadian Tire store, to put himself through university. After graduation, he was offered the job of manager at the store in Steinbach, Manitoba. (The Auto Centre Plus concept was never rolled out across the country, although two stores, in London and Toronto, are still in operation.)

Working one's way up the ladder at Canadian Tire is a good way to see the country. Steinbach is a dry community with many churches and where a man is considered strange, Young found, if he's over 21 and isn't married, with a couple of kids. He was about to move on after two years when the dealer asked him to stay to help manage the transition from a 5,200-square-foot store to a new one of 28,000 square feet. "It was an amazing experience because I was able to learn all the things that I wasn't so good at. Managing a high-volume small store and running a larger store [requires] a different skill set."

With his economics background, Young could have obtained other work, but he was hooked on Canadian Tire because "it doesn't feel like work. There's never the same day twice. You're only limited by your imagination and your ability to think things through. And we can effect change in a dramatic way on everything from how we merchandise product inside a store, how much space we give it, and so on. It's astounding to me, the psychology behind what we do."

Canadian Tire has a habit of bringing promising young talent into the corporation for a spell before awarding them a dealership. One day, the Steinbach dealer, Gary Manks, called Young in and told him, "You're going to work for the corporation."

He wasn't asked if he wanted to but he understood that this was the next step on the road to becoming a dealer. His job was retail support manager for the Prairies and it paid $10,000 less than the job he left at Steinbach. But it was a good learning experience and also a good move for his personal life — it was at the Canadian Tire headquarters in Toronto that he met his wife-to-be, Shelley.

"I was able to see the best of the best, in terms of operations, and the worst of the worst," Young says of his store visits and audits. "And out of that, you gain a lot of insight, and what you really learn is that the dealer can be a very effective tool to drive the organization. The best stores have the best teams. It's the leadership skills of the dealer combined with the business skills and the knowledge and experience to drive the organization."

Young would walk into one of the 28 stores in his territory and announce to the dealer, "I'm going to be your best unpaid manager." And if a dealer would argue with him about an idea he was proposing, he would say, "I'm younger than you, and someday you're going to retire and I'm going to take your store and I'll do it then."

The dealers liked Young and became his "ambassadors." Later, they supported Young's campaign to become a dealer himself. In 2001, he finally got his store but not before undergoing the gruelling two-day interview process in place at that time, involving seven one-on-one interviews. The interviewers were executives from different areas, including the heads of distribution and petroleum. If one voted no, the applicant still got his dealership. But if two were against it, the application was rejected.

The selection process needs to be tough, says Young. "The only way the dealer system flourishes is by having supremely committed individuals with a proven ability to grow sales and profit."

The reason he was assigned to Thompson, an 800-kilometre drive north of Winnipeg, is that 22 others had turned it down. The weather, with temperatures averaging colder than minus 20 degrees Celsius during the winter months, is a deterrent. But the real reason Thompson is a hardship post for a Canadian Tire dealer is the labour shortage. Young couldn't compete with the wages the local nickel mine was offering, and so attracting and retaining good people — especially the skilled technicians needed in the service department — was a major headache. He had to develop special skills — ones that weren't taught in dealer school in Toronto — to get and keep the people he needed.

"One of the key competencies of a dealer is the ability to adapt to the circumstances," Young says. "You've got to think creatively."

When he arrived, he discovered that the car service department lacked both mechanics and counter staff. Young launched an aggressive recruiting campaign. He even recruited among his customers. Clerks selling auto parts were told to be on the lookout for customers who seemed to know something about cars. They would ask, "Are you an auto technician?" If the customer was, he would be told, "Hold on a second, somebody here wants to speak with you."

The employee would call Young, who would rush down and escort the customer to his office. "I'd get them there for an hour or more, whatever it took, and wouldn't [let them] leave until they agreed to work for me," he says.

But he still couldn't find locally all the mechanics he needed, so he recruited employees from Nova Scotia, the Northwest Territories, Red Deer, Winnipeg, and Hyderabad, India. The latter location produced B. Poorna Chandra Raju, known as Raj, who had worked in a Mercedes-Benz dealership in India. The immigration authorities allowed Raj into the country because Young had first advertised across Canada without success.

Young has vivid memories of Raj's arrival in Thompson. "This poor guy got off the plane and it was 32 [Celsius] below zero. He'd never seen snow before. All the guys called him 'Frosty.' Even in the shop, for the first three months, he wore thermal underwear, and he had these little cotton gloves on his hands. We had an oil burner in the shop, so there was plenty of heat, but he would sit there and he would shiver all day long. And his teeth would be chattering. It was painful to watch. But he did a phenomenal job for us."

By the end of his three-year stay in Thompson, Young had doubled the number of technicians in the service department from 5 to 10. For other positions, Young recruited one of his sisters, who was living in Mexico, and another sister from Toronto, along with his wife's brother. He knew he had to sell more than a job in a northern town. He told potential recruits, "'I'm not going to give you a job, I'm going to teach you a career.' I would be their counsellor, their confidant. Every day I took a different employee for lunch."

In 2004, Young switched to another northern Canadian Tire outlet, in Espanola, Ontario. The staff were members of the Communications, Energy and Paperworkers Union of Canada, making Espanola the only unionized store in Ontario. By the time Young left in 2007, it was no longer unionized, although Young says he did not try to talk the employees into quitting the union.

"The staff chose freely that they no longer wanted that representation. We were able to articulate to our staff a relationship built on trust. The trust was earned by investing in their welfare. The first thing we did when we took over the store wasn't merchandising or investments on the retail floor, it was cleaning and painting the lunchroom and putting in better washrooms. We invested in technology to make their jobs easier and we hired more staff.

"They didn't need the union protecting their job security because I was hiring and hiring. We were able to remerchandise the store and put on significant sales growth, year after year. They were able to see first-hand that we could provide for them in a way a union could not."

The initiator of the decertification vote was an employee who had worked in the store for 24 years. She had benefited from profit-sharing for the first 14 years but hadn't received any for the past 10 years, since profit-sharing is not included in a union contract. "She was able to show the rest of the staff how much she had in her

CANADIAN

Driving

Tires Parts Service

auto
parts & service

A Fresh Start!

profit-sharing account and that she hadn't had a penny put into it in 10 years. That was a very compelling reason why the union was decertified."

His next, and current, store — a brand new store in an out-of-the-way location in a large urban area, Kitchener-Waterloo — was another different experience. The policy of buying more land than is immediately needed has served Canadian Tire well and it continues to do so to this day. Young's store was surrounded by farmers' fields and road construction made access to it difficult. A customer told Young that Canadian Tire was his favourite store but he wasn't coming often because it wasn't convenient. By that, he meant that the other stores he and his wife visited on their shopping night were close together, whereas the new Canadian Tire was off by itself in another direction.

"People don't shop stores as much today as they shop an area," says Young. "It's because they're so time-starved. So if your store is not part of a group, you're at a disadvantage." In recent years, the area around Young's store has attracted other retail businesses and so the traffic at Canadian Tire has picked up.

Most dealers are keen to move up from a small store in a small town to a bigger one in a major urban area. The dealer can make more money in a larger store but the trade-off is that the local status of a Canadian Tire dealer diminishes as he moves up. In a small town, he is an important figure in the community, with easy access to municipal officials. In a big city, he's just another storekeeper.

"In Espanola and in Thompson, if I wanted information about something, I could talk to the [civic leaders] and get the information almost instantaneously. The reason is that we were the third-largest private employer in the region — not just in the town, in the region. We were a big fish in a small pond. In Espanola, we would deal with 700 organizations a year. Why? Because everybody did business with us."

In both of his small-town stores, Young enjoyed a 28 per cent market share in what is sometimes called "CTTM," or Canadian Tire–type merchandise. In an urban centre in Ontario, a good share would be half that. In Waterloo, says Young, "we're a guppy in a shark tank. It's a different experience." Whereas in the small town, the dealer is known as the owner, most urbanites don't realize that Canadian Tire stores, unlike Walmart or Home Depot, are locally owned. Young has put up signs in his parking lot saying, "Thank you for supporting a locally owned and operated family business."

He doesn't see clear sailing ahead. Competition is stiffer than ever, costs keep rising, and customers are increasingly more demanding. "Our generation of dealer will need better skills — better human relations skills, better technology skills, better merchandising skills, better understanding of financials, leadership, and competition. We've got less margin to make mistakes, and will likely make less [profit] than our predecessors."

He figures freight costs and staffing costs are up about 65 per cent over the past decade. Yet prices haven't gone up accordingly. An oil filter, to cite a basic Canadian Tire product, costs around $4, the same price as 25 years ago.

Still, there is nowhere other than Canadian Tire he would rather be. Young expects Waterloo to be his last store. The city, with its diversified economy, educational institutions, and proximity to Toronto, is his idea of a perfect location. Apart from a lawn-cutting business he ran as a teenager, Young has never worked anywhere else and doubts that he ever will. "Canadian Tire is the one thing in my life that's never let me down."

ADAM BUCCI became a Canadian Tire dealer in 1974. The store was in the ski town of Sainte-Agathe-des-Monts, in the Laurentians, north of Montreal. At 1,500 square feet, it was minuscule. It also had a problem: it was crammed with stuff nobody wanted to buy.

The merchandise had been accumulated by two previous dealers. The one Bucci bought the store from had not wanted to discard it, since he had paid for it, so he left it on the shelves and in two warehouses. "In those days, people stayed in a store maybe a year and a half to two years because the company was expanding so fast," Bucci says. "Whatever mistakes the first guy made, they just carried on, because why get rid of it? If you throw it out, you don't get paid for it a year later when the new guy comes in and you're selling your scrap."

Nothing is perfect, including Canadian Tire's dealer system, and here was a case where the system created a perverse incentive: a novice dealer had clung to worthless, unsaleable merchandise in the knowledge that another novice dealer was going to take over his starter store and would be forced to pay him for it. This was bad for both the corporation and, whether he realized it or not, the dealer, as a store full of things nobody wants is going to have a hard time increasing sales.

Bucci was having none of it. Just because he had paid for a lot of junk didn't mean he had to keep it. He tried giving it away, but that didn't work, and recycling wasn't yet the norm. So he carted it to the dump. The previous owners had been English speakers who had not understood that the demand for large-size footwear is limited in a French-speaking town like Sainte-Agathe-des-Monts — francophone Quebeckers are smaller on average than other Canadians. Bucci took about 500 pairs of large-size boots, ski boots, and skates to the dump. "Who wears size 12 in Quebec?" he asks. A lot of out-of-season seasonal stuff, like lawn furniture, also went.

Bucci wasn't happy about having to throw away unused merchandise that he had paid good money for. He was almost crying as he discarded it, but the positive effect on his business was immediate. "All of a sudden I had space," he recalls. "Before I had very limited space for the stuff that sold. Now the customers kept buying more and more, because it was there."

The store had annual sales of $457,000 the year before Bucci bought it. When he left two and a half years later, sales were $1.3 million and the store had made a profit for the first time. Bucci had discovered a powerful retailing philosophy so simple that even a small child can understand it: if you want your customers to buy things, fill your store with things they want. It's a philosophy that guided him through a successful 35-year career.

In the end, getting rid of the outdated merchandise saved money, since he no longer had to rent two warehouses to store it. It also made his retail operation more cost-efficient: "When you have more of what sells on the sales floor accessible to the customers, the clerk is not spending his time trying to find something the customer needs."

A store today would be less likely to have a large amount of old, unwanted products, since items that don't sell are classified as discontinued and are devalued. After two years they are worth nothing, so an incoming dealer would not have to pay for them. Typically, a dealer marks down something that isn't selling. Then he marks it down even more. If still on the shelf after that, he throws it out. Some dealers display clearance sections full of such items, while others prefer not to.[5]

The Canadian Tire policy of starting new dealers off in small stores ensures that they become acquainted with all aspects of the operation. "You do everything when you're in a small store," says Bucci. "You're the cashier, you're the floor-washer, you're the maintenance man." As a result, Bucci was well prepared when he made the jump in 1976 from the small store in Sainte-Agathe-des-Monts to a brand new one eight times as large in Terrebonne, just outside Montreal. In 1976, the corporation offered much less support to dealers than it does now. "When I opened the store in Terrebonne, I had 40 feet of electrical products. You sat in front of the shelf and said, 'What am I going to put where?' And you kind of designed what the store was going to look like. Whereas today, every four-foot section is predetermined, product by product, hook by hook, shelf by shelf, so you could take anyone off the street, show them the picture, and they could do it."

Both Canadian Tire and its customers changed during Bucci's three and a half decades as a dealer. Just under 100 per cent of the Terrebonne customers were French speakers. Using these customers as an example, he said that, in the past, they didn't think through the purchase. "A customer would come in for tires and

The newly completed store in Terrebonne, Quebec, 1977.
Adam Bucci (centre) at a product review meeting, 1979.

say, 'What's your best tire?' And you'd say, 'This is my best tire.' And he would say, 'That's what I want.'" But over the years, the consumer became choosier. Now he or she picks out the tire that's appropriate for the kind of driving and mileage it will be used for, and it might be the cheapest rather than the most expensive.

Bucci was an activist dealer, always looking for ways to make Canadian Tire better. He organized a course for Canadian Tire's Quebec mechanics. He rented a location, obtained equipment from suppliers, and hired a master mechanic to enhance the skills of technicians from around the province. He was chairman of the "forecasting group," which met with the marketing executives at home office every few months to estimate sales volumes and discuss which products would or would not be big sellers. Bucci says about 30 per cent of dealers are involved in such activities, effectively working as consultants to the corporation. He served on many committees and, in 1994, became president of the dealers' association.

Not surprisingly, he does not agree with the two CEOs who thought the dealer system was unnecessary. The average CEO of a large company serves in that position for only about five years or so, Bucci points out. "And what's the life expectancy of a dealer? Thirty years. When all of your marbles are on the table, you're going to want to make sure that whoever's running the company is making the right decisions. So thank God for the dealers in this company or the company would be out of business. I say that very humbly.

"As a dealer, you want to make as much money as possible. So when the person at home office who is responsible for the marketing is not doing a good job, you're going to bloody well tell him. He's not your boss. Whereas if you were the manager and the guy did a lousy job, you couldn't say anything. Or you could, but then you'd be looking for a job somewhere else."

The outspoken attitude of dealers means that the corporation gets high-quality information. The dealers *have* to be frank: the actions of key people at home office, such as the marketing staff or the buyers, have an immediate impact on their stores. "If the buyer does not do a good job, my volume goes down, my profits go down, and it also affects my employees because I share my profits with them. So the feedback from the stores to the corporation is a lot more aggressive [than it would be in a store run by a salaried manager]."

Bucci served on the Canadian Tire board of directors for five years, as one of three representatives of CTC Dealer Holdings, which owns a slice of the company's voting stock. The dealers acquired some of those shares during their takeover bid in 1986. Even though the bid failed, it was a good outcome for the dealers, he thinks,

▶ Steve McLean and his wife, Leighann, show off the Breakaway Challenge Cup awarded to their store and staff by Canadian Tire Corporation for providing an extraordinary customer experience, October 2010. The smallest store in the Canadian Tire chain, the Nipigon, Ontario, store took the prize in the Small but Mighty category.

because it assured them of three seats on the board. It means the CEO can't just say whatever he wants to the other, outside directors. The dealers provide a reality check from the front lines.

▼

CALGARY DEALER JOE DAND, a former Canadian Tire corporate executive, has been part of dealer selection panels and found that the selection process, no matter how rigorous, is not foolproof. "Guys I thought were going to be great bombed, and guys that I was a little worried about turned out to be great," he says. "I don't think selecting a candidate is something that's easily measurable.

"Our best Canadian Tire stores are probably the best retail in North America. Our problem is that the gap between our top stores and our bottom stores is probably the greatest in North America. That's the thing that we fight. That's what keeps senior executives in Canadian Tire awake at night. How do they get all of our stores to be as good as our best stores?"

It may be that the best retailers are born, not made. There is an art to retailing that can't entirely be taught. Dand thinks his father, Al, is a born retailer. Al Dand, 76, has been a Canadian Tire dealer for 40 years and, as of 2012, was operating the store in Red Deer, Alberta. "He loves it," says his son. "He doesn't have a computer. He spends all of his time on the floor talking to staff and customers."

Part of the reason for the quality gap is that Canadian Tire doesn't have cookie-cutter stores. "That's why we've got some that are really, really good," says Joe Dand. "A lot of it comes down to ability and desire and drive and passion and skill, and some guys don't have all of those attributes. There's no single best way to do it, and sometimes that hurts us with the average guy or the below-average guy, because there isn't just one answer. They've got to feel it, and know it, and touch it, and some guys can do it and other guys can't."

Like Justin Young, Joe Dand started his Canadian Tire career early. His father had the store in Dartmouth, Nova Scotia, for 17 years. Joe fetched carts and assembled bicycles. He worked his way around the store before becoming general manager. Al then took over a large store in Calgary's south end, and Joe became general manager there. One of their first initiatives was to increase the height of the displays in the aisles, the theory being that more goods on display would translate into more sales. It did and the store's sales grew rapidly.

The success of the Calgary store caught the attention of home office; Joe was

▼

brought east in 1994 to take charge of the new store program being launched by Steve Bachand, who had become CEO the year before. His job was to spearhead the implementation of Bachand's program to enlarge and remodel Canadian Tire stores from coast to coast. He was only 25 years old at the time.

"I had a lot of confidence that probably bordered on cockiness, and that's exactly what they needed because we were a very staid, old, bureaucratic company that needed to change a lot. I probably wasn't the typical employee, but I was quite successful at getting stuff done because I didn't know how big companies functioned, so I just did things the easy way as opposed to the proper way. We got a lot accomplished in a very short period of time."

Dand and Wayne Sales, then senior vice-president of marketing, travelled to the United States to look at what the most successful stores there were doing. They visited famous national stores as well as smaller, regional chains, searching for good ideas Canadian Tire could adopt. These included wider aisles, innovative layouts, new ways to associate different products, and specialty fixtures.

"If someone had a nice way to display baseball gloves, then we'd copy it. That's the great thing about retail — you can see a good idea anywhere. Retail's all about

▲ The Calgary South store in 1979 carried more skis and toques than could be found at the average store in Ontario.

▶▶ A Canadian Tire store nestled in the Rockies, Canmore, Alberta, 2012. This store is LEED certified and uses geothermal heating.

realizing it's a good idea and just copying it." He also followed the example of his father, who relied on gut feel. "You tried something and if it felt good, you did it, and if it didn't feel good, you didn't do it, you tried something else."

In 1994, Joe Dand was part of the team that made the changes that enabled Canadian Tire to withstand the challenge from the U.S. invasion. But the retail environment keeps changing — the advent of social media as an important means of communication is one example. Complacency would be fatal. "I think we're probably at a point in the history of the company," says Dand, "that we've got to make some big change."

▼

IN A COMPANY LIKE WALMART, in which the corporation owns the stores and appoints managers to run them, an ambitious store manager wants to work his or her way up to a senior job in the corporation. Canadian Tire offers an opposite career path. Owning a Canadian Tire store is an interesting and profitable career, and so ambitious corporate executives are eager to get out of the executive suite and into a store of their own.

Some, like Joe Dand, make only a brief stop in the corporation. Others stay much longer. Bob Hougham and Peter Edmonson, veterans of the Dean Muncaster era, toiled in senior corporate jobs for 17 and 13 years respectively. Elwin Derbyshire, who hails from a Canadian Tire family, worked in the corporation for four years before acquiring his first store. His father, Donald Derbyshire, was turned down when he applied in the late 1950s to start a Canadian Tire store in Westport, Ontario, a town near Kingston. The company thought Westport's population of 700 was too small to support a store. He opened a Western Tire store instead and, by the early 1960s, when his annual sales were at $100,000, he reapplied to Canadian Tire, was accepted, and switched the banner on his store.

Elwin wanted to be a Canadian Tire dealer too but he didn't have the $40,000 that was necessary at the time to become one. After graduating from Queen's University in Kingston, he taught high school for an annual salary of $5,800. That wasn't enough to save for a dealership, so after one year he switched to selling life insurance. In 1968, he joined his father, who was then operating a Canadian Tire store in New Glasgow, Nova Scotia. Elwin was general manager of the store and his younger brother, Dale, who was still in school, was a part-time employee. In 1970, when Donald Derbyshire took over a store on the west side of Toronto, Elwin accompanied him.

After two years at that store, he began the process of applying for his own. But just then the corporation needed someone to take the reins of the dealer training program. Elwin, with his teaching and store experience, fit the bill. It was a six-month course, involving in-store placements and seminars at home office. That period was a busy one for Canadian Tire, with lots of dealers retiring and new stores opening. In four years, Derbyshire put 75 new dealers through the program and into their first stores.

Sometimes the transition was difficult. Some new dealers had occupied senior executive posts in large corporations and had never worked in retail. Others were retail veterans who had been managing large Woolco or Zellers stores that did $20 million in annual sales. They suffered culture shock when they found themselves in charge of a small Canadian Tire store doing $1 million a year.

After leaving the corporate ranks, Elwin followed a classic Canadian Tire career path. In 1977, he got his first store. It was in Perth, an Ontario town of 6,000 located halfway between Ottawa and Kingston. The next stop was a big city, Edmonton, where he operated a large store as well as a satellite in Vegreville, Alberta. His final stop, in 1990, was Kingston, where he launched a brand new store, Kingston's second. In his 22 years there, he has expanded his store three times, from 27,000 square feet to its current size of 90,000 square feet. Annual sales went from $8 million to a peak of $41 million. It is one of the top 10 stores in Canada in sales volume and was tops in the country until the corporation placed a third store in Kingston.

The remarkable growth is attributable to population growth on Kingston's west side and to Derbyshire's success in employing the Bucci philosophy of filling the store with things people want to buy. "I've always been a very aggressive buyer," Derbyshire says. "I believe the biggest part of customer service is having the product. Customers come to Canadian Tire stores with the intent to buy. People will go to a mall on a Saturday and shop. They will walk around and look at various stores. When you drive into the parking lot of a Canadian Tire store, you came for some purpose. That doesn't mean you won't wander around. But you came to buy a hammer or rake or whatever. Our job is to make sure we have what you came for. I call it 'trip assurance,' and we work very hard at that."

Although Canada may not need many more Canadian Tire stores, that needn't mean an end to growth, Derbyshire says. Stores can continue to increase sales if they are convenient and appealing to customers. That means lots of parking and a lavish display of merchandise. "We started this store at $12 million and now we

do $40 million and that's because we had the parking and the space to display the merchandise and handle customers."

The Derbyshire family carries the retailing gene going back to Elwin's grandfather who had a five-and-dime store in a small Ontario town. Brother Dale, who operates a store in Barrie, is the third member of the family to become a Canadian Tire dealer. Elwin's son Jason is business manager of the Kingston store. Another son, Mark, stocked shelves in the same store while growing up. Later, he owned an ice cream company. After that, he worked for the Canadian Tire Dealers' Association, where he developed a training program for store employees. Then he became a star in the corporate world, rising to his current position as president of Holt Renfrew.

Canadian Tire is known for low prices, whereas Holt Renfrew is known for the opposite. But Elwin Derbyshire believes Canadian Tire shouldn't be afraid of offering a broader assortment that might include high-priced merchandise. "We have to keep challenging the market," he says, giving a patio furniture set as an example. "Our best one used to be priced at $200. Now we can sell $800 to $1,000 patio sets."

He doesn't minimize the challenges Canadian Tire faces from tough competitors. For example, Walmart has the advantage of uniformity in its chain of stores.

"Walmart can take a display in one store and repeat that in their other 300 stores. We can't do that. I may have 60 feet for a certain product line and another store might have 12 feet." On the other hand, because Canadian Tire operates small stores as well as big ones, it can operate profitably in small towns that can't support Walmart's big boxes.

His job as a dealer never fails to hold his interest. "If I had stayed a teacher, I'd have been retired 10 or 15 years ago," Derbyshire says. Now 68, he has no plans to retire. He has seen many changes in a 44-year Canadian Tire career and is optimistic about the future. "The dealers feel appreciated and important, and the trust is back again. I think we're going to see some great things in the next few years."

▼

ERIC SELLORS had an early relationship with Canadian Tire. He grew up in downtown Toronto near the flagship store then operated by Fred Billes. He and his friends liked to hang out at the store and were often asked to leave. They also rode their go-karts down the hill behind the store. "Freddie would come over and chase us away," Sellors recalls with a laugh.

As a young business executive he decided to get involved with Canadian Tire in a more formal way. Like many others who aspire to become Canadian Tire dealers, he wanted to be his own boss. He was vice-president of marketing for Warnaco, an apparel company, when he applied to be a dealer in 1980. He was accepted but had to wait two years because, at the time, Canadian Tire wasn't building many new stores and few established dealers were retiring.

"Every four or five months, Peter Edmonson, who was vice-president of dealer relations at the time, would call me. And he'd say, 'Are you still with us? You going to hang in there?' And I was really impressed with that. The guy really cared about people."

Sellors's first store was in the Ontario town of Acton. It was profitable, but Sellors considers the four and a half years he spent there too long. "I came from a job where I was travelling around North America and now I'm in this little town in a little store of 1,800 square feet and those four walls close in pretty quickly on you."

The first year, he admits, he didn't know what he was doing. Fortunately, John Williams, a dealer in nearby Milton, was available to offer advice. "If it weren't for John, I probably would have gone the way of some of the guys I started with and wouldn't be here today," Sellors says.

▼

Because of the lack of mobility then in Canadian Tire, Sellors felt stuck in Acton. He told Peter Ligé, who had taken over from Edmonson as vice-president of dealer relations, that unless he was offered a bigger store, he would quit. "About two months later, I'm at the store and it's a cold snowstorm in March and Peter calls and says, 'I've got a store for you. It's in Chatham, New Brunswick, and it loses $300,000 a year. We're terminating the dealer in two days. You can't go look at the store and I don't have time to send you any of the financial information. Do you want it? I've got to know in half an hour."

Sellors said, "I'll take it."

He arrived at the store in April 1987. "It was the best thing that could ever happen to me because everything was wrong. There was no merchandise on the shelf, the staff were awful, it was filthy. You would never have believed that any company could have let it get to what it was."

Being handed a poorly run store was good because it gave Sellors a chance to show what he could do. What needed to be done was obvious. He cleaned the place, put merchandise on the shelves, and showed the staff that he meant business. "One day, the first week I was there, there was a lineup at the cash and I saw it from my office. I grabbed a cash tray, ran down the stairs, opened a lane, and started ringing customers through."

The staff was amazed to see the owner at the cash. "It told them I cared about the business. That store made my career because when I went in, it was doing $2.4 million a year, and when I left two years later, it was over $5 million."

In 1989, Sellors was offered another, bigger challenge. Ron Roberts, director of dealer finance, called to say that the company was going to build a store in Sherwood Park, an affluent suburb of Edmonton. It would be 20,000 square feet, which was considered large at the time, and was expected to lose $500,000 a year at the start.

A friend, Terry Douglas, dealer at a nearby Alberta store, told Sellors it was an outstanding opportunity and urged him to accept. (Douglas later became a Canadian Tire director; he was killed in a plane accident. His daughter Meaghan is married to Sellors's son Kevin.)

In 1990, Sellors moved west while the store was under construction. He rented a trailer to use as an office for interviewing job applicants. Contrary to home office's calculations, the store was a money-maker from day one. "It was a phenomenal store," says Sellors.

He thought Sherwood Park was a good place to raise his young children and

Raymond Gagné and his staff proudly display their 2009 Award of Excellence outside their Longueuil, Quebec, store.

planned to stay. But two years after opening the store, he got a call from Jim Ryan, who had replaced Peter Ligé as vice-president of dealer relations. A suburban Toronto store run by Gordon Gilchrist, who was also a Progressive Conservative member of Parliament, was going to be replaced and the corporation wanted a new dealer for the new store it planned to build.

The store is in one of Toronto's roughest areas. "Every day there were thieves running out with VCRs or whatever they could steal," says Sellors with a grimace. Making Sellors even more unhappy was home office's decision not to build a new store after all. Adding yet another reason to worry was the entry at that time of Walmart and Home Depot into the Canadian market. "I remember reading the headlines 'Canadian Tire Is a Dead Duck,' 'Canadian Tire Is a Deer in the Headlights.' And I was thinking, 'What have I done? My whole life is wrapped up in this thing.'"

Then Ryan called again with an offer to take over from Gordon Gilchrist yet again, this time in Oshawa, Ontario. He went there in 1995 and, four years later, opened a new store. The store was a big success.

Sellors decided that Canadian Tire, and its dealer system, had been good to him and that it was time to give back. He had been active on various dealers'

Experienced climber Dan Culver holds a Canadian Tire flag at the summit of Mt. Everest, marking the first time a commercial flag has reached the top of the famous mountain. Prior to the 1990 climb, which made Culver the first British Columbian to summit Mt. Everest, he led over four dozen store staff from the Vancouver group of associate stores on Outward Bound–style rock climbing expeditions. The group of 21 Lower Mainland stores contributed to the Everest expedition.

Members of the Canadian Tire team, consisting of employees, dealers, families, and friends, who raised $332,000 for Jumpstart by climbing Mt. Kilimanjaro in 2009.

association committees and he was ready to run for president of the association, which he did successfully in 2001. His preoccupation in that role was the negotiation for a new contract between the corporation and the dealers. The existing contract was a simple, short document that had worked, says Sellors, because there was trust between the two parties. That trust diminished during Dean Groussman's period as CEO, and the dealers decided they needed a contract that was more precise in setting out the financial split of profits between them and the corporation.

Keith Gostlin, a dealer in Kelowna, British Columbia, was lead negotiator for the dealers. "That was a pretty tough time," Sellors says. "There was a lot of fighting. But we were able to put together a really great contract for dealers and I think for the corporation." The new contract, finalized in 2004, in contrast to the slim booklet that preceded it, is 270 pages long.

Once the contract was finalized, Sellors made one last move. The company was building a vast new store on Sheppard Avenue, in north Toronto. Although it was destined to be one of the top stores in the chain, several dealers had refused the opportunity because of its size — 86,000 square feet of retail space — and the risk such a large investment entailed. It also has a Mark's Work Wearhouse outlet connected to it in the same building.

One of the more memorable characters who influenced Sellors and other veteran dealers was the late Ron Roberts, director of dealer finance. "He was like the warden to all the new dealers," says Sellors. He was also famous as a non-stop smoker. Recalls Elwin Derbyshire: "Maybe you hadn't had a good year and Ron wanted to talk to you; people used to joke it was important to bring in a packet of cigarettes because he might be easier on you if you gave him a smoke."

Dave Urso, a dealer in Bowmanville, Ontario, recalls being interviewed in Roberts's office. "He would never butt out a cigarette. The ash would be about three inches on the cigarette. He'd come up really close and he'd smoke and talk to you, and you would be afraid that ash was going to drop on your leg."

What Roberts contributed, besides smoke, was accountability. "I always felt like I couldn't fool Ron," says Sellors. "He'd look at my financial statements and he knew the numbers backwards and forwards. And he knew who were the guys who were performing and who weren't.

"He was like God. He would say, 'Okay, you're going to get this store so you're going to need X number of dollars.' If for whatever reason you came close to that cap and you had to go back and see him, you better make sure you had some answers for why you need additional funds."

Sellors was a novice dealer in 1986 when the dealers made their takeover bid for Canadian Tire Corporation. He's glad it didn't happen. A Canadian Tire dealer has a strong ego, but 475 strong egos would have had problems agreeing on how to manage a multibillion-dollar corporation. "I think it would have been terrible, it would have been a disaster. It's actually scary when you think about it."

▼

CANADIAN TIRE'S vice-president of dealer finance called dealer Dave Urso one morning in April 1997, and he wasn't happy. The previous night Urso had thrown a cocktail party attended by some 500 people to celebrate the opening of his new store in Woodbridge, a Toronto suburb that was home to a large contingent of Italian Canadians. Tables containing lavish offerings of hors d'oeuvres, a roasted pig, and other edibles occupied the centre of the store. Ice sculptures of the Canadian Tire triangle decorated the entrance.

Owen Billes remembers it well. "The store was located in what was back then basically the middle of a field. It seemed like we were in the middle of nowhere, but I've never seen a grand opening like it. It looked like an Italian wedding."

Murmurs of disapproval were heard at home office. Wasn't it all a bit extravagant for Canadian Tire? The vice-president of dealer finance told Urso, "People are concerned about how much you spent on this party."

Urso said, "How much do you think I spent?"

"Well, based on what I saw last night, you had to have spent at least $30,000 to $40,000."

"Well," said Urso, "actually I spent $3,500."

The party was staged as a favour to Urso by the same company that had done his wedding. "I only paid for the food. I didn't pay for anything else. It was probably the most elaborate party ever at Canadian Tire for under $5,000."

It turned out to be a good business move. "It created a real buzz in the community," recalls Urso. "And the store just took off from day one, in spite of all the competition. In the first three to five years, we were in the top 15 stores in volume."

Getting a good deal on a great party wasn't the only way Urso was unusual. He had stayed at his first store, in Picton, Ontario, only four months. When the company decided to build a new store in Woodbridge, 20 more-experienced dealers gave it a pass. For Urso, it was an opportunity to move from a 5,000-square-foot store to one more than 10 times as large, so he jumped at the chance.

Urso began his career in the corporation in 1984, working first in the dealer finance group and then as manager of the profit-sharing plan. For a while he worked as a manager for a dealer in the Toronto area and then went back to the corporation for five years, working in store systems and as a retail support manager before acquiring the small store at Picton.

After Woodbridge, the next stop was the massive 76,000-square-foot store that opened in Bowmanville, east of Toronto, in 2011. There he is getting a chance to try out some new ideas, such as a "party pit stop" where customers can buy piñatas, balloons, and other party supplies. The store is one of several automotive concept stores that have been launched as part of the company's drive to recapture its status as Canada's leading store for auto service and supplies. The store has a drive-in reception area, four express lube bays, and an auto detailing service. There is also a shuttle to take customers home or to the office while their cars are being serviced.

Urso, who is 51, runs one of Canadian Tire's most advanced stores. Yet he is also a link to the past: during his time in the corporate office, he got to know Myrel Pardoe, a legendary figure from the early years. She joined the company in 1932, when it consisted of one store at the corner of Yonge and Isabella in downtown

▲ Dave Urso, 2009.

Welcome to Canada's #1 Choice for Auto Service

Check In - Pick Up

▲ The new "automotive store of the future" in Bowmanville, Ontario, offers best-in-class customer-focused automotive service and advanced retailing tools, including interactive kiosks to help customers select the right parts for their vehicles. It also carries a full range of household and sporting goods.

Toronto, and stayed for 71 years in various secretarial positions. "She was sort of the grandmother of Canadian Tire," he says. "If you wanted to find out something about a dealer or certain people in the corporation, she knew about everything. She knew about the history, she knew about everything that went on."

▼

BOB HOUGHAM joined Canadian Tire in 1968, working first as a buyer and then in marketing. He worked his way up to the post of director of advertising. Then he spent three years in a lost cause — as vice-president of marketing for White Stores, during Canadian Tire's unsuccessful attempt to break into the U.S. market. "After that debacle, I thought I'd had enough corporate abuse after 17 years, and decided to take a franchise," he says.

His first store was in Forest, a town of about 2,800 people near Sarnia, Ontario. "It was a teeny-weeny store that exploded in the summertime when the tourists came to the Grand Bend area. In winter it was the dance of the living dead."

The smaller the store, the harder the dealer's job is. "The first store is a lot of stress," explains Hougham, "because there's no infrastructure, so the dealer answers the alarm calls at night and also has to make sure that everything is set up and works. I was probably working 80 hours a week. Once you have a bigger store and a good general manager who's keen and understands the game, the load on the dealer becomes considerably less."

Although a corporate veteran, Hougham, who retired in 2009, found that as a dealer, he was often in opposition to the corporation. "It's always been a rocky road between the franchise dealer and the corporation," he says. "The friction was a good thing. The corporation put on restraints and price controls and some kind of discipline and got rid of bad dealers, and the dealers would put pressure on the corporation and [so] bad corporate people disappeared."

Later he moved to Dryden, a pulp-and-paper town in western Ontario. While dealers need to be responsive to the needs of the local market, the corporation wants Canadian Tire stores not necessarily uniform but recognizable as Canadian Tire stores wherever they are. Hougham recalls with displeasure a corporate emissary who thought "all Canadian Tire stores from coast to coast should look exactly the same so the customer would know where to find stuff on the shelf. Well, that's just fine, except that you can't put the same amount of fishing gear in downtown Toronto as you would in Dryden. Half my store was fishing gear because that's

what people there did. And this guy was complaining that I wasn't giving kettles enough space." While at Dryden, Hougham also operated two satellite stores in the northern communities of Red Lake and Sioux Lookout.

Hougham thinks the three American CEOs — Dean Groussman, Steve Bachand, and Wayne Sales — did not fully understand the dealer system. "They thought a dealer should be standing at a salute like a store manager would at a Kmart. And when they didn't get that kind of response they were very hard to give feedback to. They always viewed it as criticism."

There's no textbook that teaches how to be a dealer, says Hougham. "It's all empathy, and doing 10 per cent of the talking and 90 per cent of the listening."

When Hougham decided to retire in 2008, he sold his store to his friend Owen Billes. For Owen, it was the next big step in a Canadian Tire career that had begun 25 years earlier when, at the age of 13, he wrote a letter to Arch Brown, the Barrie dealer, asking for a summer job and saying he would be happy to do anything, from sweeping the floor to stocking the shelves. The Barrie store was the closest one to Shanty Bay, where he spent the summers. Brown hired him and took him at his word — his first three days on the job were spent sweeping the warehouse floor. He continued working summers in the Barrie store before joining the corporation in 1992.

His first job was in dealer changeovers, which involves facilitating the transfer of a store from one dealer to another. His role was to assess the value of the inventory and fixtures that the new dealer was going to buy — an excellent way to get to know Canadian Tire and how it works. "You count all the assets and manage the counting of all the inventory. You are there for a week and you count literally every shelf, shelf hook, bracket, beam in the warehouse — everything the dealer owned.

"And then you actually produce a book of all the assets in the store, and it's everything down to office supplies — everything that makes a business run that is owned by the associate dealer. Then you go back and do the inventory. Everything's counted, everything that isn't 100 per cent perfect, so if you have ripped packaging and stuff, that's pulled out. The idea is, when the new dealer takes over his first day, the store should be in perfect condition. I don't imagine any other company in the world does this."

The new dealer pays for the assets and the inventory and nothing else. "He should be buying a perfectly clean store, with everything sorted out nice and neatly, able to find anything that he wants, so he knows he's getting full value for his money," says Owen.

Touring the country during the early 1990s was a course in the history of the company for Owen. "A lot of the older dealers were still around, and I got to meet them and see how they did things. There were all kinds of quirky stores, like the one in Saskatoon that had a warehouse in the lower level but no elevator. There was a hole cut in the concrete floor and a forklift in the basement. If you wanted to get stuff up, the forklift would lift it up and push it through the hole." Staff had to be careful to avoid the hole — it was a long drop down. The store no longer exists.

After his stint in the changeover department, Owen worked in several other corporate areas, including distribution, automotive marketing, new business development, and petroleum. Being a Billes wasn't necessarily an advantage during Owen's corporate career. Even before he started, the head of the changeover department was told by a more senior executive that he had good news and bad news. The good news was that he was getting a new employee and it wouldn't affect his annual budget. The bad news was that the new employee was a Billes.

"There was a perception that someone with my last name was going to be a spy and report everything back to the family and the board. I had friends that wanted to apply at Canadian Tire and they would ask if they could use me as a reference. I would say to them, 'You can if you really want to, but you have to understand that people are going to judge you.' And I had a friend who did use me [as a reference], but he was told when he was hired that they didn't appreciate spies in their department and to be careful.

"So it wasn't always a smooth ride. I guess the difference is, when you're management, you're trying to move up. You have targets to hit, and you'll do things to hit your bonus and not necessarily the right things to do, even if they're right for your little area. And I would say, 'Well, why don't we just do the right thing?' because I didn't care about making my bonus and getting ahead. I never wanted to be the CEO, that was never my thing."

Owen's preference was to do the right thing for the company even if it was not necessarily the right thing to win the biggest bonus. "That was probably the difference between me and a lot of other people, and sometimes it didn't work out so well. I always came out on the losing end. Even if I could show financially how things we'd done made a positive impact, I did not end up doing well by it."

There was an obvious solution to this problem and that was to become a dealer. "You're in the store, you do your own thing, and you know right away whether you've done good or you've done bad — customers will tell you."

As a changeover consultant, he had been in many stores. He had worked in four stores, including the Toronto flagship and Dave Urso's in Woodbridge. But nothing had prepared him for taking over his own store, in Welland, a town in the Niagara region of southern Ontario, in the fall of 2008.

He had first met Bob Hougham as a child on a visit to Texas when Hougham was working at White Stores. Later Owen managed the changeover when Hougham took over the Welland store. "I can remember being overwhelmed by the Welland store because, at the time, it was one of the 'Cadillac' stores. I was so excited for Bob because he was getting this great store."

Now the store was changing hands from Hougham to Owen Billes. It was an easy changeover, since they agreed not to go through the inventory. "I trusted Bob and I was keeping his general manager. The general manager wasn't going to stiff me in Bob's favour because he'd have to explain it to me the next day. And we all had a great relationship anyway.

"We did the changeover on a Thursday, and then Friday was the first day of operations under me, so there was lots of excitement with the accountants in and out all day and the dust settling. And I got to the end of the day and everybody went home, and it was just surreal standing in the dealer's office, now my office, that I had been standing in years before. I remember thinking, 'What do I do now?' and then I thought, 'Oh, I have a store. I can walk around on the floor.' So down I went, and I was walking around, poking around, and sort of wondering what I'd gotten myself into."

Unlike most dealers, Owen Billes did not start in a small store and demonstrate his abilities there before moving up to a bigger one. Other dealers do not have mothers who are controlling shareholders of Canadian Tire Corp. It facilitated matters that Hougham did not announce he was retiring, attracting the interest of other dealers wanting to move to a large store. Corporate management informed the dealers' association of what was occurring and there were no objections. There

▲ Owen Billes with his long-standing Canadian Tire employees, 2012: (from left, front row) Owen Billes, Gerry White (43 years), Lorraine Paolone (38 years); (middle row) Alma Sault (19 years), Elaine Brear (19 years), Vicki Courtney (19 years); (back row) Joe Sammons (18 years), Mike Dockrill (31 years), Sandra Fortier (35 years).

was general agreement, Owen says, that "I was one person who would be allowed to jump the queue."

Canadian Tire was part of Owen's life from early childhood. He remembers the gold Cadillac his grandfather, A.J., had at his summer place at Shanty Bay when Owen was just four years old. Dealers who visited him also drove Cadillacs. Owen was fascinated by the *V* trunk emblem on these cars. "In my mind, that was the same thing as a triangle, so somehow Canadian Tire had something to do with making Cadillacs."

Shortly after he took over, the Welland store was replaced with a brand new one that had been under construction. It is located in a shopping plaza that also contains a Walmart and a Rona. The proximity of the competition is good for Owen's business: a cluster of stores attracts customers.

Owen Billes has been successful in making Welland one of the top-rated stores in customer satisfaction. Business is good, despite high unemployment in the region thanks to plant closures. Because of who he is, Owen could have hung about home office doing "odds and sods," points out Stephen Wetmore. Instead, he took on the challenge of operating a store in a depressed market — a "gutsy move" because he risked looking foolish if he failed.

"His work ethic at the store blows me away," says fellow dealer and friend Justin Young. "He is there six, seven days a week. There is not a line between him and the staff. When he is actively in the store, he is a part of them. He works with his employees. He is humble and approachable, and the team loves him."

Like Young, Owen Billes is always looking for ways to improve customer experience. For example, both have introduced hand-held computers that show staff exactly where products are located, either in the store or warehouse, so that they can be retrieved quickly. He also uses more old-fashioned methods of customer satisfaction, such as presenting mothers with hanging flower baskets on Mother's Day.

He knows that Canadian Tire's retail offering, from spark plugs to tulip bulbs, is somewhat eccentric. On trips outside Canada, he doesn't even try to explain it; when asked, he says that Canadian Tire sells tires. But some customers have strong feelings about what Canadian Tire should sell. When the new Welland store opened, it was one of the first to experiment with food. It carries a convenience store offering of milk, eggs, bread, pop, and potato chips, as well as canned and frozen food, but no produce or other perishables.

"Old-timers would come in and say, 'Canadian Tire shouldn't sell food, it's just not right,'" Owen recalls. "So I said, 'You might have a point, but could you imagine an automotive store that started selling housewares and sporting goods and garden stuff? Now that would be pretty weird.' And they would say, 'You have a point, but I still don't think Canadian Tire should sell food.'"

In fact, the wide assortment of goods and the diversity among stores is an asset. For its competitors, Canadian Tire is a moving target. Says Billes: "It's really hard to go after Canadian Tire in one way because Canadian Tire goes at things 485 ways."

The Dealer Convention

CANADIAN TIRE'S DEALERS
have been getting together since 1941, when they first met in Toronto to discuss matters of mutual interest. Since then, the Dealer Convention has evolved into an annual event, organized by the corporation one year and the Canadian Tire Dealers' Association the next. Corporate-sponsored conventions are held in Toronto; dealer-sponsored ones in some other city. The convention, which runs from three to five days, is a chance for the dealers to hear from senior executives and majority share-holder Martha Billes about the corporation's strategies and initiatives. An important feature of the convention is the Products Parade in which vendors show off their latest wares and encourage dealers to order them for their stores. The welcoming party, closing banquet, and other social events offer plenty of opportunity for dealers and corporate representatives to exchange ideas and information informally.

▲▲▲ A reception for the 1960 Dealer Convention is held at the Yonge and Davenport store.

▲▲ Dealers touring a service bay are shown the latest in automotive diagnostic equipment, 1953.

▲ The women help out during the 1960 convention. Gladys Billes is standing in the middle. A "Ladies Day" program was organized for the dealers' wives, starting in 1955.

▲▲ A 1958 business panel, officiated by Mayne Plowman. A.J. Billes is fourth from the left.

▲ Dealers tour the recently expanded Sheppard Avenue Distribution Centre, 1963.

▲ ▲ ▲ A.J. Billes makes his grand entrance on a "turtle" at a presentation commemorating 25-year dealers. The theme of the 1963 Dealer Convention was "Behold the Turtle."

▲ ▲ Dealers' wives arriving for specially tailored business sessions as part of the 1967 Ladies Day program.

▲ Dealers and their wives make their way to their hotel via the convention bus, 1974.

▲ ▲ Products Parade, 1983. The first took place in 1963.

▲ ▶ A Coleman display and lawnmower demonstration at the 1979 Products Parade.

▲ The 2011 Award of Excellence presentation: a proud moment for dealers and their families.

▲ Gala night at the 2006 Dealer Convention in Calgary.

 GAS⁺

 CANADIAN TIRE
FINANCIAL SERVICES

 ESSENCE⁺

 SERVICES FINANCIERS
CANADIAN TIRE

CHAPTER EIGHT

Canadian Tire today—and tomorrow

CHRIS HADFIELD, the first Canadian to leave a spacecraft and float freely in space, likes Canadian Tire so much he wrote a song about it.

Hadfield is an engineer, former fighter pilot in the Royal Canadian Air Force, and an astronaut. In 2001, as part of a mission to install a Canadian-built robotic arm at the International Space Station, he performed two spacewalks. When he's earthbound, he likes to write and perform music.

The Canadian Tire tune, reports his brother Dave, who is also a singer-songwriter and gets a co-credit on the song, came about when Chris was a test pilot in the air force and sent on an exchange posting with the U.S. Navy in Maryland, where he rented a farmhouse. Dave later wrote about what happened next:

"He looked around, decided to do a little sprucing up before the furniture arrived, and hopped in the car to go buy some paint and brushes and thinner and so on.

"As he started the car, he realized he didn't know where to go! Anywhere in Canada there's a Canadian Tire within reach — a national, unifying institution. But is there such a thing in the States? He didn't know."[1]

Chris Hadfield might have gone to the closest hardware or paint store. But, in

▶ The paint department in Ottawa's Orléans store, one of two new Smart stores launched in 2008. This latest store concept aims to improve operating productivity while creating a comfortable and inspiring shopping experience for customers.

the absence of Canadian Tire, he felt so "disoriented" that he went back into his house and wrote the song, which ends this way:

Well I stand in the rain and I wait for the bus,
Then head to the office — I suppose 'cause I must.
There's work on my desk in a gigantic pile,
But I'd rather spend time in the sporting goods aisle.
There's only one problem that might lie ahead;
If this store should go broke I'd be better off dead.
So dig out your wallet and be the next buyer.
And go to Canadian Tire.[2]

It's hard to imagine any other Canadian business, except perhaps Tim Hortons, inspiring a song from a customer. Maureen Sabia and others describe Canadian Tire as "iconic." It is certainly true that Canadian Tire is more than just another hard goods store: it has cultural significance to millions as an integral part of the Canadian landscape. Following the demise of Eaton's and the acquisition of Hudson's Bay Co. by an American, Canadian Tire is among the few remaining Canadian-owned national retailers.

The Canadian competitors have been replaced by American ones. The big U.S. chains have noticed the vibrant Canadian retail market and they want a piece of it for themselves. And so they just keep coming.

▼

STEPHEN WETMORE succeeded Tom Gauld as CEO in January 2009. Previously, he had been CEO of Bell Aliant, a telecommunications company, and had also worked in health care and transportation. Trained as an accountant, Wetmore had been a member of Canadian Tire's board since 2003. Michael Sabia (Maureen's brother), who had worked with Wetmore at Bell Canada, sized up the skills he brings to Canadian Tire this way: "He's a master at being able to find his way through some pretty complex problems where there are a lot of differing and competing interests."[3]

Those are good qualifications for a Canadian Tire CEO. In her speeches, Martha Billes often talks of the meaning of the Canadian Tire triangle. Created from a doodle by her father, A.J., it symbolizes the "successful partnership among the corporation, the dealers, and the Billes family."[4] Wetmore's job is to maintain harmony and unity among the three sides of the triangle.

Unlike some of his predecessors, Wetmore avoids conflict, summing up his management style with a story about a homeowner and a paper boy. The paper boy was always in a hurry; sometimes the paper would wind up under the car in the driveway or under the hedge but never at the front door where the homeowner wanted it. The homeowner shouted at the paper boy but to no avail. He complained to the newspaper and things improved — for a couple of days. Then the paper was under the car again. So the homeowner decided on a change of strategy: he bought a basketball net and put it next to the front steps. The next morning, the paper boy said "Cool" and tossed the paper through the net, landing it right on the porch where the homeowner wanted it.

"And that," says Wetmore, "is how you have to manage Canadian Tire. There's no sense screaming. That's just not the way the place works. You've got to lead and

figure out what decisions you can make to try to get the big machine to go where you'd like it to go because *it* wants to go there."

Living — Playing — Fixing — Driving. Those four words are emblazoned on the front of many Canadian Tire stores. "They are the four pillars that underpin the brand," says Wetmore. "The pillars have to be as strong as they can possibly be. If you make the pillars strong, then the triangle is strong."

When the Billes brothers opened Hamilton Tire and Garage in 1922, their business was all about one of those pillars: driving. Automotive remains the foundation of the business, accounting for about 25 per cent of total sales. But when Wetmore arrived, it was in trouble. It had lost $70 million in sales to online competitors. And its auto service ranked 39th out of 40 brands in the 2011 customer satisfaction survey compiled by J.D. Power, a market research company. "We did beat BMW though," Wetmore says. "They were number 40."

He can joke about it, but that doesn't mean he was prepared to put up with it. Wetmore acted immediately. He took everything connected to automotive and grouped it together under the direction of one executive. The new automotive division now includes the auto service centres, tires, auto parts, auto accessories, 300 gas bars, 85 PartSource stores, and the Roadside Assistance program. To manage this automotive behemoth, Wetmore selected Allan MacDonald, a former Bell executive.

Although a newcomer, MacDonald understands the importance of automotive to Canadian Tire's history and brand. "The triangle to Canadian Tire is what the mouse ears are to Disney," he says. "Disney can grow into theme parks and computer animation but Mickey Mouse is always at the core. Automotive remains the core of Canadian Tire."

▲ Bowmanville's expansive
service bay is part of the new
Ontario store's automotive focus.

MacDonald starts from a strong position. "There is no other mass retailer in the world that has our automotive presence," he points out. Canadian Tire sells more tires and batteries than anyone else in Canada. And it has 5,500 service bays. To put that number in perspective, Pep Boys, one of the biggest service chains in the United States, has 7,000 service bays for a population 10 times as large as Canada's.

The auto business is more complex than it used to be. There are 5,000 types of tires, and Canadian Tire was losing sales because too often it didn't have the ones that customers needed, when they needed them. MacDonald decided it was essential that each store knew which tires were most often purchased in its particular area. Using data from provincial motor vehicle departments, the automotive division created a tire assortment for each store based on the cars in its trading area. As a result, the typical store can satisfy the needs of about 90 per cent of the cars in its market.

As well, Canadian Tire launched an online tire store. Customers can turn on their computer or smartphone and order tires to be picked up at their local Canadian Tire store. Significantly, 99 per cent of those tires are installed by Canadian Tire's mechanics. Fewer and fewer people can install a set of tires or do an oil change

▲ The new Smart store concept features specialty boutiques within the stores that offer customers a large assortment of innovative products. The auto safety boutique (above), where auto and child safety elements are brought together in one area to provide a more complete experience for the customer, is unique to the Bowmanville store.

on their own car, yet most automotive stores, including Canadian Tire, have been designed for the automotive enthusiast. MacDonald wants to continue to satisfy the needs of the amateur mechanics while also appealing more to the average person who doesn't know much about what's under the hood.

The plan is to build on the categories in which Canadian Tire has credibility. Thus, while Canadian Tire is not the place to shop for the latest in computer technology, its expertise in anything to do with automotive makes it the place to go for mobile communications such as a GPS. Similarly, new parents wouldn't think of going to Canadian Tire to outfit the nursery, but they would go there to buy their baby's car seat.

MacDonald's ABSM team, short for "automotive business support manager team," consists of 33 experts who act as intermediaries between the corporation and the stores on automotive issues, organizing training and informing the stores about new products. "The more complex a service or product, the higher the margin," he explains. "Our ABSMs are in the field to help dealers manage some of that complexity."

The reason for Canadian Tire's poor showing on the 2011 customer satisfaction survey was not that cars weren't serviced well but that the counter personnel did not interact well with customers. One of the goals of the ABSM team is to make Canadian Tire the place to go for information and expert advice on cars.

When the big U.S. stores first announced they would enter Canada in the early 1990s, some people within the corporation thought Canadian Tire had to change. Maybe the existing format was dated. Maybe, someone suggested, it should become a warehouse store like Home Depot. Canadian Tire had experimented with warehouse stores and they weren't successful.[5] "We realized our strength lay in our uniqueness and we had to enhance it to compete," says Maureen Sabia. "Canadian Tire has a huge recognition among most Canadians. We don't want to lose that by aping Home Depot or Walmart."

There are many speciality automotive chains, but only Canadian Tire offers everything. "We are the only national company that can do complex repairs of virtually any make or model," says MacDonald. "That is very precious." Wetmore agrees. "Automotive," he says, "is the number one underpinning of the brand."

That's why Canadian Tire needs dealers like Keith Gostlin, who runs a store in Kelowna, B.C. Gostlin is one dealer who has never needed a push from the Toronto home office to focus on the automotive side of the business. A dealer for 45 years, he is a car fanatic — he takes part monthly in racing events at the wheel of his British-made Radical. The car has a V8 engine with 460 horsepower and reaches speeds of 290 kilometres an hour. Although, at age 69, he is usually the oldest

driver on the track, he doesn't think that's a big deal — the late actor Paul Newman was still racing in his 80s.

Gostlin has been racing cars for 40 years. "I've been in shops where professional racers have their cars serviced, and they are absolutely pristine, like operating rooms. I've taken that back to Kelowna. I think we have one of the cleanest auto service centres in Canadian Tire."

It also features some of the company's most experienced technicians. Two of his 12 auto technicians have been with Gostlin for about 30 years and two others for 20 years. He runs his own apprenticeship program to train technicians.

If a customer wants to go somewhere else while her car is being fixed, Gostlin calls a taxi at the store's expense. "It's a relationship business. I don't want anyone coming to me and saying they are dissatisfied with service they received. We ask them when they leave [with their car], 'Is there anything we could have done better today?'"

He says the company "lost focus for a few years where automotive wasn't given a high level of importance. I think we are overcoming that now. Some of our competitors can do an oil change or replace your wiper blades. But nobody else does automotive except us. It's a challenging business. It's easier to just put goods on the shelf and not worry about training technicians. But it's what makes Canadian Tire special."

▶ Keith Gostlin's Kelowna, B.C., store opened in October 1981.
▲ Keith Gostlin races his Radical at the Spring Mountain Motorsports Ranch near Las Vegas, January 2012.

$49.95
Mastercraft 'Pro' Hockey Outfit

See item #11, Page 230 for full details on this quality skate
and a wide range of values for every player . . . . 5.88 to 69.9!

PARLEZ-VOUS FRANCAIS? VOIR PAGE 147

HOT Products

HOT PRODUCTS

Exciting, New and Exclusive

This winter, Canadian Tire Retail (CTR) is working hard to differentiate itself from competitors by selling exciting, new and exclusive products that help parents with kids get started.

Hockey's Not Over Yet!

Hockey fans, look no further - CTR's LeGolie (83-4541) is the ultimate hockey item of the year. This automated inflatable goalie lets customers play Canada's favourite sport on ice or on the street. Operated by remote control and run on a track system, LeGolie has random movement capability to truly challenge those excited hockey players.

Let's Get the Movie Started!

"Are we there yet?" Parents can say good bye to this familiar question with the new Mobile DVD Player (35-2520). Exclusive to CTR, the Mobile DVD Player with Headrest Mounting Bracket appeals to customers who want the flexibility of a DVD player that can travel with the family on long car trips or plane rides. Complete with an anti-shock system, built-in FM modulator which allows customers to play the audio through their car stereo system and 7" widescreen colour display that provides smooth viewing, the Mobile DVD Player also comes with a cigarette lighter adapter for unlimited viewing time.

INCREASING REVENUES by providing better service on the automotive side is one way Canadian Tire can grow in an existing business. Another way to grow is to acquire other businesses in areas the company understands. "If the triangle is strong," says Wetmore, "it can go to other businesses." Playing is one of the four pillars; Canadian Tire has been selling sporting goods since 1935. It is the largest retailer of hockey equipment in the world.

Wetmore saw Canadian Tire's existing strength in sports as an opportunity for growth. The Canadian Tire stores specialize in entry-level equipment. They don't sell the sports apparel that large sporting goods stores do. It was time, Wetmore decided, to "play in the whole space," time for Canadian Tire to become "the authority in sports in Canada."

And so, in 2011, Canadian Tire closed a deal to acquire Calgary-based Forzani Group for $771 million. Forzani, Canada's largest sporting goods retailer, operates 500 stores under several retail banners, including SportChek, Atmosphere, and Sports Experts. It had been targeted by potential suitors for years but it wasn't for sale. Canadian Tire made a generous offer. "We had done a ton of work and were able to put a good price on the table," said Michael Medline, who led Canadian Tire's acquisition team and has since taken over as president of FGL Sports, as Forzani is now known.

Forzani was launched in 1974 when an offensive lineman on the Calgary Stampeders named John Forzani, along with three of his teammates, opened Forzani's Locker Room, a 1,200-square-foot sporting goods store, in downtown Calgary. It grew by acquisition, absorbing several of Canada's best-known sporting-goods-store brands until it was the biggest in that category in Canada.[6] Forzani, who had been chairman, accepted Canadian Tire's offer because, he explained, he liked the idea of selling to a Canadian company in the same business.

Moreover, the Forzani Group needed deep pockets and the prestige of a large enterprise to realize its ambitions. It was having difficulty attracting top talent to the Calgary head office — despite being Canada's premier sports retailer, Forzani was viewed as too small by ambitious executives.

As for store expansion, Forzani would have liked to double the size of its downtown Calgary store and open similar sports megastores in Toronto and Vancouver but it didn't have the money to do it. The deal with Canadian Tire gave Forzani two key ingredients it was missing: economies of scale and the resources necessary to grow faster.

▲ Michael Medline, president of FGL Sports, 2012.

◀ Hockey is a core part of life in Canada. It's also a core part of Canadian Tire. In 1935, the new sporting goods department first featured camping gear. A winter sports line of hockey equipment followed six years later: (from left, top row) Welland, Ontario, store, 2008; (second row) Montreal's Boulevard de l'Acadie store, 1973; Canadian Tire staff hockey team, 1950s; (third row) 1970 fall/winter catalogue cover; an employee newsletter showcasing hot products for 2004; KOHO hockey display at the 1988 Products Parade; (bottom row) the "wall of skates" at the Welland store; hockey boutique in the Cambie Street, Vancouver, store, 2011.

SPORTCHEK

YOUR BETTER STARTS HERE™

If the deal was good for Forzani, it was also good for Canadian Tire. The reason it paid a healthy premium over the market price was that Forzani is an excellent business. The sports category as a whole in North America has annual growth of between 1 and 3 per cent. Forzani aims for 10 per cent, a target its biggest banner, SportChek, has achieved.

And Forzani complements Canadian Tire's existing business. In hockey, for example, it offers high-end equipment, such as a $649 pair of skates, that Canadian Tire stores do not usually carry. Canadian Tire's hockey customers are generally beginners and younger players, whereas Forzani attracts more advanced players between the ages of 16 and 35.[7] In another sport, golf, Canadian Tire stocks entry-level clubs, whereas Nevada Bob's boutiques in the SportChek stores have the latest in golf technology.

FGL Sports gives Canadian Tire access to "younger, wealthier customers," says Medline. It also gives it access to shopping malls, where 75 per cent of SportChek stores are located. And it gives Canadian Tire a connection to the 16-to-35 age group that it didn't have before.

Medline says Canadian Tire is committed to supporting sports in Canada, "from the grass roots to the elite." This commitment could involve sponsorship of amateur sports federations whose members use products sold by Canadian Tire and FGL. It could also reach all the way to the pinnacle of amateur sports, the Olympics. "We would love to become a premier sponsor of the Canadian Olympic teams," says Medline.

Although Canadian Tire and FGL both sell sporting goods, there isn't much overlap. Canadian Tire's sporting goods aisles contain only equipment. But equipment represents only 28 per cent of Forzani's sales; the rest is footwear and apparel. "There is almost no impact when an FGL store opens near a Canadian Tire," said Medline. "It's a different customer and a different price point."

Still, the Canadian Tire dealers might have been concerned to see the corporation acquiring stores competing in the same category. To alleviate any fears, Wetmore and Medline gathered a small group of dealers early in the acquisition process to inform them of the proposed transaction and explain that their stores would not be affected. The dealers reacted positively. "They recognize that without a strong corporation they don't have a strong business and they're going to have to enable us to be more nimble," Maureen Sabia says. "Even some of the older dealers supported our deal on Forzani in a way I would never have envisaged 10 years ago. They would have fought tooth and nail against it."

◀ SportChek's new brand message, "Your better starts here."

In fact, the deal is beneficial to the Canadian Tire dealers because it increases the corporation's purchasing clout with suppliers. For example, says Wetmore, Canadian Tire can persuade brand name vendors to provide entry-level products for the Canadian Tire chain, a request those vendors might have rejected before the Forzani purchase.

Acquisitions such as FGL Sports will be an important part of Canadian Tire's future. But the Canadian Tire stores remain the heart of the business. Millions of Canadians recognize the triangle logo and feel at home in the big store that fixes your car and, while you're waiting, sells you plumbing and electrical equipment for your do-it-yourself project, a microwave oven, some dog biscuits, a dozen golf balls, a bag of bird seed, and some fertilizer for your lawn. That's the store Chris Hadfield sang about, the one that's just a 15-minute drive from 90 per cent of the Canadian population.

Mike Arnett, who was president of Canadian Tire Retail for almost six years before switching to corporate development in 2012, says the company has two main objectives for the stores: to increase revenues and to improve the customer experience. These two objectives are closely connected.

Canadian Tire adds about four new stores every year, unlike some other retailers that are adding stores more rapidly. Canadian Tire has chosen to enlarge or replace stores in existing locations rather than add new ones. "Most of the communities that are large enough to support a Canadian Tire store already have one," Arnett says.

As of 2012, Canadian Tire Retail has four sizes of store — A, B, C, D — which are larger than the "Class Of" stores of the 1990s. The biggest Class Of was 52,000 square feet, whereas the current largest stores are between 70,000 and 80,000 square feet. The B stores are in the 60,000-square-feet range. The C stores are in the 35,000 to 55,000 range, and the D stores are around 30,000 square feet. In addition, Canadian Tire has introduced a 15,000-square-foot design for the smallest markets. These small stores differ in both layout and product assortment from the larger ones. For instance, they have little space for elaborate displays of large items.

Arnett agrees with the Calgary dealer, Joe Dand, who observes that the best Canadian Tire stores are the best retail outlets in North America, while the gap between them and the worst stores is the largest of any chain. "It's partly to do with the business model," he suggests. "In traditional corporate-run stores, performance is more regulated and more disciplined, and the store managers are accountable to a district manager, who ensures that standards are met. Canadian Tire has never operated that way." The corporation does send executives to the stores to

◀ SportChek offers a wide selection of high-end fitness clothing and sporting goods.

◀ In 2002, Canadian Tire introduced an assortment of 12 core barbecues, all exclusive to Canadian Tire. At the same time, the company offers a new barbecue top-to-bottom warranty program, an industry first.

▲ Canadian Tire executives visiting the Winners offices in 2012 are presented with a barbecue to commemorate the companies' 10 years as business partners: (from left) Jack Xie, director of Winners; John Salt, senior vice-president of supply chain; David Hong, president and CEO of Winners; Maureen Sabia, chairman of the board of Canadian Tire; James Hou, president and founding partner of Winners; Paul Thompson, director, supply chain operations, Asia; Pat Sinnott, strategic advisor.

THE FOUNDING Billes brothers always insisted that success for Canadian Tire must also mean success for the manufacturers that supply the products sold in its stores. The company's close ties to its suppliers continue, and there is no better example than Winners Products Engineering.

Winners, the largest manufacturer of barbecues in the world, owes its existence to Canadian Tire. It all started, recalls James Hou, one of the principals of the company, in the spring of 2001 when he had dinner in Shanghai with some Canadian Tire executives. One of them, Christina Leung, director of Pacific Rim operations, mentioned that Canadian Tire couldn't find a reliable source of barbecues in China.

Back in his home base of Toronto, Hou discussed barbecues with a Canadian Tire buyer. "What would you want for a Canadian Tire customer looking to buy a barbecue?" he asked.

The buyer ticked off his wish list and, within three months, a new company, Winners, was producing barbecues at a former sink and bathtub factory in Guangdong, in south China. The first units, bearing Canadian Tire's Master Chef brand, were shipped that fall.

The business grew quickly. As of 2012, Winners was producing 2.5 million barbecues a year under several major brands, including Coleman, Cuisinart, and Broil King. Its products are sold in North America, Europe, Australia, and South Africa.

"Our relationship with Canadian Tire is unique," says Hou. "No other retailer in North America is as integrated with their barbecue vendor as we are with Canadian Tire. We've had that since day one."

In other circumstances, it would be risky to launch a new business on the basis of a deal with just one customer, but Hou and his partners understood Canadian Tire's

power in the retail marketplace and that gave them the confidence to go ahead.

Hou was born and raised in Toronto. He had a previous business relationship with Canadian Tire as a supplier of auto parts. The president and CEO of Winners, David Hong, had lived in Toronto for nine years; he told Canadian Tire's chairman, Maureen Sabia, that he visited a Canadian Tire store every weekend. "We all understand the place that Canadian Tire has in Canadian culture," Hou says.

Winners continues to work closely with Canadian Tire on product development of the company's Master Chef barbecues. Other Canadian retailers have asked the company to develop similar house brands for them, but Winners has declined. "Canadian Tire is our chosen channel in Canada and we consider ourselves very lucky to have this relationship."

assess performance but, says Arnett, "it's more of a coaching relationship than it is direct accountability."

Arnett started Canadian Tire's online business in 2000. As has been the experience of other stores, it hasn't turned out as expected. Retailers thought online sales would be 5 to 10 per cent of the total within a matter of a few years but, as of 2012, in Canada they are less than 2 per cent, compared with 7 per cent in the States. "One of the challenges that Canadian Tire faces in online selling, unlike some of our competitors, is just the convenience of the stores," Arnett says. In other words, you don't need to go online if the Canadian Tire store is just a 15-minute drive away. Furthermore, some products, such as books, computer software, and groceries, are well suited to being purchased online, as the customer doesn't need to see them before pulling out her wallet. "You don't need to touch and feel a case of bottled water," Arnett points out. "But people want to put their hands on a lot of what we sell."

▲ Now and then: (left and bottom right) a new, large store in a suburban Halifax mall, 2011; (top right) a downtown street-fronting Halifax store, 1970.

▶▶ The Saint-Jérôme, Quebec, store, with its easy-to-read signage, the reintroduction of the "race track" — the main aisle that loops customers through the store — and high walls and ceiling, is an impressive example of the Smart store concept's design enhancements that help customers navigate easily.

Canadian Tire and auto racing

▲ Jacques Villeneuve, Canadian Tire's first sponsored driver, poses with a picture of the two-litre Italian-built Osella that he drove in 1982.

◥ For the 1983 racing season, Jacques Villeneuve drove a five-litre Frisbee, previously driven by Al Unser Jr., the 1982 Can-Am winner. The car's graphic was created by Bernie Freedman.

1959 A.J.'s son, David Billes, drives his Corvette in club racing and gets involved in driving and building racing cars.

1968 David Billes starts Performance Engineering Limited, which designs and builds high-performance automotive racing engines. That year, he purchases a McLaren M8C and reworks it in the shop before the car, driver John Cordts, and team enter the competitive Can-Am Racing Series.

1982 Canadian Tire sponsors its first car and crew in the $2 million Can-Am Racing Series.

Jacques Villeneuve, the 1980 and 1981 Formula Atlantic driving champion, becomes the first driver sponsored by Canadian Tire.

1983 Jacques Villeneuve, sponsored by Canadian Tire, wins the Can-Am Racing Series driving a five-litre car. He is the first Canadian driver to win at Mosport and to win the Can-Am Racing Series. David

Billes's company, Performance Engineering Limited, manages the racing team.

1984 Canadian Tire becomes corporate sponsor for the Formula 2000 Racing Series.

Jacques Villeneuve races in the Indy 500 and the Championship Auto Racing Teams (CART) Series.

1985 Jacques Villeneuve and the Canadian Tire Racing Team win at Elkhart Lake, Wisconsin — the first time any Canadian driver has done so in the CART Series for Indy-type cars. The Canadian Tire racing team (with driver Johnny Parsons) captures fifth place in the Indy 500. Canadian Tire withdraws sponsorship of the CART IndyCar Series at the end of the year.

1986 Richard Spenard, sponsored by Canadian Tire, is the most successful race driver of the year, winning the Canadian Tire Formula 2000 Championship and the Players Challenge Series.

▲ A custom March Cosworth 85C Indy car grabbed the attention of Whites customers in Mesquite, Texas, and provided a great photo opportunity, July 1985.

▲ Powered by two-litre, four-cylinder engines, the typical F2000 car produces 140 horsepower and a top speed of 240 kilometres per hour.

1987 Richard Spenard wins the Rothmans-Porche Challenge Series and finishes fourth in the Players Challenge Series. Motomaster sponsorships include:

- Motomaster Pro Formula 2000 Series (a featured attraction at the 1987 Molson Toronto Indy),
- Motomaster Players Challenge Team with Richard Spenard and Ron Fellows,
- Jacques Villeneuve and the Motomaster Pro snowmobiles racing team (Villeneuve wins fourth world snowmobile title),
- Spenard-David Racing School,
- Nissan School of Advanced Driving,
- Rothmans–Honda Motorcycle team (associate sponsor).

1988 Canadian Tire sponsors a team of stunt car drivers for a cross-Canada tour. It also continues its sponsorship of Richard Spenard.

1989 Canadian Tire claims two championship titles and 14 other victories in car racing, giving it the most wins of any Canadian sponsor.

1990 Richard Spenard wins both the east and west Players LTD/GM Motorsport Series; David Empringham finishes second overall.

1991 The Eastern Motomaster racing team finishes on a winning note with Richard Spenard posting his fifth victory.

1993 A Motomaster racing vehicle, driven by David Empringham, wins the Players Formula Atlantic Championship.

1994 A Motomaster racing vehicle wins the Players Formula Atlantic Championship for a second time.

▲ David Empringham won back-to-back championships in the Players Ltd/ GM Motorsport Series in 1993 and 1994 and was considered the "winningest" driver at the time.

▲ David Empringham (far right) and his racing team were a winning combination.

◥ Greg Moore racing in the Detroit Grand Prix, 1996.

▲ Players GM Champion Series, 1994.

▲ Ron Fellows (centre) and Patrice Brisebois (right) at a 2010 Montreal NASCAR Canadian Tire Series event.

1996 Canadian Tire is a first-time Molson IndyCar and Indy Lights sponsor. Drivers Greg Moore, David Empringham, and Claude Bourbonnais make up the Players racing team. David Empringham wins the Indy Lights Series.

1997 The Canadian Tire Motorsports program sponsors seven drivers competing in five racing series. Peter Gibbons wins the Super Series Eastern Championship in his first year as Canadian Tire's CASCAR driver.

1999 Peter Gibbons and the Canadian Tire race team win the CASCAR Super Series National Championship.

2000 Peter Gibbons is the CASCAR National champion for the second time.

2002 Peter Gibbons continues as Canadian Tire's sponsored driver.

2006 The National Association for Stock Car Auto Racing (NASCAR) announces the creation of the NASCAR Canadian Tire Series. Scheduled to launch in May 2007, the series includes a multi-year sponsorship agreement with Canadian Tire.

2007 Cayuga International Speedway Park hosts the first NASCAR Canadian Tire Series race on May 26.

2008 Canadian Tire announces a sponsorship agreement with reigning NASCAR champion Scott Steckly, an 18-year veteran of auto racing. He wins four races during the 2008 championship season.

2010 The NASCAR Canadian Tire Series runs 13 races coast to coast throughout the summer, from Antigonish, Nova Scotia, to Vernon, British Columbia. Canadian Tire announces a new sponsorship arrangement with Canadian racing legend Ron Fellows.

2011 At Kawartha Speedway, Scott Steckly races his Canadian Tire Dodge to a second-place finish in the NASCAR Canadian Tire Series season finale. Steckly secures the points championship for the second time in four seasons.

2012 Canadian Tire announces a long-term partnership with Mosport International Raceway, a renowned racing facility in Bowmanville, Ontario. The track is renamed Canadian Tire Motorsport Park.

▶ Opening weekend at Canadian Tire Motorsport Park, May 2012. Racing fans cheer on Canadian Tire–sponsored driver Scott Steckly (bottom right). Motorsport Park has been a major venue for professional motor racing for over 50 years.

IN A SPEECH to Canadian Tire's annual general meeting in 2011, Stephen Wetmore recalled a National Association for Stock Car Auto Racing (NASCAR) race in Montreal at which Canadian Tire gave away 20,000 hats at the entry gate. The hats had no words on them — just the Canadian Tire triangle. One of the American drivers was baffled.

"If you're going to give out so many hats, why not put your name on it?" he asked.

"We don't have to," replied the Canadian Tire representative. "Every Canadian knows what the triangle means."

Outstanding brand recognition in a country that has few famous brands of its own is a huge asset for Canadian Tire. It didn't happen overnight and it didn't happen by accident. "It has been the culmination of decades of building our authority in our categories," said Wetmore. Canadians recognize the triangle because Canadian Tire serves a purpose in their lives.

"For generations we have been the company you rely on to make sure your car is ready for winter, or for summer, or for taking your children to school. We've been there every Christmas when your kids were young — and every Christmas when your kids have brought home your grandchildren. We're the place where you outfit your lawn with skeletons and cobwebs at Halloween ... We have outfitted generations of kids for hockey ... We've provided most of the bikes for that first bike ride ... We've outfitted entire families for memorable camping trips ... And we remain a Saturday morning destination for the entire family." Wetmore sums it up by defining Canadian Tire as the "purveyor of Canadian dreams." That is its purpose.

An award-winning television commercial created by the Detroit agency W.B. Doner in 1989 depicted a young boy on a Prairie farm who longs for a bike he has seen in the Canadian Tire catalogue. He cuts the picture out of the catalogue and carries it with him everywhere. He never dares ask for it, but one day his father astounds him by lifting a brand new bike out of the pickup truck. It was one of the most memorable TV spots in Canadian marketing history.

Kids still get their first bikes at Canadian Tire but, in the 21st century, it happens differently. The young boy today would have seen the bike on YouTube rather than in a printed catalogue. He may have asked family members to email his birthday money to a PayPal account he set up to save for it. He would have compared prices on the Internet. His parents may have done some research of their own, going online to find out about value, performance, and safety.

An electronic discount coupon, downloaded by Canadian Tire to Mom's phone, might help pay for the bike, and the money earned on the Canadian Tire loyalty

▶ Canadian Tire's "A Bike Story" television commercial received the 1990 Bessie Award as the number one English-language commercial in Canada.

Some things
from Canadian Tire
are priceless.

card might be used for a light, a bell, and other accessories. If anything goes wrong, Canadian Tire will hear about it that night on Twitter or Facebook. "Our retailing world," sums up Wetmore, "is in transition."

In order to manage that transition successfully, both corporate management and dealers understand they must work together as a team. They must use their time and energy doing battle with their competitors, rather than with each other. Unlike certain of his predecessors, Wetmore is a believer in the dealer system. So is Maureen Sabia, who sees it as the most powerful legacy of the founding Billes brothers.

"The brothers were entrepreneurs, starting off in a little garage with no money at all, staying up at night to keep the fire going to keep the tires warm," she says. "A.J. believed men like himself and his brother were the kind of people he wanted to involve in this enterprise called Canadian Tire. All the business gurus told them to have store managers instead, but he believed in these businessmen. So the entrepreneurial spirit has always pervaded the company."

Wetmore sees his job as leading rather than imposing. The result, he said in his annual meeting address, is "the best working relationship with our dealer network that we can remember — a relationship built on trust and commitment to breaking down anything that stands in our way of making quick decisions in the interest of our customers."

Dave Deplaedt, a Saskatoon dealer who is president of the Canadian Tire Dealers' Association, agrees. The corporation has always consulted dealers but sometimes it was just as a courtesy, he says. "Now they are asking us because they really want to know, and they have respect for what we have to say."

Change is buffeting the retail industry, but Deplaedt argues that it always has. "Twenty years ago, Canadian Tire had these tiny 5,000-square-foot stores. Now you hardly ever see one under 40,000 or 50,000 square feet. We have recreated ourselves dozens of times since J.W. and A.J. started this company."

Canadian Tire is the only major national retailer that uses the dealer model, says Deplaedt, and that is a competitive advantage in helping it manage rapid change. "It's the understanding of the local market, the energy and effort you put in, the level of passion and interest. You can't imagine the difference between owning a store and managing a store."

▼

"THE FUTURE IS HERE and it's staring us in the face," says Stephen Wetmore. The impact of technology means that "you have to move faster and faster and faster." The future of Canadian Tire depends on the answer to one simple question: Can it adapt?

"Our whole world is upside down. Our customers are radically changing, so our current methods of retailing all have to adapt. How do you do returns? How do you order?"

He worries about his daughter Stephanie laughing at the sight of the Canadian Tire flyer on the kitchen table. "Dad, do people still read that?" she said. "If I wanted something, I'd just get on the Internet, find the cheapest price, and get it sent to the house. Why would I go into the store to buy pots and pans?"

In the early years of the 1990s, Canadian Tire faced what could have been a devastating challenge from powerful newly arrived competitors. It defended its territory successfully by enlarging, remodelling, and upgrading its network of stores. Twenty years later, it faces a different kind of challenge. "Now we have to build the technology structure to compete in a totally reinvented retail environment," says Wetmore.

New communications media are eating away at consumer loyalty. Whereas Chris Hadfield might say, "Let's go down to Canadian Tire and check out the barbecues," a member of the younger generation goes on her mobile phone, checks out the barbecues for sale within a five-kilometre radius, and then chooses the one she wants at the best price.

"The customers are in control," says Wetmore. "They use Facebook to put products on shelves and to take them off. If you get a thumbs up, it stays there; if you get a thumbs down, [it's taken] right off the shelf. Customers are influencing pricing and marketing methods. They're arriving in stores often with more product knowledge than our sales associates ... This is a totally new direction where nobody has been and Canadian Tire certainly hasn't been. It's a very different world."

"The customer now manages the brand as much as we do," agrees Cliff Hammell, an Ottawa dealer who is vice-president of the dealers' association. "Look at what

Small market store in Hearst, Ontario, 2008, the first such store to open under the new retailing concept designed especially for small communities. With automotive, hardware, home, sports, seasonal, and a full-size Mark's, the focus is on providing customers with a one-stop shopping experience. Over 100 communities have been identified as potential sites for this concept.

▷ Canadian Tire make a generous contribution of over $23,000 during the 1983 cerebral palsy telethon.

△ Canadian Tire dealers sponsor many stampede events, including the Strathmore Stampede, 2012.

Canadian Tire dealers Ted Mangnall and Tim Tallon present a $60,000 cheque to city councillor Sarah Doucette and the City of Toronto for the reconstruction of the Jamie Bell Playground in High Park, May 2012. Mike Holmes (third from left) and his staff led the reconstruction project. The entire rebuild process was filmed for a fall 2012 episode of *Holmes Makes It Right*.

"Now we have to build the technology structure to compete in a totally reinvented retail environment." — Stephen Wetmore

happens around the world when people get together on social media. They can bring down governments. Companies better pay attention."

Previously, it was not easy to communicate with customers about products. Now the customers educate themselves. The successful companies will be the ones that best manage their relationship with this new breed of informed consumer, says Hammell. "When someone can stand in your store and look at prices within a five-kilometre radius, the disciplines of how you execute and how you pay attention to your prices and your warranties and how you deal with upset customers become more important than they've ever been."

Dealers closely connected to their communities give Canadian Tire an advantage other stores don't have. Kelowna's Gostlin is part of a Canadian Tire family. His father and uncle were dealers and so is his son Daniel, who runs a store in Kingston. When it opened in October 1981, Gostlin's Kelowna store was the first Canadian Tire in the B.C. Interior. Few of the local residents had ever heard of Canadian Tire. When Gostlin went to a federal employment office to hire some cashiers, an employee there couldn't understand why he needed so much space and so many employees just to sell tires.

Kelowna got to know what Canadian Tire was all about pretty quickly. Back then, he recalls, "our prices were by far the best in town. Today you've got competitors that won't allow that to happen." He has to compete by making sure he has the things his customers want. "The core business of automotive, hardware, housewares, and seasonal — we have always stayed true to that." He also works hard at service, such as free home delivery for items that won't fit in a customer's car.

Gostlin's parking lot usually gets swept every morning before the store opens. If that doesn't happen, Gostlin hears about it from his customers. "They have high expectations of us," he says. "They expect us to maintain a very high standard." For him, complaints aren't necessarily a bad thing. It means his customers care about "their store."In its 90 years of continued growth, Canadian Tire has never forgotten its connection to Canadians, from the famous, like singing astronaut Chris Hadfield, to the kids who will get their first bike someday at a Canadian Tire store. As it continues to grow, it will retain that connection because it retains the values

▶ Dave Malcomson receives his 25-year service pin from Martha Billes at the 2009 Dealer Convention in Toronto. Owen Billes, Stephen Wetmore, and Maureen Sabia (facing) look on; Peter Kilty, of Dealer Relations, is on the left.

instilled in it by the founding Billes brothers. There's nothing complicated about it, as A.J. liked to say: "Do unto others as you would have others do unto you, and you can't go far wrong." Another way to express the same idea might be: Be nice to your customers. It's good for business.

In March 2012, an arsonist set fire to a playground in High Park, in the west end of Toronto. The fire destroyed a unique wooden play structure that for many years had provided hours of safe adventures for small kids. "This was much more than a playground," said Sarah Doucette, the city councillor for the area. "This community came up with the idea for it, put their money into it, designed and built it." Many of the children worked on the design and construction.[8]

The community began collecting money to rebuild the playground. That effort got off to a strong start when Canadian Tire donated $60,000. This act of generosity was not done for publicity. It was done because it was the right thing to do, a way to give back to the community, one of hundreds of communities across Canada that are the basis of Canadian Tire's success.

As A.J. taught, you have to keep trying new things. That's especially true in today's retail world, where the competition is relentless. Canadian Tire bought Forzani as part of its growth strategy, but there was also a defensive aspect to the acquisition: if Canadian Tire hadn't bought it, some U.S. chain might well have, just as Target snapped up Zellers.

Martha Billes was a strong supporter of both major acquisitions. "She doesn't get stuck in the past," says Medline. "She's open to evolving the company, and that has been a big part of our success."

Although Canadian Tire remains a widely held public company, control rests in the hands of Martha Billes, who retains a majority of the voting shares.

"With the prudent streak I inherited from my father, I have been preparing my son, Owen, for the enormous responsibilities that lie ahead for him." — Martha Billes

Maureen Sabia argues that the presence of a controlling shareholder provides stability and certainty. Management can implement its strategies without being distracted by investors more interested in quick stock market gains than in the long-term viability of a great company. This does not mean that Canadian Tire is a one-person show. Martha Billes does not attempt to manage, and she insists that the board of directors be composed of people with strong opinions who speak their minds. During board meetings, she most often waits until her colleagues have spoken before voicing her opinion.

Martha's relationship with her father was always close. In 1962, while on a Mediterranean cruise, he wrote to her, saying, "You know, Martha, you are our rock — you always come through for Mother and me in the end. We depend on you." As the daughter of Canadian Tire's co-founder, she is the most important link to the company's colourful past. Speculation that used to appear in the press about who might buy her controlling block of voting shares has disappeared. She has made it clear that her son, Owen, will inherit control. In her speech to the 2007 Dealer Convention, she said she hoped to be part of Canadian Tire for many years to come, "But with the prudent streak I inherited from my father, I have been preparing my son, Owen, for the enormous responsibilities that lie ahead for him."

In an interview she pointed out that, before becoming a dealer, Owen did several jobs in the corporation. As a dealer he runs a store that is a top performer. And he has the advantage of being bilingual. "I think it says something wonderful about our great company that the third generation is completely committed to and engaged in its success and in its future," she told the dealers.

The first generation is not forgotten — on a wall in the original flagship store in downtown Toronto is a portrait of J.W. and A.J., the two brothers who spent so many productive years at that location. Yet the store itself is now in a new, modern building that speaks to the future.

In one of her convention speeches, Martha recalled her father being asked the secret of his success. He said, "Striving always to make things better." If Canadian Tire remembers that simple secret, it will continue to be Canada's store.

▸▸ The Orléans, Ontario, Smart store, also known as a Concept GPS store, opened in November 2008.

Canadian Tire companies

GAS+

CANADIAN TIRE
FINANCIAL SERVICES

ESSENCE+

SERVICES FINANCIERS
CANADIAN TIRE

PartSource®
The Parts. The Pros. The Price.

Jumpstart
Bon départ

Mark's

L'ÉQUIPEUR

SPORTCHEK

sports experts®

INTERSPORT®

ATMOSPHERE

national sports®

★ SNOW ★ SKATE ★ SURF ★

Hockey Experts

MotoMaster SINCE-DEPUIS-1933

Mastercraft

Broadstone GEARED FOR LIFE OUTDOORS · PRÊTS POUR LE PLEIN AIR

debbie travis

for LIVING

NOMA

LIKEWISE

YARDWORKS

Garrison TM/MC

blue planet

DENVERHAYES

DAKOTA

WINDRIVER OUTFITTING CO.

AGGRESSOR

dri-Wear

HEALTH PRO

DH≡U35

T-max Heat

DH3

ispiri

ARMOUR-FLEX

X-TOE

TARANTULA ANTI-SLIP ON ICE · A safer way to walk on ice.

Quad Comfort
CURVE-TECH

FRESH TECH

TARANTULA

Hyper-Dri HD1 · Hyper-Dri HD2 · Hyper-Dri HD3

DENVERHAYES SOFT

ENERGETICS · THERMALECTRIC · ARASHI

FIREFLY

CAPIX

matrix

MILLENNIUM THREE · NAKAMURA · McKINLEY

PRO TOUCH

ULTRA WHEELS

VIC

TECNOPRO

Acknowledgements

LIVING THE CANADIAN DREAM exists because Maureen Sabia, chairman of Canadian Tire, decided that the company's fascinating history should be captured and preserved in book form. She insisted on a frank and comprehensive account of the Canadian Tire story, one that described difficult times as well as triumphant ones. Throughout the project, she offered invaluable support and advice.

The book could not have been written without the enthusiastic participation of almost 70 former and current corporate employees, dealers, and others who were so generous in sharing their memories, insights, and, in some cases, historical materials, including old photographs. Sadly, two of them, Dean Muncaster and Alan Warren, died before the book could be published; both gave hours of their time to this project.

Researching 90 years of history is no easy task. Fortunately, I had plenty of support. Martha Billes provided a wealth of material from her personal archives and also from her remarkable memory; she was never too busy to answer questions about the history of the company and the family that created it. From among the others who provided archival material, special mention must go to William Vincent, who provided a box full of letters, internal newspapers, news clippings, and other documents.

Archivist Bev Brereton of the University of Western Ontario helped locate materials in the early weeks of the project, as did Marjorie Copeland and Cristina Giovanniello of Canadian Tire. Corporate archivist Siân Madsen unearthed tapes of interviews with such eminent past Canadian Tire figures as A.J. Billes and Arch Brown. Working with book designer Linda Gustafson, Siân ransacked the company archives for photos, catalogue covers, and other visual material. She also researched and wrote captions and the sidebars on logos and signage, tires, and auto racing.

Thanks also to the capable team of transcribers who transferred hours of interviews from tape to print: Nicole Salter, Meghan Walsh, Heather Stonehouse, Catharine Chen, and Shlomit Kriger. And to the many staff members of Canadian Tire, Mark's, and FGL Sports, who found additional visual material to help illuminate the story.

Linda Gustafson and her colleague Peter Ross took full advantage of the rich visual history of Canadian Tire, choosing the images that would best bring the story to life. They designed the book, creating a seamless combination of text and image. In her role as book producer, Linda oversaw the project right up until the finished volumes rolled off the presses.

Editor Judy Phillips has a special talent for exposing points that need explanation or elaboration. In doing so, she helped to clarify a complex story.

Finally, the author would like to thank his in-house editor, Judy Stoffman, for her support, encouragement, and research assistance.

Daniel Stoffman

Notes

In the following notes, names appearing alone, with no reference to a document or page number, indicate an interview with the author. Any direct quotation in the text that is not noted also comes from an interview with the author.

CHAPTER ONE: YOUNG MEN IN A HURRY (pages 1–29)

1 A.J. Billes, recorded interview by Marjorie Billes, Melrose Baptist Church, Toronto, January 28, 1992, analogue tape, Canadian Tire Corporate Archives, Toronto.

2 Fry & Co., Toronto, "Canadian Tire Corporation, Limited," August 14, 1944, Canadian Tire Corporate Archives, Toronto.

3 Martha Billes. Henry Thomas Billes was born in December 1859 in the London borough of Lambeth.

4 William Stephenson, "History of Canadian Tire" (unpublished manuscript, 1972), 15.

5 Ian Brown, *Freewheeling* (Toronto: Harper & Collins, 1989), 14.

6 Martha Billes.

7 Hugh McBride, *Our Store* (Canadian Tire Corporation, 1972), 44.

8 Fry & Co., August 14, 1944.

9 A.J. Billes, DVD interview, August 1992, Canadian Tire Corporate Archives, Toronto.

10 Quoted in Dan Proudfoot, "Retire? Not This Wheeler Dealer!" *Toronto Sunday Sun*, April 18, 1982, s3.

11 Martha Billes.

12 For example, see *The Globe*, March 4, 1922, 8.

13 A.J. Billes, DVD interview, August 1992.

14 A.J. Billes, Melrose Baptist Church interview, January 28, 1992.

15 Ron Base, "Wheel of Fortune," *The City* magazine (*Toronto Star*), June 3, 1979, 11.

16 Larry Collins, "The Store That Grew Like Topsy," *Reader's Digest*, July 1977, 69.

17 Martha Billes.

18 A.J. Billes, Melrose Baptist Church interview, January 28, 1992.

19 Province of Ontario, 1927, Canadian Tire Heritage Collection at the University of Western Ontario, Western Archives, London, Ontario.

20 Martha Billes.

21 Michael Bliss, *Northern Enterprise* (Toronto: McClelland and Stewart, 1987), 288–89.

22 Base, 13.

23 A.J. Billes, *Some Thoughts and Proposals on Profit-Sharing*, Canadian Tire Corporation internal document, 1985, Canadian Tire Corporate Archives, Toronto.

24 A.J. Billes, DVD interview, August 1992.

25 A.J. Billes, recorded interview, July 7, 1994, Canadian Tire Corporate Archives, Toronto.

26 Stephenson, 58.

27 Martha Billes.

28 A.J. Billes, recorded interview, July 7, 1994.

29 A.J. Billes, DVD interview, August 1992.

30 Martha Billes.

31 This and the preceding two quotations are from A.J. Billes, Melrose Baptist Church interview, January 28, 1992.

32 A.J. Billes, Melrose Baptist Church interview, January 28, 1992.

33 A.J. Billes, DVD interview, August 1992.

34 I. Brown, 34–35. The preceding "a crowning achievement" quotation comes from Brown, 23.

35 Canadian Tire Heritage Collection, Western Archives, London, Ontario.

36 A.J. Billes, Melrose Baptist Church interview, January 28, 1992.

37 Quoted in Stephenson, 65.

38 "Mac McNish Retires," *Canadian Tire Associates Review*, June 16, 1972.

39 Pierre Berton, *The Great Depression* (Toronto: Penguin Books, 1990), ix–x.

40 A.J. Billes, DVD interview, August 1992.

41 Mayne Plowman.

42 Martha Billes.

43 McBride, 35.

44 Martha Billes.

45 Jos Wintermans.

46 Tommy Rye.

47 Martha Billes, speech at Canadian Tire Dealer Convention, October 10, 1997.

48 McBride, 32.

49 Marjorie Billes, A.J. Billes Melrose Baptist Church interview, January 28, 1992.

CHAPTER TWO: THE ROLLER SKATING YEARS (pages 31–71)

1 Mike Filey, *Toronto: The Way We Were* (Toronto: Dundurn Press, 2008), 76–77.

2 Martha Billes.

3 Stephenson, 71.

4 A.J. Billes, Melrose Baptist Church interview, January 28, 1992.

5 "Historical Highlights," Canadian Tire website.

6 Martha Billes.

7 Bill McCullough.

8 Mayne Plowman; Martha Billes.

9 Arch Brown, recorded interview, February 16, 1997, Canadian Tire Corporate Archives, Toronto.

10 Gary Coniam.

11 Bill McCullough.

12 A.J. Billes, DVD interview, August 1992.

13 Stephenson, 97.

14 A.J. Billes, Melrose Baptist Church interview, January 28, 1992.

15 Ibid, 82.

16 Fred Sasaki.

17 Alan Warren, interview with author.

18 Martha Billes.

19 Mayne Plowman.

20 A.J. Billes, DVD interview, August 1992.

21 Ibid.

22 Alan Warren, *A Snapshot of My Life* (privately printed, 2003), 52–53.

23 Martha Billes.

24 Hugh Macaulay.

25 Dean Muncaster.

26 "Drugs: The Dangers of Chloromycetin," *Time*, 16 February, 1968. http://www.time.com/time/magazine/article/0,9171,837894,00.html.

27 A.J. Billes, Melrose Baptist Church interview, January 28, 1992.

28 Arch Brown, recorded interview, February 16, 1997.

29 Tommy Rye.

30 Stephenson, 105.

31 Martha Billes.

32 A.J. Billes, DVD interview, August 1992.

33 Jeffrey Smith.

34 Quoted in McBride, 63.

35 Fred Sasaki.

36 Martha Billes.

37 "Canadian Tire Money," *TCV* 4, no. 4 (1997): 14. Canadian Tire newsletter, 75th anniversary edition.

38 Stephenson, 124.

39 Mayne Plowman.

40 Quoted in Collins, 70.

41 Jeffrey Smith.

42 McBride, 75.

43 A.J. Billes, Melrose Baptist Church interview, January 28, 1992.

44 Canadian Tire annual reports.

45 Jeffrey Smith.

46 Ibid.

47 Arch Brown, recorded interview, February 16, 1997.

48 Alan Warren, interview with author.

49 A.J. Billes, Melrose Baptist Church interview, January 28, 1992.

50 Dean Muncaster.

51 A.J. Billes, "Training Dealer Seminar — April 9, 1975," Canadian Tire Corporation internal document, 2.

52 Ibid., 4.

53 Fred Sasaki.

54 Rosemary Speirs, "Canadian Tire's Profit-Sharing Turns Workers into Capitalists," *Toronto Star*, June 21, 1975, D10.

55 Jeffrey Smith.

56 James Dunlop, "The Pension Fund with the Big Payoff," *Toronto Star*, June 5, 1971. There is additional coverage of profit-sharing in subsequent chapters.

57 Martha Billes.

SIDEBAR: CANADIAN TIRE MONEY
(pages 60–63)

* A.J. Billes, Melrose Baptist Church interview, January 28, 1992.

† Dakshana Bascaramurty, "Hands Off Our Funny Money," *Globe and Mail*, February 22, 2011, L1.

‡ Jamie Simpson, "How to Outsmart a Thief in Mexico: Carry Canadian Tire Money," *Globe and Mail*, January 20, 2007, T6.

** "CIBC ATM Dispenses Canadian Tire Money," *Toronto Star*, December 2, 2004, D6.

†† Quoted in Leanne Delap, "Toronto Musician Raises Enough Canadian Tire Money to Record Live Album," *Toronto Star*, May 17, 2012.

CHAPTER THREE: THE DEAN OF CANADIAN TIRE (pages 73–111)

1 Dean Muncaster.

2 Ibid.

3 Martha Billes.

4 Dean Muncaster.

5 David Foot and Daniel Stoffman, *Boom Bust & Echo* (Toronto: Macfarlane Walter & Ross, 1996), 18.

6 Rich Hobbs.

7 Dean Muncaster.

8 Ibid.

9 Bob Hougham.

10 Quoted in Stephenson, 184–86.

11 *Traction*, Canadian Tire employee newsletter, June 1974.

12 Dean Muncaster.

13 Fred Sasaki.

14 Steve Bochen.

15 Dean Muncaster.

16 Larry McFadden.

17 Warren, *A Snapshot of My Life*, 71–72.

18 Al Cox.

19 Dean Muncaster.

20 *Traction*, June 1974.

21 Paul Goldstein, "Hardware Stores Catering to Handy Women," *Globe and Mail*, April 22, 1985.

22 Arch Brown, recorded interview, February 16, 1997.

23 Robin Law.

24 Jeffrey Smith.

25 A.J. Billes, Melrose Baptist Church interview, January 28, 1992.

CHAPTER FOUR: NEW HORIZONS
(pages 113–45)

1 Vern Forster.

2 Clyde Farnsworth, "Nice Degree — Go Away and Use It," *New York Times*, January 5, 1992, 1.

3 Vern Forster.

4 Matt Mucciacito.

5 Dean Muncaster.

6 Martha Billes.

7 "Canadian Tire Sells Interest in McEwan's," Canadian Tire press release, July 21, 1982.

8 Dean Muncaster.

9 Martha Billes; Gary Philbrick.

10 Gary Lamphier, "Hard Lessons from the U.S.," *Financial Times*, March 25, 1985.

11 Dean Muncaster.

12 Quoted in "National Tea, Loblaw's, and Related Chains," www.groceteria.com.

13 Martha Billes.

14 Tony Reid, "Canadian Tire in U.S.? It Sure Looks Good to Me," *Toronto Sun*, December 13, 1981.

15 This and the preceding quotation are quoted in D. Peter Vanderlee, "CanTire's Entree to the U.S. Market," *Financial Times*, January 18, 1982.

16 Quoted in Canadian Press, "Canadian Tire U.S. Acquisition Could Cause Problems — Analyst," *Toronto Star*, December 17, 1981, B15.

17 Quoted in Vanderlee.

18 Bob Hougham.

19 Dick Nolan, "Canadian Tire Rolls the Dice on Its White Stores Gamble," *Automotive Chain Store*, March 1984, 31.

20 Bob Hougham.

21 This and the preceding quotation are quoted in Paul Goldstein, "Canadian Tire Ousting Head of White Unit," *Globe and Mail*, August 8, 1985.

22 Robin Law, Canadian Tire press release, February 28, 1986.

23 Bob Hougham.

24 Rod McQueen, *Can't Buy Me Love* (Toronto: Stoddart, 2001), 99.

25 A.J. Billes, letter to John Bourinot, May 27, 1987.

26 Canadian Tire news release, June 6, 1985.

27 Maureen Sabia.

28 Fred Sasaki.

CHAPTER FIVE: WHO'S IN CHARGE HERE? *(pages 147–73)*
The struggle for control of Canadian Tire was a subject of intense interest and was followed closely in the press. Many newspaper articles were consulted by the author in the process of reconstructing this complex drama. Not all can be listed here but it should be noted that the work of Kenneth Kidd in the *Toronto Star* and Karen Howlett in the *Globe and Mail* was particularly useful.

1 Martha Billes.

2 Robin Law.

3 Ibid.

4 Stephenson, 165–66.

5 Warren, *A Snapshot of My Life*, 80.

6 Wayne Lilley, "It's Loyalty vs. Dollars in Canadian Tire Battle," *Toronto Star*, June 26, 1983, H1.

7 *Control of Canadian Tire*, Canadian Tire Corporation internal document, 2–3.

8 Ibid., 5.

9 Dean Muncaster, letter to employees, June 24, 1983.

10 *Control of Canadian Tire*, 7.

11 Paul Goldstein, "Billes Family Ponders Next Move as Imasco Ends Bid for Canadian Tire," *Globe and Mail*, June 28, 1983.

12 Robin Law.

13 Kenneth Kidd, "Bad Blood," *Toronto Star*, January 24, 1988, F1.

14 Canadian Tire directors' circular, December 22, 1986.

15 Canadian Tire directors' circular, December 23, 1986.

16 Theresa Tedesco, "A Dynasty in Turmoil," *Maclean's*, January 26, 1987, 33.

17 Jack McArthur, "Canadian Tire Takeover Is a Horror Story," *Toronto Star*, December 5, 1986.

18 Bruce Alexander, "Canadian Tire Sale May Mark End of Era," *Globe and Mail*, December 6, 1986, 1.

19 John McLeod, "Finally, Someone Stands Up for Small Investors," *Toronto Sun*, December 11, 1986, 79.

20 Diane Francis, "Group Pledges to Fight Bid for Canadian Tire," *Toronto Star*, December 11, 1986.

SIDEBAR: THE CANADIAN TIRE DEALERS' ASSOCIATION *(pages 172–73)*
* Sandy MacDonald quotations are from Sandy MacDonald, "Birth of an Idea," undated essay.

CHAPTER SIX: THE NEW WORLD OF RETAIL *(pages 175–219)*
1 Canadian Tire news release, signed by Bill Hicks, vice-president personnel, June 6, 1985.

2 Rosemary Sexton, *The Glitter Girls* (Toronto: Macmillan, 1993).

3 Eric Sellors.

4 Wayne Sales, taped interview with Hugh McBride, February 24, 1997.

5 Ibid.

6 Dave Urso.

7 Wayne Sales, interview with author.

8 Elwin Derbyshire.

9 Jim Ryan.

10 Jos Wintermans.

11 Marina Strauss, "Canadian Tire Makes Surprise Mark's Work Wearhouse Bid," *Globe and Mail*, December 20, 2001, B1.

12 Brian Hutchinson, "Blumes Put the Mark in Work-Wear Marketing," *Calgary Herald*, December 22, 2001, E1.

13 Wayne Sales, interview with author.

14 Martha Billes.

15 Bruce Wilson.

16 Gary Philbrick.

17 Bruce Wilson.

18 Tom Gauld.

19 Ibid.

20 "Options Success at CTFS," *Team Canadian Tire*, Winter 2005, 3.

21 Art Arai memo, n.d.

22 Quoted in Malcolm Gladwell, "Creation Myth," *The New Yorker*, May 16, 2011, 52.

23 *Traction*, May 1976.

24 Canadian Professional Sales Association posthumous induction of A.J. Billes into the Sales Hall of Fame, November 3, 2005, Fairmont Royal York, Toronto.

CHAPTER SEVEN: ADVENTURES IN DEALERLAND *(pages 221–63)*
1 A.J. Billes, letter to John Bourinot, May 27, 1987.

2 Daniel Stoffman, *Partners in Success: Boston Pizza and the Art of Franchising* (Richmond, B.C.: Boston Pizza International Inc., 2005).

3 All quotations from Brown in this chapter are from Arch Brown, recorded interview, February 16, 1997.

4 This and the preceding quotation are from Marg Bruineman, "Local Business Pioneer Dead at 81," *Barrie Examiner*, November 17, 2009.

5 Justin Young.

CHAPTER EIGHT: CANADIAN TIRE TODAY – AND TOMORROW *(pages 265–95)*
1 Dave Hadfield, www.hadfield.ca/Waltz/Canadian_Tire.html.

2 Ibid.

3 Quoted in Jordan Timm, "Canadian Tire: Fixing a Flat," *Canadian Business*, April 25, 2011.

4 Martha Billes, speech at the Canadian Tire Dealer Convention, September 16, 2007.

5 Keith Gostlin.

6 FGL website.

7 Maureen Sabia.

8 Tim Alamenciak, "Man Charged in High Park Playground Arson," *Toronto Star*, March 24, 2012.

Index